The Psychology of Human Freedom

Malcolm R. Westcott

# The Psychology of Human Freedom

## A Human Science Perspective and Critique

Springer-Verlag
New York Berlin Heidelberg
London Paris Tokyo

Malcolm R. Westcott
Department of Psychology
York University
North York, Ontario, M3J 1P3
Canada

Library of Congress Cataloging-in-Publication Data
Westcott, Malcolm R.
    The psychology of human freedom : a human science perspective and
critique / by Malcolm R. Westcott.
        p.    cm.
    Bibliography: p.
    Includes indexes.
    ISBN 0-387-96809-1
    1. Autonomy (Psychology)    2. Social psychology—Methodology.
3. Science and psychology.    I. Title.
    BF575.A88W47    1988                                                        88-19994
    155.2—dc19

Camera-ready copy provided by the author.
Printed and bound by Edwards Brothers, Inc., Ann Arbor, Michigan.
Printed in the United States of America.

9 8 7 6 5 4 3 2 1

ISBN 0-387-96809-1 Springer-Verlag New York Berlin Heidelberg
ISBN 3-540-96809-1 Springer-Verlag Berlin Heidelberg New York

*This book is for my own gentle band of freedom fighters —*
*Page, Frodo, Andy and Virginia.*

# Appreciations

A project that has been in progress more than a dozen years accrues a sizeable number of debts along the way. It is delightful to think that these can be paid off substantially merely by acknowledging them. They range from relatively anonymous conversations in a common room, pub, or airplane, to formal and serious criticism, to hard cash. They are variously easy or difficult to identify and acknowledge.

I want to thank the Canada Council and the Social Sciences and Humanities Research Council of Canada for support through Leave Fellowships in 1975-76 and in 1982-83. These made possible some long-term concentration on the project. I have also received consistent support from the Social Sciences and Humanities Research Council Small Grants Programme and the York University Faculty of Arts Small Grants Programme for many facets of the research and writing of this book.

I appreciate the contributions of my students, both graduate and undergraduate, who have served as research assistants, critics, or collaborators, in tasks ranging from library research to data gathering, to computer programming, to arguing, to proof reading. Some have written extensively on human freedom in course papers, theses, and dissertations. With their permission, I have drawn liberally from their work. More or less chronologically, they are Joel Oxman, Kenneth Enns, E. Mark Clare, Trudy Beaulne, Sharon Tothill Madill, Tony Merante, Peter Shermer, John Dunbar, Greg Taylor, Ivana Guglietti-Kelly, and Perry Klein.

As heavyweight critics and supporters, I want to thank the members of the Toronto Interest Group in Epicritical Research (TIGER), who in real life are Kurt Danziger, Gerald Cupchik, Rolf Kroger, Ian Lubeck, David Rennie, and Linda Wood. Following good dinners, they have repeatedly hassled me appropriately on many points in many chapters of this book. They have demanded justification for the unjustifiable, and have curbed many of my excesses. I have reserved the right to retain others, and remain responsible for them.

The President and Fellows of Wolfson College, Oxford, gave me a wondrously warm and productive welcome when I was a Visiting Fellow there in the Michaelmas Term of 1975. Never, before or since, have I felt as free to pursue my academic interests as I did then. In addition, the Warden and Fellows of Wells Hall, University of Reading, provided me accommodation and support, as did Roy Davis and the Department of Psychology when I was a Visiting Professor there in the autumn of 1982. Both of these sojourns into academic withdrawal served me well, providing time, solitude, and the opportunity to converse and consult with such provocative colleagues as Bernard Babington-Smith, Brian Farrell, and Rom Harré.

I thank the many persons who wrote protocols on their experiences of freedom and who were ultimately included or not included in the data, as well as those students from Victoria Park Secondary School in North York and the members of Living and Learning in Retirement who agreed to be interviewed. I thank them for their time, their interest and their candor.

Finally, I thank Zehra Ali Kahn, Kay Rosseau, and Tere Tilban-Ríos for shepherding the manuscript of this book through word processing, in many editions and in several languages.

Toronto                                                M.R.W.
February 6, 1988.

## Permissions to quote

The following have granted permission for me to quote and to reproduce figures and tables from the works indicated:

The Society of Authors, on behalf of the Bernard Shaw Estate: Shaw, G. (1931). *The complete plays of Bernard Shaw*. London: Constable and Company, Ltd.

Lawrence Erlbaum Associates, Hillsdale New Jersey: Westcott, M. (1985). Volition is a nag. In F. Brush and J. Overmier, (Eds.), *Affect, conditioning, and cognition: Essays on the determinants of behavior*.

Franciscan Herald Press, Chicago: Zavalloni, R. (1962). *Self determination: The psychology of personal freedom*. Chicago: Forum Books.

Mouton and Co., The Hague: Lee, D. (1963). Freedom and social constraint. In D. Bidney, (Ed.), *The concept of freedom in anthropology*.

Ross Parmenter: Parmenter, R. (1980). *School of the soldier*. New York: Profile Press.

The Canadian Psychological Association: Westcott, M. (1978). Toward psychological studies of human freedom. *Canadian Psychological Review, 19*, 277-290.

The Journal of Mind and Behavior: Westcott, M. (1982a). Quantitative and qualitative aspects of experienced freedom. *The Journal of Mind and Behavior, 3*, 99-126.

The Journal of Mind and Behavior: Westcott, M. (1984). Natural science and human science approaches to the study of human freedom. *The Journal of Mind and Behavior, 5*, 11-28.

Tony Merante: Merante, T. (1984). The phenomenology of freedom: an empirical study. Unpublished manuscript. Department of Psychology, York University, Toronto.

Greg Taylor: Taylor, G. (1986). A phenomenological investigation into the structure of experienced freedom. Unpublished B.A. Honours Thesis. Department of Psychology, York University.

# Table of Contents

# Introduction

In this book I pursue three goals. The first is to describe what has been learned about human freedom through psychological research. The second is to provide a conceptual and methodological critique of the large body of that research which has been conducted within the framework of a positivist natural science experimental social psychology. My third goal is to offer a contrasting human science approach to the study of human freedom and to illustrate its use in empirical study.

For more than twenty years psychologists have investigated the conditions under which people are seen to be free, the conditions under which they report feeling free, the psychological consequences of interference with behavioural freedoms, and to a lesser extent, how it feels to feel free. Empirical findings on each of these facets of human freedom have arisen in quite separate research traditions, and they are brought together here for the first time.

During the same twenty years, a general critique of the dominant positivist natural science approach to complex human phenomena has been growing. Although it has escalated recently, this critique has firm roots that go back to the turn of the century. I review this general critique and apply it specifically to the study of human freedom — surely a complex human phenomenon, more complex, ambiguous, and paradoxical than most of us imagine.

Similarly, for about twenty years, human science perspectives on human psychological processes have been developing. These also have roots of a far greater age. The human science perspectives are various, but they all respect the human being as agent, they all attend to reports of human experience as evidence, and they all recognize that human action and experience are normally invested with meaning and are historically and culturally situated. They argue that psychological processes must be studied with an appreciation of the conceptual, historical, and cultural settings in which they are lived and commonly understood.

Consequently, in Part I of this book (Context) I begin with two chapters on conceptual, cultural, and historical views of human freedom. Chapter 1 draws mostly from philosophy and examines various meanings of freedom, their complexities and contradictions. The free will issue is explored as a central feature of this "conceptual labyrinth". Chapter 2 draws largely on history and anthropology, and reviews different conceptions of freedom arising in different times and different places.

With some light cast on the context, Part II (The Nat Sci Variations) introduces psychological research. It is concerned with two well-established psychological research programmes rooted in the natural science conception of social psychology. Chapter 3 focusses on psychological reactance — the motivational and behavioural consequences that arise when an individual's behavioural freedoms are threatened or eliminated. Chapter 4 explores the literature on the attribution of freedom — the circumstances under which observers attribute freedom to the actions of others or to their own actions. The conceptual bases and the findings of these two lines of research are examined both on their own terms and from the human science perspective.

In Part III (Metaconsiderations) I step back from the specific issue of human freedom. In Chapter 5 I review the more general critique of the positivist natural science approach to complex human experience and action. Some alternative human science perspectives are described which promise greater fidelity to the human phenomena which are the subject matter of social psychology.

Part IV (The Hum Sci Variations) presents three chapters of studies of human freedom which are informed by these human science perspectives. Chapter 6 deals with two kinds of personal reports of experienced freedom. One is a sustained autobiographical study and the other is a presentation of a large number of solicited reports of experiences with freedom — both its presence and its absence. In Chapter 7 I describe the development and use of theory-based systematic surveys of the conditions of experienced freedom. Both quantitative and qualitative analyses are employed, and some cross-cultural findings are included. Chapter 8 presents a number of interview studies of experienced freedom carried out by my students and me. Although the informants are drawn from a single historical and cultural setting, they range widely in age from the early school years to retirement. Similarities and differences between the various age groups are explored,

Part V (Further Facets of Human Freedom) includes only Chapter 9. Here I emphasize once again the context of human freedom with reference to a variety of contemporary problems not previously discussed. Included are concerns about technology and privacy, freedom and well-being, circumstances of extreme privation, and some fundamental paradoxes.

I have dealt with human freedom as an individual human phenomenon, and have avoided much reference to specific political or social systems. I have tried to include a variety of perspectives and a variety of kinds of evidence, and to indicate how these different kinds of knowledge might be valuable in enhancing human freedom. I have been impressed repeatedly that human freedom means many different things, is in conflict with other human values, and is culturally and historically situated.

*********************

When I began this study of human freedom, some years ago, I quickly learned that the empirical psychological research on the topic was quite circumscribed, but the background supporting literatures were virtually boundless. I considered these literatures arising outside psychology — in history, philosophy, and anthropology — very important because they form the context for our understanding of the phenomena in question. Necessarily, I have been selective in my treatment of these, but fortunately, some broad analytical schemes have been provided by philosophers, so my selectivity has some order in it. I have also been selective in examining the psychological literature, focussing mainly on empirical work. Some readers will find that I have omitted sources they consider absolutely fundamental, but they will also find some sources which are novel, and I believe, illuminating.

Be forewarned that I do not refer to Hegel, Marx, Weber, or Durkheim; nor to Rawls, Adam Smith, Jefferson, or Malcolm X. On the other hand, I do refer to Berlin, Cranston, Adler, Sartre, Malinowski, Lee, and Fromm. I do not refer to May, Rogers, or Freud; but I do refer to Brehm, Steiner, Parmenter, Zavalloni, G. B. Shaw, and Solzhenitsyn. A bibliography on the subject of human freedom can be built in many ways.

Some readers will be jarred by my mixed methodologies. That is as should be, because I speak two languages and they interpenetrate. Just a few days ago a student whom I have known for many years told me that some years ago he had voiced the view that "Westcott speaks phenomenology with a strong behaviouristic accent." And it is true. Early in my career I spoke behaviourism like a native, having learned it at the knee of Richard Solomon, for which I am eternally grateful. I knew Hull's variables better than I knew the Ten Commandments. Now I speak self-taught phenomenology, but I cannot, nor do I want to, divest myself of the fresh air that behaviourism and positivism blew through a set of very musty attics more than fifty years ago.

At the same time, I am no longer satisfied with fresh air that is devoid of the voices of people, their experience, their satisfactions, and their strife. So I speak these two languages, wear two hats, perhaps have two heads.

I have found this project enormously exciting and perplexing. I hope the reader can share the excitement and tolerate the ambiguity.

# PART I: CONTEXT

# 1 A Philosophical Foray

## The plan

In this chapter I will attempt to sample coherently from the nearly endless philosophical literature on freedom. I will make reference to schemes proposed by Cranston (1967), and by Gibbs (1976), to a broad integrative abstraction proposed by Adler (1973), and to some other analytical schemes which I have extracted from various authors and have found useful. I will lead a side trip into the issue of free will, because it is fundamental to notions of human freedom, but I make no pretense to resolving this issue. Finally a glance at the sweeping ubiquity of human freedom proposed by the existentialists will give an additional dimension to the conceptual labyrinth of this diversified topic. The focus will be on a conceptual analysis of freedom, dealt with at varying levels of abstraction, and we will see that capacity and non-interference are fundamental in such an analysis, with some attention paid to discipline as a necessary feature.

## Conceptual issues

Certainly the prime literature on human freedom arises in a philosophical context, or more accurately, in a variety of philosophical contexts. Philosophical treatments of society, law, politics, ethics, and so on, are all, at one point or another, concerned with human freedom. This tradition is thousands of years old. Yet psychologists writing on freedom have, with rare exceptions, simply ignored the wealth of serious thinking generated by philosophers, and have opted for more-or-less simple minded and easily operationalized definitions of freedom. Typically, these definitions do scant justice, and perhaps do major violence, to the phenomena said to be under investigation.

In most of what I believe to be the major psychological works so far concerned with human freedom (Brehm, 1966; Brehm and Brehm, 1981; Fromm, 1941; Lefcourt, 1973; Skinner, 1971; Steiner, 1970; Wicklund, 1974) there is barely a handful of references to serious philosophical sources, and most of these are simple extractions of a definition here and there. The same can be said for the anthropological literature, (Bidney, 1963; Lee, 1959; Malinowski, 1944) with rare exceptions. I exclude my own work from this list of major contributions for reasons of modesty and for the reason that I have specifically attempted to take philosophers seriously as having something to say to psychologists.

So this chapter is devoted to providing some philosophical background concerning human freedom. It is necessarily selective and various, and those lines of reasoning which seem to be of minimal importance to psychology are treated only briefly; other lines of reasoning which seem particularly germane to the psychological study of freedom are treated at greater length. This can be no more than an introduction, inasmuch as the full treatments in the philosophical literature run to many volumes (e.g., Adler, 1973; Berlin, 1958; Cranston, 1967; Gibbs, 1976) and none of these even claims to be exhaustive. The philosophical literature is by no means a completed body of work, nor does it have clear-cut boundaries. Parent (1974b) published on "recent" work in the area, covering perhaps the preceding 15 years, and referred to 19 sources; Ofstad (1967) provided a bibliography of more than 200 references in English alone on the free will problem between 1954 and 1965.

Surely these philosophers have something to say about the nature of human freedom, whether human freedom be considered a true ontological state or whether it be considered an illusion. Whether psychologists want to investigate freedom as a subjectively determined state, which when threatened, yields motivating properties (cf. Brehm, 1966; Brehm and Brehm, 1981; Wicklund, 1974) or explicitly as an illusion which has important antecedents and consequences (Lefcourt, 1973; Steiner, 1970), as an experience (Westcott, 1978, 1981, 1982a) or as a pernicious myth (Skinner, 1971) they surely should have some detailed idea of the dimensions of the concept, the phenomenon, the experience, as elucidated by thoughtful scholars for thousands of years.

8

A very high level of abstraction was used to sort out the meanings of the term freedom in a project carried out by the Institute for Philosophical Research, under the direction of Mortimer Adler, and published in two volumes in 1958 and 1961 (Adler, 1973). The list of works cited and reviewed runs to 40 pages, and this project was able to reduce the various treatments of freedom to three main formats:

1. Circumstantial freedom of self-realization — which focuses on the circumstances of non-interference and the availability of both options and the capacities to pursue them. This is the format of freedom we most generally think of — the existence of circumstances in which one can fulfill desires.
2. Acquired freedom of self-perfection — which means attaining a state in which one "wills what one ought" or truly desires the good, or alternatively, reaches a state of perfection where one is free from all desire. This is less often immediately thought of in everyday life, but is certainly common within the framework of various religious or political ideologies.
3. Natural freedom of self-determination — which focuses on the capacity to initiate action, to make choices; in fact, under favourable circumstances, to be the genuine master of one's actions.

Adler claims that "We have found no theory that cannot be classified as consisting in either (a) one of these conceptions exclusively, (b) two or more of these conceptions as distinct, or (c) a single conception that combines two or more aspects of freedom which other theories conceived as distinct freedoms" (Adler, 1973, p. 589).

In the selective presentation of specific views which follows, we will see these three themes repeated in varying forms and combinations as they become more concrete. There are specific formulations of human freedom to suit every taste, but as Adler points out, there is a limited number of themes.

### Assumptions

It appears that there are three fundamental assumptions which unite the philosophical literature on freedom: first, there is a commitment to one or another free will doctrine; second, there is an assumption that human life goes on in the context of some social organization; third, there is a belief that the expression of free will is a desirable thing, and should be inhibited in the least possible degree by society.

The first of these, the commitment to free will, is a very controversial issue in itself, and it is necessary to address this issue in its own right, which we will do subsequently. We do not propose to "settle" the matter; we explore some of its dimensions.

While all philosophical discourses which consider freedom to be real, assume some form of free will, some capacity to initiate or terminate action, they do not all take the time to explore or defend this assumption. Many theorists take it purely as an assumption, neither proved nor provable, but useful for further theorizing.

The second general assumption — the existence of society as fundamental to human life — needs little discursive support in the contemporary world. The empirical evidence is that people do live in groups, and in those societies where philosophy is practiced, the groups are of ever increasing size and complexity. This fact gives rise to many practical problems in the realm of political and social freedom, and it also gives rise to the fact that while freedom is taken to be a fundamental good, it is continuously in competition with other values which arise in social groupings.

The third assumption, that the expression of free will in a social context is good, has many facets, and the different facets of this assumption lead to the different details of political and social philosophy — from the extreme libertarian philosophy of Rousseau through the more middle ground of J. S. Mill to the totalitarian philosophies of fascism. In these different positions, the expression of individual freedom is accorded very different priorities, and a detailed analysis of the nature of freedom appears only in those philosophies which give it a relatively high priority.

Given these three assumptions (free will, social grouping, desirability) as fundamental to philosophical considerations of freedom, consider next some of the conceptions generated. Philosophers in this area are not particularly rigid about their terminology, but we hope to emerge from this foray into what Gibbs (1976, ch. 1) calls a "conceptual labyrinth", with some useful distinctions.

## Some basic concepts

Perhaps the philosophical considerations of freedom can be split into two major groups: characteristics of the human individual and characteristics of the environment. Central to the former group, personal characteristics, is what Gibbs calls "optative freedom" (1976, p. 17). Basic optative freedom is the capacity for human beings to be the origin of actions — to choose, genuinely, what they will do. It is the power to act or to forbear from acting. Optative freedom is not simply a human being as the locus of causality, the biological machine which processes the historical and contemporaneous information and renders an output. Optative freedom is sometimes called "free will", and it appears that any sensible discussion of human freedom must arise on the foundation of optative freedom. This state of affairs calls for an exploration of the free will issue before we can go on to discussions of other aspects of human freedom.

## An exploration of free will

Westcott (1977) has pointed out that there are three levels of questions with respect to free will and only one of them has been addressed systematically. The first level is the metaphysical level, concerned with universal truth about the existence of free will and the consequent relations between free will and responsibility; the second is the theoretical question about the role of free will as an element in any theory of explanation of human behaviour; the third question is the psychological question about the origins and consequences of the experience of free will. The first is properly the business of philosophers and they are busily at it — as busily today as they were a hundred years ago. The second is the business of psychological theorists, and they have barely begun to scratch the surface of that problem (cf. Shotter, 1975). The third is the business of empirical psychology — the systematic exploration of a widespread human experience, whether conceived as reality or as illusion. Psychologists have not turned much attention to this problem either, but are beginning to find respectability in such an endeavour.

The first question is whether there is, properly, any such thing, state, or set of processes that can be called optative freedom or free will. Subsequent to that, the question must be addressed as to whether the issue is a real one or a pseudo issue, and after dealing with that we will return to our main theme of human freedom.

There are several lines of argument which are brought to bear on the question of free will. Many of them are used on both sides of the dispute, but there are some which weigh heavily on one side or the other, exclusively. First are the theological arguments concerning the nature of God, and man's relationship to God. If God is seen as omniscient and omnipotent, and the controller of the universe, then every act of every person is determined by God. There is no will other than God's will, and free will in individual men is a false presumption. Cranston (1967, p. 84) points this out as a fundamental tenet of Calvinism, and notes that people went to prison for expressing a belief in free will during the 16th century. On the other hand, the omnipotence of God may be accepted, but coupled with the notion that in human affairs the will of God works only through the will of man. God, in his omnipotence can supply or refuse to supply volition and the conditions which He knows (through His omniscience) will result in an expression of free will in a particular direction. Thus the acceptance of omnipotence and omniscience of God can result in the conclusion that all human events are predetermined, or alternatively, that free will operates, deftly managed by the will of

God. The full presentation and critique of these arguments is a matter for theologians and is of marginal interest to the present work.

A second view of marginal interest is the argument from morality. If there is no free will, that is, if an individual has no power to choose a higher goal over a baser goal, if whatever road chosen is fully determined by preceding events, none of which were chosen by the apparent agent, then there is no basis for morality, no substance to ethics. William James found this intolerable and opted for free will from this ground, plus the ground of his own experience — an argument to be dealt with below. The acceptance of a full determinism of human behaviour, in which neither praise nor blame can be attributed, in which no choices of the higher or the lower course of action are, or can be, made is seen as a mockery of the highest forms of human life and civilization.

However, in the free will position, the application of praise or blame, and the subsequent consequences of reward or punishment are almost universally thought to have some effect on behaviour — especially those behaviours which are subject to moral and ethical judgment. This expectation, then, shows so-called free will to be subject to manipulation, and not, in fact free. If this were not the case, then the use of rewards and punishments with respect to morally relevant behaviour would be pointless.

In contrast, virtue is said to be its own reward: moral actions taken through free will cannot be influenced by reward. But immoral actions, carried out through the exercise of free will should be similarly impervious to manipulation. While I have never seen this argument put forward seriously, the usual high rate of recidivism of criminals and the dismal record shown by almost all rehabilitation programmes may well be an argument for free will.

A third view on the matter concerns reflexivity — that a belief in determinism must itself be determined, and as such, cannot be the product of open rational deliberation. Rationality requires that a person be able to explore, appreciate, and weigh evidence, and come to conclusions, freely, on the basis of rational consideration of the evidence. If there is no free will, there can be no rationality of this kind, and a belief in determinism is not rational. The argument cuts the other way, of course: From a fully deterministic point of view, a belief in free will is similarly determined and is no more rational or irrational than a belief in determinism. But a belief in free will can at least make possible the argument that such a belief can be reached through the use of free rational deliberation. The determinist is seen to have no hope of open rationality, nor can he have any illusions about it; the person who espouses a free will position can at least argue that his position is rational.

The most common determinist position argues that all events are the result of efficient causes which are, in principle, identifiable, and however complex the mix of determinants, they make up the efficient causal matrix. Rarely is the *one-cause-one effect* notion invoked, although much of the empirical evidence cited for causal relations in behaviour is of this simplified variety. In human action *in vivo* such a state of affairs is rare, so under ordinary conditions it is not possible to trace the deterministic relations between causes and effects. This state of affairs may be elaborated by a free will theorist to assert that the impossibility of prediction in natural states is not only a practical problem, but a problem of principle. If it is possible to make predictions only under artificial conditions, how can one assert that it is possible, in principle, to make full and correct predictions under all conditions—a requirement of the determinist position? From this perspective the determinist position is seen to fall by demanding more of itself than it can deliver, either in fact or in principle.

Not so, the determinist argues, for the universe is a natural system, and natural systems, including human behaviour, are lawful and determinate. The fact that concrete predictions about human behaviour are most successful in highly controlled situations does not detract from the principle that human behaviour is equally predictable in natural situations. In fact human behaviour in natural situations is highly predictable, albeit with less precision, and is predictable from a knowledge of prior causal determinants; in principle, a full description of determinants in any situation would yield full and correct prediction. Agreed, this may not be possible in practice, due to the constraints of the time course of events, but the principles of the position are not altered.

But let us focus for a minute on the fact that prediction in natural situations, and indeed in highly controlled laboratory situations, always shows variation and error. Psychologists ordinarily attribute these variations to individual differences, or to some undetected variation in the conditions of an experiment from time to time, or to errors of measurement. Human beings are too complex to be interchangeable one for another, as atoms of iron are interchangeable, so we try to randomize selection of subjects so that systematic biases do not creep in. But we cannot avoid the fact that people are different, often in entirely unknown ways. If additional knowledge were available, so that individual differences could be eliminated, if our conditions could be more perfectly controlled, and if our measurement techniques were more precise, there would not be variation, and there could be perfect prediction.

But what of the indeterminacy at the most fundamental levels of the universe? With the delineation of the principle of indeterminacy at the subatomic level, Eddington (1935) argued that a doorway was opened for free will in human behaviour. The principle of uncertainty is often described in two ways: First, and most accurately it has to do with the fact that the measurement of the position of a particle interferes with the simultaneous measurement of the acceleration of the same particle, and vice versa, so that when one measures one feature, one must remain uncertain about the other. The second version of uncertainty, is concerned with some residual randomness in the activity of sub atomic particles such as the specific rate of emission of radioactivity. It should be evident that the first conception of uncertainty has nothing whatever to do with the possibility of human free will, and the second contrasts determinacy with randomness. This second contrast is fetching, on the surface, but upon examination it just won't wash. In human behaviour we are concerned with determinacy versus free will, and behaviour to be explained by free will is not random. Free will behaviour is often highly systematic, persistent, and may defy all of the apparent determinants which "should" control it. In addition freely willed behaviour is quite predictable to the actor, before the act is carried out. If one wants to use the indeterminacy principle in physics as the analogue of free will, then free will behaviour must be random, whimsical, accidental, unplanned, unsystematic, explicable neither by the actor nor the observer. Such a notion of free will completely robs it of any bearing on morality or ethics or of any peculiar relation to the human species. When human behaviour becomes significantly random or unpredictable, we begin to invoke a special set of determinants, such as madness, demons, drugs. The principle of indeterminacy has nothing to do with free will in human behaviour. (cf. Stebbing, 1937; Westcott, 1977).

There are arguments from experience: I feel perfectly confident that I could have written this sentence differently, had I decided to do so. And I could have decided differently. Everyone has that kind of experience in the making of decisions, both large and small. I engage in rational activity, I weigh evidence, I seek new evidence, I take account of my preferences and the costs anticipated in a choice, and I choose. In some cases the choice is forced upon me and one side or the other becomes very heavily weighted ("Your money or your life...") but nonetheless, I choose.[1] Religious martyrs and political heroes have shown that one can choose what appears to be the greater evil to themselves in pursuit of a higher principle. One is certainly pressured to give over one's money to preserve one's life, but one has still made the choice. And it could have been different. Under less stressful conditions we frequently experience ourselves as the origin of our acts (de-Charms, 1968). We purchase a necktie, select from a menu, and we know that we are making the decision, that we could have chosen the red rather than the blue, the mousse rather than the sorbet, the chips rather than the mash.

These daily experiences are very convincing of the reality of free will, but they lend themselves to a deterministic analysis, as well (Westcott, 1977). Experiences of free will may appear as such because one does not have a full grasp of the deterministic sweep of the origin of one's preferences, of the shifting weight of the various arguments which can be marshalled for one course of action over another, nor of the changing evaluation of the costs and payoffs anticipated. Further, a free will position must argue that one could have made a different choice *under precisely the same conditions*. If one engages in deliberation, each sweep of consideration forever changes the conditions under which a decision subsequently is "made". That is, if I am to choose between two alternatives, my first set of considerations may lead to a tentative decision to do "A" under conditions "X"; but my second consideration is made under changed conditions, for now the conditions of choice is "X" plus the fact of having made the first tentative decision "A". In this kind

---

[1]Jack Benny seemed to have more trouble with this choice than most people have.

14

of rational decision making, subsequent considerations are not, cannot be, made under precisely the same conditions. A final decision is made under its own unique set of conditions, different from the conditions under which previous tentative decisions were made. Thus, there is not even a theoretical testing ground for the proposition that a different decision could have been made under the same conditions. In effect, you can't step in the same decision making river twice.

Campbell (1938) argues at length for the free will, or libertarian position, and derives most of his evidence from experience in moral choice situations. He points out that all of the forces of both heredity and prior environment contribute to, and determine what he calls formed character, and this complex determines a situation in which genuine moral choice is made. But he goes on to argue for the effort and agony which leads, or can lead, one away from the alternative which might be most strongly determined by formed character and toward the alternative which is morally right. He does not imply that following one's formed character choices is always following a low road, but it is always the easier road. Who can deny the personal experience of the effort of will — sometimes succeeding, sometimes failing? Campbell also makes clear that a determinist critique of this viewpoint and the evidence in support of such a critique depends on an entirely external point of view which denies the very existence of the only kind of evidence which can support it. The opposition to Campbell's view arises on the assumption that all events *must* be the result of some preceding events and that there is no possibility of genuinely creative, self-initiated acts. Therefore, all the experience of effort of will must simply be discounted as illusory. Campbell's position, of course, is that there can be, and are, creative self-initiated events — acts of will which are influenced but not determined by prior events. While Campbell's argument is primarily in defense of free will, he does not argue that all acts are free, nor that no acts are determined; he argues that some events, specifically weighty moral choices are free acts. And that is quite enough to establish the existence of free will, without preempting all deterministic accounts of behaviour.

In summary, then, we have outlined several kinds of arguments brought to bear on the reality of free will or optative freedom:

1.  The arguments from theology concerning the omniscience and omnipotence of God. We have seen that such arguments can be used on the side of free will or the side of determinism in human behaviour.
2.  Arguments from morality, that free will is necessary for ethics or morality to make any sense. However, we have noted that a consequence of this position, the meting out of rewards or punishment with the intention of supporting or modifying behaviour which is ethically relevant implies that free-will behaviour can be modified, which hardly makes it free.
3.  Arguments from reflexivity, namely that the determinist must accept the fact that his belief in determinism is determined, and could not

be arrived at rationally, through free consideration and evaluation. Of course the determinist would argue that the free-will position is arrived at in the same way.

4. Arguments from naturalism, namely that the entire universe, including human behaviour, is a lawful system and that no undetermined force such as free will has a place in it. This argument is almost exclusively on the side of determinism.

5. Arguments from indeterminacy in physics which assert that even at the sub-atomic level phenomena are not fully predictable, and thus free will is possible. This argument is rejected because of what is seen as a false analogy: the contrast in physics is between predictability and randomness, while in human behaviour it is between predictability and some other highly organized action which violates external predictions. Further, while human behaviour under conditions of so-called free will may not be predictable to the outside observer, they are predictable to the actor, as agent, before action is taken.

6. Arguments from experience, the ubiquitous feeling that one is the origin of one's actions and under a particular set of circumstances one could have done differently. This is dismissed as the result of an actor's simple unawareness of the chains of determining causes which have led to the present action. Further, it is argued that the same circumstances can never, in principle, repeat themselves: as one engages in deliberation, the occurrence of each step modifies the context in which a subsequent step occurs. The conditions of decision making just won't hold still to allow an argument that an individual could have done other than what was done, in the particular circumstances: the same circumstances simply do not recur.

As one can readily see, none of these arguments is anything like air-tight or totally convincing for either side. Is it the case, then, in the great free will/determinism sweepstakes, that ya pays yer money and takes yer choice? Even that may not be necessary, since there is a third position generally known as "compatibilism", but sometimes called "reconciliationism" which argues that the two so-called opposing doctrines are compatible or can be reconciled so that both are true. Such distinguished philosophers as A. J. Ayer (1963), Patrick Nowell-Smith (1948), and even David Hume (1978) have contributed to this discussion. Most of the exploration is within the framework of problems in ethics, responsibility, and moral judgment, and is based on very careful (sometimes elusive) analysis of language use. Sometimes the argument is put forward in a relatively formal logical progression, arguing for the compatibility of progressively more contentious assertions (Canfield, 1962).

In contrast to the formal logical progression, Ayer (1963) argues that the contention between causality and freedom is troublesome because it is inappropriate. Rather, he argues, freedom should be contrasted with *constraint*. "Now we began with the assumption that freedom is contrasted with causality:

so that a man cannot be said to be acting freely if his action is causally determined. But this assumption has led us into difficulties and I now wish to suggest that it is mistaken. For it is not, I think, causality that freedom is to be contrasted with, but constraint" (p. 278). The question as to whether a behaviour is free or not is not whether the action has any cause at all, but whether it has a special sort of cause. He says that determinism requires only that behaviour be explicable in terms of causes and that actions have many different kinds of causes: some are deliberations, some are constraints. Causation means only that two events occur in some sort of relation to each other; all else, he says, is metaphor. In effect, he adopts an explicitly Humean conception of causality — mere co-occurrence — and admits any sort of cause into the causal formula: we will have to decide if the particular cause renders the action free or constrained.

Certainly it is the case that our satisfaction or dissatisfaction with the resolution of the issue is fundamentally dependent upon how we *talk* about it. Ayer has translated what seemed to be an ontological issue into an epistemological one.

This is not a very satisfactory conclusion to those of us outside discipline of philosophy, those of us who want some guidelines for our views of human behaviour. We may be very naive to want to know whether there is or is not free will, or at least whether a view which accepts or rejects free will is more or less productive and advantageous than its alternative.

Can a dispute which yields such mixed and unsatisfactory support on either side, be a real issue? Or is it a pseudo-problem? To try to deal with this, it is necessary (as where isn't it necessary?) to delineate very precisely just what is being debated. There are many notions of free will, and there are alternative notions of determinism — such as hard and soft — and it may be quite trivial to debate the omnipotence of God versus the principle of uncertainty, or the necessity of the freedom of will for the sake of morality versus the regularity of the universe.

When one is arguing fundamental metaphysics, it appears that one must argue that the universe is lawful, and that effects flow invariably from causes, or that alternatively, in human affairs there is a discontinuity between past and future — that the human being can intervene and produce effects which could not be predicted from a complete knowledge of antecedent events. We have to distinguish between an external observer and an actor in this case, because, as I have already argued, one often can predict accurately one's own actions even when an observer cannot. It is also true that one may explain unpredicted actions as being at one extreme more-or-less random or at the other extreme as being "very wilful" — that is, highly organized and persistent and counter to the usual determinants of an action (cf. Westcott, 1977).

William James opted for a possible discontinuity between past and future (Murphy, 1971, p. 251; Viney, 1986) and the occurrence of an autonomous act of choice when decisions are made. When decisions are made which seem to be reasonable, in keeping with the evidence available, ethical, advantageous, and so on, we are not troubled by a connection between past and future; we don't raise the question of will or wilfulness. It is only when the decision seems to be out of keeping with an observer's assessment of the evidence, or when a choice is made to an individual's disadvantage that the question of free will arises. We will be discussing this later on, in some detail, in the section on attribution.

However, when an individual engages in decision making, the experience of will may be present or absent — depending on the circumstances — and the experience of will is heightened as the alternative courses of action become more nearly similar, and when there is clear conflict between the two courses of action and both are attractive, even if for quite different reasons. For example, my desire to play golf this afternoon vs. my obligation to finish a manuscript. A genuine conflict, but it would be difficult to assess the valence of these two alternatives on any single scale.

Certainly no one claims that our decision-processes are entirely autonomous of the evidence brought to bear on them, nor independent of our own past history of decision making, nor of our values, nor of coercions which might be part of the evidence. If decisions were entirely "wilful", that is, independent of all prior conditions, behaviour would surely be entirely unpredictable, even chaotic — behaviour wouldn't make any sense. So the connection between past events — determinants — and future actions — consequents — cannot be denied. The problem is the nature of the connection between these: Does the consequent flow directly from the antecedents, inevitably, if we just knew all the antecedents, or is there a necessary peculiarly human step, which might or might not be taken?

The arguments mounted so far concerning the reality of free will — pro and con — are concerned with exactly that: reality of free will. The effort is to establish that there is or is not such a process, thing, force, or whatever. They are arguments about the ultimate nature of reality, and particularly the nature of human beings. They are not about what might be worthwhile ways of looking at human behaviour, they are not about how best to explain human behaviour, they are trying to get at ultimate truth, and they beg the question as to whether there is one truth or alternative truths. Clearly, there is one truth concerning free will: either *it is* or *it isn't*. Compatibilism attempts a resolution of this antinomy and attempts to find grounds upon which it is legitimate to say that human behaviour is both freely willed and determined.

This may be done by arguing that an individual's desires are determined, but the turning them into acts is freely willed. That is, there is a step from desire to action which is mediated by the free will. This point of view certainly squares with the fact that we do not always do what we want to do, and that the relation between desires or motives and actions are not the same relations as between causes and effects. The matter of concern is not acts. The matter of concern is choice or decision: acts are only seen as praiseworthy or blameworthy if they are seen to be the consequences of choices or decisions.

After reviewing a variety of these attempts to reconcile the positions of determinism and free will, Cranston (1967, p. 105) is not encouraged. He is satisfied that there appears to be no satisfactory way of reconciling the belief in freedom of the will with the scientific assumption of predictability of all natural processes.

Ultimately the question is recast into the problem of predictability, and he argues that there are certain kinds of acts which are not, in principle, predictable. He describes the problem of gathering and processing sufficient information so that a prediction of an event can be made before it occurs, and he finds that there are many events for which this could not possibly happen — an event would have occurred before one could have developed a prediction (p. 118). In part, this may be a product of the time he wrote, before the ready availability of computing devices which far exceed human computational speeds. However, this practical consideration is not important, anyway. One can readily take a model, enter the appropriate parameters and "predict" events which have occurred thousands of years ago. It is not the point of getting out the prediction before the event occurs, but getting the model to predict events as they have occurred, without knowing that they have occurred. If I am prepared to use such a method for the prediction of the last general election, the only information I must exclude from my prediction is the information as to the actual outcome, regardless of how long after the election I can actually produce the "prediction".

But there is one kind of situation in which the unpredictability seems especially vexing: creative acts and inventions. Is it really possible that someone with knowledge of all the necessary prior conditions and characteristics of an inventor could predict what was going to be invented? If so, without knowledge of the invention ultimately produced, the predictor would become the inventor. This, I think, is a special problem, unless we move back from the business of specific prediction, and rely on probabilistic prediction: I predict that inventor X will develop a process for long-life storage batteries of light weight and low cost, knowing the details of the individual's training, prior interest, successes, concern with economy and so on. Even if we follow the development process through from these background facts to the step by step change, do we reach a point where specific prediction of the details of the storage battery is possible? Actually, it seems that the answer is no.

Remember that the question of the freedom of the will was recast in terms of predictability. Does this apparent failure of predictability with respect to creative acts, such as inventions, endorse freedom of the will? I think not, inasmuch as many events such as inventions are the consequences of dogged pursuit of lines which others have not followed, or alternatively, the product of a sudden observation that some quite unplanned combination of elements or processes served the need of the overall plan. While the pursuit of a line of inquiry is certainly purposive, and while the serendipitous observation is in a context of search, neither of them is what we would ordinarily call wilful. Will, as we have already seen, seems to involve some sort of effortful struggle, and this is not the same as planning or context.

At this point, it is appropriate for me to withdraw from the philosophical contest concerning free will and determinism. There is no one view which is universally accepted, of course, and the development of positions and arguments goes on unabated (cf. Dennett, 1984; Watson, 1982). Suffice if this excursion has helped to illuminate some of the issues and provide a context for the study of human freedom. After all, that is the purpose: to provide a context which indicates that there are many lines to the pursuit, and that it is not likely that one will show itself to be the best.


## Return to human freedom


We now return to philosophical considerations of freedom after this excursion into the more specific question of free will. As noted before this side trip, a study of human freedom as an ontological state seems to require a commitment to one or another form of optative freedom as a base, that is, a commitment to the notion that human beings actually do choose, actually initiate action, and do not simply serve as organic computing systems which tote up balance sheets and register a decisive imbalance in favour of one alternative over another.

So we move on to what Gibbs calls *conative freedom*. Conative freedom is a state of affairs in which at least one alternative is attractive or desirable. Choosing between evils does not represent conative freedom. With a single alternative, one can choose to do or to not do, but if the single alternative is not attractive, one can make this choice — one can exercise optative freedom, but conative freedom is not involved.

Gibbs follows with *elective* freedom, as encompassing all the above — the capacity to make genuine choices, the presence of at least one attractive alternative — and adds the presence of more than one alternative which is attractive. One can still choose to do or to not do, but more importantly, one can chose among attractive alternatives. Finally, we come to *natural freedom* which becomes evaluative as well as analytical. Natural freedom encompasses all of the above as prior conditions, but in addition, it is the use of these in the pursuit of the good life, specifically, the development of one's maximum potential. Natural freedom is not the untrammeled pursuit of just any goals, but the pursuit of good goals.

Gibbs argues (p. 23) that the pursuit of one's drug addiction is not included in natural freedom, even though all other features may be present, and he argues this on the ground that the individual is not developing his highest potential, but rather, is destroying himself. In my own view, it seems a more appropriate argument, if one wants to exclude such acts from natural freedom, to question whether the basic optative freedom is present. Indeed, an addict may initiate the pursuit of drugs (optative freedom), may know they are available and attractive (conative freedom) and may even find a variety among which to choose (elective freedom). The problem arises because Gibbs overlooks, as part of optative freedom, the capacity to *not act*, as well as to act. He implies this, when he describes the optative freedom of an individual under duress—that even when one is threatened, one has the optative freedom to not comply, but he fails to make the forbearance as important to optative freedom as he makes the initiation of acts. This strikes me as a more telling argument, and avoids the value judgment of what is or is not a good goal. While we might find religious or political martyrs engaged in activity which ultimately leads to their destruction, we are likely to see them as engaged in free behaviour because of the moral or ethical quality of what they are doing. They may have the choice of recanting or death—optative freedom is present, but conative freedom is not, for neither alternative is attractive. But there may still be natural freedom, in that martyrdom may well be seen as the highest point of one's existence and development. Some of the highest principles of human behaviour are mounted on self-sacrifice.

So the problem comes down to one of the values being pursued, and Gibbs seems rather more sanguine than I am as to these value judgments being shared. For example, he demeans the pursuit of exploitation and tyranny as if everyone agrees that they are bad; he lauds the freedom to seek out stout and oysters as if there were no principled vegetarians or abstainers in the world. Additionally, there is the question of internal compulsion, of whatever sort. While he has tended to downplay the optative freedom to forbear (and this is central to many conceptions of free will) we have examples of highly principled persons who do not claim optative freedom for their behaviour. Quite apart from the drug addict, Luther said "Here I stand—I cannot do otherwise. God help me. Amen!" (Bartlett, 1955, p. 86). Have I lost my optative freedom when I conclude, on the basis of principle, that I cannot bring myself to injure another? Again, the paradox: to use one's optative freedom to do *this* rather than *that*—or that rather than this - leaves one without the option.

So here is one reasonably diversified concept of freedom, including several analytical steps, some value judgments, and some problems. As with notions of free will, there is no universally accepted definition or analysis, and the purpose here is to provide a background in variety. There are concepts to suit every taste.

### Some additional ideas

We can move to some conceptions which do not carry the moral tone of Gibbs' work. It is possible to describe conditions of freedom, supporting the value that the expression of freedom is a social good, and maintaining the caveat that social goods are not necessarily compatible with each other.

There is the most fundamental notion of "negative freedom" or as it is often called interchangeably, "negative liberty". Berlin (1958, 1969) has written at length about negative freedom but the notion is a very old one. It is simply the condition of being left alone to do as one wishes without interference from any legitimized source. This conception assumes that one has the capacity to do as one wishes. It is also a negative definition in that it is *freedom from*. It is the elemental condition under which humans are expected to be able to express their wills and fulfill their desires, and it is often argued that any social organization should operate so as to maximize this freedom from interference. It will be useful to call this notion negative "liberty" rather than "freedom", and to retain the term "freedom" for something more elaborate which we will take up a little later (cf. Parent, 1974b).

The next conception to note is the conception of "rights". Rights are said to be operative when a society acts, either collectively, or through appropriate agents, to ensure or guarantee that the negative liberties which are not interfered with by official bodies are also not interfered with capriciously by private individuals. We move from the "liberty" to walk down the street without official interference to the "right" to walk down the street, when the governmental authorities assure us that no one else is allowed to interfere with our doing so either.

It is at this early point in the progression that absolute negative liberty begins to be eroded, and some proscriptions on behaviour are introduced. The basic constraint is that one may express or enjoy complete liberty only as long as one does not interfere with other people expressing or enjoying the same. However, two different persons with the desire to occupy the same point on the pavement at the same time, or to possess the same diamond necklace at the same time must inevitably come into conflict: Our laws and judicial system come into being to control and adjudicate these conflicting liberties. It is also at the point of ensuring "rights" that other social goods begin to conflict with liberty, whether the competitors be equality, justice, economic growth, or whatever (cf. Friedenberg, 1975).

The next consideration which comes into making freedom progressively more complex has to do with "opportunities" and "resources". It is here that philosophers begin to identify liberties and freedoms as being "meaningful" or "meaningless", by exploring whether an individual can actually make any use of the liberties and rights guaranteed. It is also at this point that various kinds of obstructions to action are considered. For example, does a man with two broken legs have liberty to go for a walk in the park? By definition, the man has both the liberty and the right to go for a walk in the park, because no outside person is allowed to interfere. However, the liberty and right are said to be "meaningless" because he lacks certain personal resources to act in accord with them. In the same way, the liberty or the right to go to the theatre is meaningless if no theatre exists. Since social and political philosophers are concerned principally with obstructions to behaviour which are purposely imposed by acts of other persons, many philosophers insist that it is proper to talk about freedom even when there is no practical possibility of an individual taking advantage of it (cf. Berlin, 1969; Parent, 1974a). That is, "meaningless" freedom can be a legitimate point of discussion.

Paradoxically, many of the conflicts which arise among social goods are the necessary result of attempts to provide the opportunities and resources to ensure that people can move from basic liberty to meaningful freedom. The conflict concerning the Official Languages Act in Canada, private medicine in Britain, and busing to schools in the United States, are all examples of a fundamental conflict between a conception of liberty and a conception of equality. Berlin points out that these conflicts seem to come as surprises, when in fact, they are inevitable. He notes "...the natural tendency of all but a very few thinkers to believe that all the things they hold good must be intimately connected, or at least compatible with, one another" (1969, p. 128). Friedenberg reiterates this point with respect to the more common understanding. He says, "Men do not become freer as the society they live in becomes more equitable. The belief that they do is a confusion resulting from the fact that equality and social justice are such great goods in themselves that people in our century tend to assume that all other great goods must flow from them" (1975, p. 155). Friedenberg explores at length the complex implications which privilege, egalitarianism, elitism, economic growth, liberty, and freedom have for each other. Every implication appears to be double-edged. One boggles at the task set for a government which proclaims its explicit dedication to three conflicting aims, such as *Liberté, Egalité, Fraternité*.

MacCallum (1967) moves the argument further along the line of increasing complexity, and argues that any intelligible statement about freedom must have three components either explicit or implicit: (1) There must be an acting agent; (2) there must be a statement about negative liberty (what the agent is *free from*); (3) there must be a statement about positive liberty (what the agent is *free to do*).

Berlin however, is very wary of this notion. He points out how easy and common it is for a society or a philosophical system to prescribe a set of explicit negative liberties and then go on to prescribe the positive liberties which may legitimately accompany them. He cites the many varieties of rational libertarianism which aspired to maximize liberty, but which did not extend even basic liberties to the irrational, the immature, or the uneducated. These were systems which assumed all constraints could wither away, that is, negative liberty could become absolute — but only when all persons were fully rational, at which time all would agree on and pursue good ends. Thus, the positive component may become expressly prescriptive, and when this occurs, when someone says what ends shall be pursued without encumbrance, the door is opened for every form of tyranny practiced in the name of magnifying freedom (Berlin, 1969, pp. xlviii, 131-134, 145-149).

But MacCallum's point is more clearly directed to the description of individual freedom than to a social or political conception of freedom promulgated as a social prescription. He makes it very clear that neither the "freedom from" statement nor the "freedom to" statement are necessarily prescriptive. They are only necessary descriptive components to make a complete and intelligible statement about freedom. In effect, he is allowing only "meaningful" freedom to qualify for the term "freedom" at all. It would appear that MacCallum has effectively translated abstract notions of freedom, which exclude the individual person, into psychological notions of freedom which include not only the acting person, but also include a concern about obstructions to behaviour. For example, he is concerned with problems of personal inadequacy, absence of opportunity, the lack of resources, natural obstructions, and so on, and his concern with the positive side of the three-part statement requires this. Such an extension of the scope of the problem is heavily criticized by Parent (1974b) as stretching the concept of freedom beyond any useful limits, and by Berlin (1969, pp. xliiiff), as blurring the distinction between liberty and the exercise of liberty. However, the human appeal of MacCallum's notion is obvious, and is the position espoused by Fromm (1941) which we will explore in the next chapter.

Some writers (e.g., Parent, 1974a; 1974b, pp. 155-158) explore the simple performance of an act as the necessary and sufficient condition for identifying freedom: if one carries out an act, it is adequate evidence that one was free to carry it out. Freedom in this form is quite independent of any explicit liberties or guarantees, but is crucially dependent upon opportunities and resources. If the sign says "Keep Out — Trespassers Will Be Prosecuted", but one climbs over the fence, the fact of entering the restricted area is evidence that one was free to do so. On the other hand, when one is legally licensed and fully equipped to take grouse, one is not free to do so unless one sees grouse and has the requisite skill to shoot one. Thus, we run the full course from the notion that freedom resides principally in negative non-interference to the notion that freedom is principally in the accomplishment of an act, regardless of interference, costs, or prohibition.

In the above paragraphs concerning notions of freedom, I have pointed out that the philosophical literature is based on three assumptions or commitments: the assumption of free will, the assumption that humans live in social organizations, the assumption that the expression of will within society is a social good. Subsequently, several levels of complexity in the consideration of freedom were described: first, the negative liberty of official non-interference; second, the rights of guaranteed protection from casual interference; third, the consideration of resources and opportunities; fourth, the ultimate expression of freedom in the conduct of acts which give witness to all the preceding steps, or may render some of them inconsequential. It would seem to be valuable to maintain the distinctions among liberties, rights, opportunities, resources, and ultimately freedom.

## A more radical view

From a somewhat different point of view we find what is certainly a radical, sweeping and extreme view of human freedom in the work of Sartre (1956). For Sartre, freedom is not a condition which can be enhanced or diminished, sought or rejected. It is not a condition controlled by forces outside the individual nor guaranteed by legislative act. Freedom is a fundamental condition of being human, or as more often put, human *being*. This is not freedom to choose from a menu or to vote for a politician, it is not freedom which can lie dormant and fail to be exercised. The very condition of human being is constant free choice — free choice in defining and symbolising situations in which one finds oneself and constant choice in one's acts which define oneself. There is no necessary continuity or security in oneself or in one's world — they are both continuously redefined by choice of interpretation and choice of acts. Humans, in virtue of their being, are condemned to be free.

Whether one actively makes choices or not, one *is choosing*. The choice may be to define a situation or choose an act on the basis of one's full phenomenological interpretation and vision — authentic choices — or it may be a choice to ignore one's phenomenology and vision and choose inauthenticity — an actively chosen passivity in the face of the world. But one *has made* a free choice, nonetheless, from which the human, in being, cannot be excused.

Thus, for Sartre there is no question as to whether humans are free or whether they choose — this is a fundamental condition of human being, a condition which recurs continuously.

Further, when one chooses a definition or redefinition of a present or past situation and chooses to define or redefine one's self through an authentic or inauthentic act, one modifies the situation for those with whom one interacts, and one is responsible for this. Freedom and responsibility are inextricably connected, and exist in the ultimate aloneness of the individual in carrying out these necessary functions of being human. The future of the self is in no way guaranteed, and must be chosen over and over. The self *is* only insofar as it chooses and acts, and it must do this.

For Sartre, there is no arguing the point. He asserts an unproved and unprovable position — much as the extreme determinist asserts an unproved and unprovable position. Both state articles of faith.

Whether *we* choose between them or opt for a compatibilist position will be acts of faith. We will conduct our professional and personal affairs more or less in consonance with the position we take — passively or actively. We will define situations or design investigations in the light of these positions, however dim or bright the light may be; our decisions will be informed by them, our explanations will be influenced by them.

Like it or not, we all take some sort of philosophical position with respect to determinism and free will. Whether we ever untangle the labyrinth sufficiently to see a direct line from entrance to exit, we should have some idea of the intricacies of the issue, or we are surely as blind men describing the elephant.


## A folk observation


In his novel, *Home Game*, Paul Quarrington (1984) recounts a conversation between Nathaneal (Golden Legs) Isbister and Dr. Dexter Sinister. The former is a baseball player, the latter an impresario and magician. In the following passage, Isbister is clearly speaking of baseball, but when Doc speaks of "the capital M" he is referring to what he calls "real magic". Isbister speaks:

"...as I was saying, I liked sports real well myself. And when I was about thirteen, I thought I knew why. I looked at it this way. God put you in a body, and He made the body subject to a lot of natural laws, you know? Like gravity and stuff. You see, Doc, I was brought up very religious, and I believed in God. And I believed in a soul. And I got to thinking that maybe the soul was like a prisoner in the body. Maybe the soul was too big for the body and was always trying to get out. And sports was well, according to natural laws, you should only be able to run so fast, right? I mean, you get your legs working, you get your muscles churning as fast as they can go, you take into account the wind against you, stuff like that, all natural and scientific, and then you know just how fast you can go. You see? But me, I figured that there was something inside you, inside your soul, that could make you go just a little bit faster. Just a little bit faster, and it didn't have anything to do with muscles or nature or anything. It was your soul doing it. And when your soul made you go just that little bit faster, well then, for that moment, you were free. Does that make any sense?"
"Indeed! It is precisely analogous to my search for the capital M. Everything I do, everything that I bid hither from nothingness and render back to the same, all that can be accounted for in mechanical terms, i.e., I do it with my fingers. Therefore, when finally it happens, and I am not doing it mechanically, then, as you say, in that moment I shall be free" (pp. 156-157).


## Retrospect and prospect


In this chapter I have repeatedly referred to the notion of human freedom as a conceptual labyrinth. It is a labyrinth with a very large number of entrances, a very large number of turnings, and no clear exit. Which reminds me of a Dave Allen story about a group of Irish tourists rioting outside the Hampton Court Maze: They couldn't find their way in.

Indeed, in discussing issues of human freedom it is often the case that we can't find our way in. At least not a mutual way in. It is the case that almost anyone who can speak at all can speak about human freedom, and do so authoritatively. But to find common ground or a common way to address the matter is not so obviously possible.

I have tried to show some of the dimensions of the problem, playing off the broad abstractions of Adler against the more detailed analysis of Gibbs, the progressive descriptions of Berlin and Parent, the requirements of Mac-Callum, and the sweeping assertions of Sartre. Surely the abstractions and requirements are proper subjects for discussion, analysis, and debate, but surely the functioning of human freedom on a more concrete level, in everyday human life also demands study.

In the next chapter, we will look at human freedom placed in cultural context, in the lives of human beings. Some of what we will look at is quite abstract and is hardly distinguishable from the philosophical treatments. But some of it will be more human and personal, and as we proceed through this book, the personal elements will become more and more salient.

# 2　Views from a Bridge

### The plan

In this chapter I will review some work, primarily by anthropologists, which views the issue of human freedom in concrete contexts. This view contrasts with the more abstract philosophical treatments. Another contrast will be seen in that the philosophical emphasis tended to be on an absence of constraint, while the anthropological views emphasize the necessity of constraints in the support of free action. Some writers, not clearly anthropologists, are included—Eric Fromm and G. B. Shaw—because their views of freedom are clearly rooted in historical and cultural process. There does not seem to be any natural progression in the views to be presented, and they tend simply to stand side by side— similar, but rarely representing refinements of each other. The views, however, share a strong concern with cultural constraints, forms, and instrumentalities as being the very mechanisms through which freedom is possible. This is a significant departure from the focus on *capacity* and particularly on *non-interference* noted in the preceding chapter. This new focus represents an elaboration of the feature of *discipline*. Once again, all three of these—

capacity, non-interference, and discipline – are mentioned in various forms, but they are explored in a complex, interactive manner.

## Some continuities and discontinuities

It is not surprising that anthropologists, historians and practical politicians would argue that human freedom can be discussed meaningfully only in a cultural setting. As a human phenomenon, freedom draws its very meaning from the context in which it occurs. It is argued that there is no possibility of a meaningful discussion of human freedom outside a concrete setting, in spite of the fact that most of the last chapter made no mention of any context whatsoever.

It is also the case that anthropolgists would be alert to the various alternative and even conflicting meanings of "free" and "freedom" which derive from the various social and cultural contexts in which the term arises; and to the manifold ways in which linguistic manipulation can distort the meaning of a concept which has such sweeping positive connotations. A very striking contemporary rendering of linguistic distortion is illustrated in Orwell's *1984* (1949) where in "newspeak", freedom, as well as a variety of other strongly valenced terms are actively distorted, merged with, and come to represent, their opposites. While this is presented as a purposeful manipulation, Leach (1963) points out how distortions can arise more subtly.

He points out how the concepts "free" and "not free" "master" and "slave" – rendered into these contemporary English terms – distort a set of relationships of ancient India described by Chanana (1960). The original concepts refer to distinct, but equally valued, reciprocal relationships in which there was a differential in advantage of one person over another, but the relationship was one in which the differential was very small. In more sophisticated societies where chattel slavery existed, the differential between master and slave was typically very great, as was the difference between free and not free. Not so in ancient India. Leach goes on to point out that even in industrial societies where chattel slavery has been abolished, the differential advantage of the most favoured members of society over the least favoured members may be greater than the advantage of master over slave in ancient India – even though in these industrial societies all persons are "free".

So the meanings of free and not free, master and slave, – that is, the concrete cultural meanings – must be seen in the context in which they occur. The fact that the terms can be translated precisely or loosely from one language to another does not mean that the meanings are the same.

Lee (1959) makes an even more fundamental point from an anthropological, linguistic perspective. She points out that it has been argued that freedom is a fundamental goal of all humankind, and that an individual or a culture must at least make the *distinction* between free and not free, between acting and being acted upon, and this distinction must have some significant role in the organization or evaluation of human experience and behaviour.

That such a distinction is generally made in literate societies is attested by the very fact of this book and the dozens of other books on the topic, however variously they may concretely conceptualize the distinction. The universality of the pursuit of freedom, in a western mold, is implied by de Charms, in his notion of personal causation. He says, "...man's primary motivational propensity is to be effective in producing changes in his environment" (1968, p. 269). He describes the difference between producing changes (being an *origin*) and being acted upon (being a *pawn*) as deriving from the universal experience of children of the growing correspondence between wishes, efforts, and results. While this sequence of experience may well be universal, the importance of this sequence may be quite different from culture to culture.

Lee (1959) provides the example of the Trobrianders, drawing heavily on Malinowski's descriptive material. She describes their non-linear reality, their non-causal views of the world. While their behaviour is certainly not random or unpatterned, the nature and origin of the patterning of behaviour is of particular interest. She says,

"Something must be said here about individual and pattern; how does an individual Trobriander enter a pattern? There are various ways in which he does so and we in our culture would distinguish them according to the principle of whether he enters automatically, or whether he does so by act of will. By virtue of being born, an individual enters certain patterns of behaviour in terms of certain people, those, for example, who are his relatives by blood or affinity" (1959, pp. 101-102).

Yet there are other patterns which as westerners we would generally say the Trobriander may enter or not enter, as a matter or choice. Lee says:

"However, I think the concept of freedom of choice is incommensurate with Trobriand value or behaviour, and, in fact, a false measure. For us, to act as we want to act necessarily involves freedom of choice, but for the Trobriander the concept is meaningless. I think the Trobriander has no more and no less freedom when he initiates than when he continues an ordained pattern. In each case, he acts as he wants to, because the act, and the pattern which validates it, holds satisfaction for him; he acts in this way because he is a Trobriand, and the pattern is Trobriand. To be Trobriand is good. 'Act of will' and 'freedom of choice' are irrelevant as principles of classification or evaluation" (1959, p. 102).

This world view should strike us as no more strange than the marginal difference between master and slave in ancient India. Nor should it be strange that the value placed on individual liberty leads the Kapauku to refuse to imprison or lock up those who offend tribal laws. Rather, the offenders may be killed, or punished—and allowed to fight back while punishment is administered—but they are not restrained, hands bound, or confined (Posposil, 1958; cited by Leach, 1963). By the same token, two very free societies, aspiring to greater freedom—England and Canada—had a greater proportion of their citizenry incarcerated in prisons in 1982 than ever before. Both nations complain, from an administrative point of view, but neither raises the question as to how increasing freedom leads to increasing incarceration.

## The necessity of constraints

Perhaps this question can be approached obliquely through Malinowski's reasoning (1944) which is adamant that the common dictionary definitions of freedom and liberty are simply wrong, as must be many of the conceptions explored in the previous chapter. Freedom as "absence of constraint" is intolerable to Malinownski, as it is to some other anthropologists. Freedom always implies structure, some constraints within which action is not only possible, but guided, so as to produce the desired results. Without a goal, without guiding constraints, freedom is chaos, hardly to be sought as a high ideal, or a context in which human life can go on. The absence of constraint is simply *not* freedom: It is chaos.

Working from an anthropological perspective—that is, real people in real societies—some kind of a balance between restraint and lack of restraint is either observed or prescribed as central to both the maintenance of continuity and the acceptance of orderly cultural change.

Keeping in mind that Malinowski wrote in the early 1940s and was deeply and personally concerned with the rise of Fascism and the fact of World War II, he saw the fact of warfare and violence as the greatest single threat to freedom, and argued that the participation in warfare, sadly, required the abrogation of a great many freedoms. He wrote with a pragmatic purpose, and it is difficult to disentangle his anthropology from his political and social philosophy. He said, "Those who attempt any definition of freedom in terms of negative categories...must be chasing an intellectual will-o'-the-wisp" (p. 59), and "To scour the universe for possibilities of freedom other than those given by the organization of human groups for the carrying out of specific purposes, and the production of desirable results is an idle philosophical pastime" (p. 95). So he set his cap for a conception of freedom which is positive and which lies within a cultural context. Much of the analysis which concerned us in the last chapter would be seen as this idle pastime—negative freedom or negative liberty.

Malinowski works from a simple definition: "Freedom can be defined as the conditions necessary and sufficient for the formation of a purpose, its translation into effective action through organized cultural instrumentalities and the full enjoyment of the results of such activity." (p. 25). This definition, of course, encompasses all of the conditions discussed in the previous chapter plus the more specific notion of "organized cultural instrumentalities" as the means to facilitate this sequence. It includes an absence of both external and internal restraints with respect to the given activity, it includes the basic capacity of optative freedom—that choices and plans can be made by human agents; it includes opportunities and resources, and access to them, and it includes reaping the consequences, described essentially in positive terms— "enjoyment of the results..." But the definition refers only to "conditions", it does not refer to actual action. Can freedom exist in a society if no one does anything with it?

If you are a continuously active planner and decider, carrying out schemes one after the other, and I am a relatively apathetic sort who occasionally makes a low-order decision and follows it through with a pretty unimaginative plan, are you more free than I? Or are we equally free because the conditions which make your sequences of action and mine equally possible pertain to us both? This is not a question Malinowski deals with, but surprisingly, he rejects Boaz's notion that a person perfectly integrated with his culture feels free (Boaz, 1940, p. 376). In at least some contexts a person perfectly integrated with his culture certainly would be acting within the terms of the definition. Malinowski rejects the validity of *feeling* free on several grounds which are characteristic of some of the weaknesses of his work: first he rejects the subjective datum of *feeling free*, because it does not fall within his "objective measurement" notion of scientific evidence; second, he rejects it because feeling free could occur under some social conditions (e.g., Nazi culture) which cannot accept, in either organization or purpose. Feeling free is no criterion of freedom, for Malinowski.

This is an awkwardness which goes through Malinowski's work. Each conception he considers is either rejected, or requires great qualification, in order that freedom does not lead to bad things. For Malinowski, the ultimate consequence of freedom must be an unalloyed good: cultural stability, security, orderly pursuit of desirable ends, tolerable degrees of innovation and change, world peace.

Similarly, Malinowski rejects Fosdick's (1939) notion that liberty involves both the availability of multiple options, and the possibility of changing from one option to another after a first has been pursued (Fosdick, 1939, p. 11). Malinowski considers this an infantile kind of whimsy which completely ignores the programmatic nature of human life and the long-term planning, pursuit, and reaping of benefits which he espouses. In the adult, this "options eternally open" is the freedom of indecision, most often seen in pathological states. And of course a definition or concept of freedom such as "...opportunity for man to make the most of himself in the fragment of the world about him" (Hamilton, 1928) is rejected because Hitler did exactly that, and tried to expand his "fragment".

So almost any definition which Malinowski rejects, he does so because it either conflicts with his own, or because it allows for some cases in which freedom leads to negative consequences. Indeed, his own definition, noted earlier, allows for a wide variety of exemplars that he would not accept. The formation of plans, the carrying through and the reaping of benefits can occur within any conceivable kind of culture, for any kind of purpose, whether it be Nazi Germany, Maoist China, or Walden II — all within the guiding constraints of the particular society which give meaning and form to human behaviour. Malinowski's point of view, further, gives scope for a variety of offensive practices: the planning of perfectly legal manipulation or exploitation of others — using the cultural instrumentalities to one's unilateral advantage. He is clear that freedom implies some efficiency and success, hence power over circumstances and over other persons. But this possibly unfortunate imbalance is hedged by reference to the fact that too much of a balance in one direction may yield the tyranny of the state or of one individual over another, while a lack of power over circumstances or persons leads to interpersonal anarchy or cultural anarchy. The subtle notion of a balance is always present, but never is there a mechanism proposed for identifying what the balance should be, or how it should be maintained.

He disposes, quite rightly, of any notion of complete negative freedom as freedom from the trammels of the body or the pressures of desire as sought in various religious systems. Almost without fail, such freedoms require extremes of discipline and training, and are not beyond culture, but are the fullest flowering of cultural traditions. Real freedom, according to Malinowski, far from being the simple and mindless absence of restraint or the picking up and laying down of alternatives "...is always an increase in control, in efficiency and in the power to dominate one's own organism and the environment" (Malinowski, 1944, p. 59).

So Malinowski leaves us with a passionate statement which attempts to be analytical, objective, scientific. He places the study of human freedom squarely in a cultural context and says that freedom can't be studied meaningfully without that context. He stands foursquare that freedom as absence of restraint is an abstract illusion and that in practice can produce nothing but the rule of anarchy and terror. It is precisely the constraints of cultural forms which make coherent action possible, and the constraints of culture which make the planning, executing, and reaping the rewards of one's behaviour possible.

## Some consequences of freedom and constraint

So it is quite possible to reconcile greater societal freedom with greater frequency of incarceration: One need only define freedom as "absence of restraint" pursued by a somewhat thoughtless populace, and greater and greater frequency of law-breaking occurs. This is followed by greater and greater incarceration. Members of society who aspire to be free and who are encouraged to think of freedom as absence of restraint are inclined to conduct their lives with greater violation of law and violation of other cultural instrumentalities which are the actual mechanisms of their freedom. This statement is consonant with Malinowski's thinking, and it is easy to see how readily this could be twisted to justify the most draconian tyranny, precisely what Malinowski abhorred.

In contrast to Malinowski's unalloyed optimism about human freedom, Muller (1963) provides a somewhat less totally optimistic view. While he points out that the first recorded use of the term or concept of freedom was in Sumer in the 24th century B.C., the kind of political freedom with which Western society seems obsessed is a very latecomer to history. Muller describes the traditional autocracies of early civilizations, and points out that "Oriental despotism" (cf. Wittfogel, 1957) provided a state of affairs which was stable and satisfactory, but had nothing to do with freedom as we understand it. Such political forms maintained China and Egypt for thousands of years as stable, yet advancing civilizations, based on the absolute authority of rulers and the provision of mystery and survival necessities for the common man. The manner in which society was organized and lived was seen as the natural, mythically ordained proper course, complete with hereditary rulers who received their power through the perfectly legitimate method of inheritance. The idea that ordinary people should attempt to change this was simply not in the air until very recent times. The abolition of slavery was more or less complete in the western world only 125 years ago, and until that time, the owning and using of slaves was thoroughly defended by philosophers, politicians and clergymen alike. That it was opposed by large numbers of people and eventually abandoned, does not negate the fact that chattel slavery was part of the positive moral order until very recently.

So, too, the idea of general civil liberty is quite new and it clearly is not the case that people have always striven for self-determination. In fact, Muller is not very optimistic that people struggle for self-determination, even now. He shares with the grand inquisitor of Dostoevsky's creation, the notion that most people still want to be surrounded by miracle, mystery and authority rather than by the demands and uncertainties they must live with as free persons. And Fromm will tell us more about that, subsequently.

The fact that we can now think of changing our world does not mean that people always could think of changes. Nor was there reason to do so. Until the later middle ages, people were as they were; they had what they had. One inherited a status and one of the divine orders was that one did not even consider altering that status. Predestination — of a civil sort rather than a religious sort — has certainly been the rule rather than the exception for thousands of years.

Many of the changes which have been wrought in the *status quo* have superficially increased "freedom", however vaguely defined, but this has been by no means an unalloyed good. For example, T. H. White (1982) points out that in the "Great Society" of the United States, slogans such as "Liberation" "Affirmative Action" and so on led to "...the centralization of federal controls on a scale never envisioned by those who dreamed the dreams..." (p. 103). The pursuit of one of the basic four freedoms — freedom from want, led to a state of affairs such that

"By 1980, 36 million Americans received their monthly Social Security checks; 22 million drew Medicaid benefits; 26 million more, Medicare; 18 million added to their budgets by food stamps; 11 million received general welfare payments; 15 million received veterans benefits; 27 million children were nourished by school lunch programs; 11 million drew from the Aid to Families with Dependent Children programs... All in all, much more than half the population of the United States depended in whole or in part on federal aid or protection" (p. 135).

Those who argue that freedom has been the primary pursuit of humankind seem to be numbered among that large number of thinkers who somehow believe that all social goods are compatible. The extensive provision for freedom from want has brought in its wake (as many who have applied for such aid can testify) endless paperwork, repeated interviews, waiting lines, humiliation, bureaucratic insensitivity, reduction to the status of being a "case", and so on. Apparently a great deal of surveillance of applicants must go on (it certainly does go on) if the freedom from want is to be assured. It is assured, obviously, at the sacrifice of a great many other freedoms — such as freedom of privacy, freedom from humiliation, freedom to live with whom one wants to live, and so on.

Throughout history, vast numbers of persons have been entirely dependent for their daily needs upon government — whether of the "Oriental despot" variety or the bureaucratic sort of modern welfare democracy. Historically, a great deal of this dependency has occurred in a context of divinely ordained order, but a good bit of it has been generated in the name of elementary freedom. We can easily see that the pursuit of one social good, such as equality, can erode another social good, such as freedom. As we have already noted, Berlin asserts "...the natural tendency of all but a very few thinkers to believe that all the things they hold good must be intimately connected, or at least compatible with, one another" (1969, p. 128). Friedenberg emphasizes this point with respect to freedom, specifically: "Men do not become freer as the society they live in becomes more equitable. The belief that they do is a confusion resulting from the fact that equality and social justice are such great goods in themselves that people in our century tend to assume that all other great goods must flow from them" (1975, p. 155).

Many of the conceptions of freedom offered in cultural context by anthropologists seem to suffer this kind of confusion. Freedom is seen as such a fundamental good that people have always striven for it — which they have not; freedom is the basis on which a society can remain stable while accepting adaptive changes — which may not be necessary; freedom, finally, must be kept in check by law and custom, lest it get out of hand and make it possible for one individual to gain excess advantage over another and disturb the balance between freedom and equality. Similarly we have conceptions of freedom which include the notion that an individual is free only when pursuing the good. This requires a massive, and ill-defined notion of what is the good. In general, it appears that the good comprises those activities which maintain the qualities of culture which have been designed as the balancers between freedom and all other social goods. This places an unwarranted burden of value judgment on the anthropologist, for as Muller points out, "We should all be able to agree that free men are not necessarily virtuous or wise" (1963, p. 272). As a matter of fact, we have reviewed viewpoints in which this agreement is clearly unattained, and virtue is inherent in freedom. With this confusion, one can argue that action which is not virtuous cannot be free; or that action which is not free cannot be virtuous; that action which is free is necessarily virtuous. This tangle is nearly hopeless and certainly does not square with the use of the notion of "free" in a contemporary western cultural context.

## Freedom and constraint for the individual

Let us see how another anthropologist attempts to sort out the tangles. Lee's (1963) general position is basically consonant with Malinowski's, but tighter, less sweeping, more personal and individually centred. Lee is by no means as certain that an individual practicing or experiencing freedom is likely to be doing something valued by someone else. She argues that freedom is only in *acting*: one can be free only by moving from *being able to* to *doing*. Freedom is in the thrust to be — in doing within the framework available. External constraints cannot prevent free expression of some kind as long as a thrust to act, and acting, occur. On the other hand, the removal of external constraints does not produce freedom if the thrust to act is not present. She distinguishes between conditions of freedom and freedom itself. The former may be affected by the presence or absence of constraints, but the latter is not.

She uses the example of Jews in Nazi concentration camps, deprived of almost every aspect of their very being. There were some who sang on the way to inevitable extermination, while others did not. Those who retained the thrust *to do* remained free, while those who had lost the will to act did not. The constraints of the situation were surely relevant to the condition of freedom, but not to the being free. This example is certainly extreme, but she goes further, describing her own life conditions — the obligations, commitments and structure of her life as home maker and as academic, as well as the structure which derives from being a member of any particular culture. She says (1963, pp. 61-63):

"In writing the preceding sentence, I observed a number of taboos and followed a number of regulations. I refrained from using obscenity or any particularly strong language. I refrained from using colloquial English. In fact I also resisted the temptation of substituting a Greek word for an English word, even though my knowledge of Greek is as good as that of English. I put in a comma where the rule of my culture posits a comma; I added an - s to "culture" by way of following the rule that more than one culture should be referred to by means of an added-s. I followed a large number of regulations pertaining to vocabulary, grammar, academic communication, etc."

* * * *

"I myself speak about slavery to time schedule. We are constrained by the date, the hour, the deadline. Yet, when I get up in the morning, how do I know what to do? How can I act freely without being ordered by someone else to do what has to be done? Actually I do act autonomously, just because I have a schedule. If I know the date and the time of day, and if I know my schedule, I know how to proceed. If it is Tuesday, November 23, I dress in time to go to teach my class at 9 o'clock. If it is Thursday, November 25, I go to my kitchen to stuff the turkey for Thanksgiving dinner. If, when I wake up, my clock says 5, I turn around and sleep some more. If it says 8, I get up. No one has to order me to get up, or to go back to sleep."

"My time schedule, the clarity of the structure within which I find myself - that is, the 'social constraint' - not only frees me from the interference of others, but actually makes it possible for me to act; that is, it furnishes me with the conditions of freedom. If I wake up after a period of amnesia and do not know whether it is October or May, twilight or dawn, Wednesday or Sunday, I am truly constrained. I am immobilized. I do not know even what to eat if I

35

am hungry. Should I have toast and orange juice, eggs and bacon, or should I have roast beef and potatoes and ice cream for desert? Perhaps I am not even entirely sure that I am hungry; that is, I am not sure that my hunger is valid and should be recognized. Should I recognize these feelings as hunger at 3:30 in the afternoon? Or should I suspect this of being the beginning of an upset stomach? Or should I simply dull the pangs with a snack?"

\* \* \* \*

"My students from non-Western societies, and even from some other Western societies, find me unbelievably constrained when they first arrive in this country. They put themselves in my place and find me intolerably coerced; but of course, they have brought their own culture with them when they have put 'themselves' in 'my' place. They look from the outside and find constraint; I from the inside find this as a way of life, a clear trail."

While her life as described is very busy, she points out that its principal features can be perceived as constraints and blockages or they can be perceived as the set of guiding structures which makes it possible for her to engage in coherent free acting. Knowledge of the time of day, having a lecture commitment, following the rules of grammar, are what make it possible for her to drive sensibly to work, to teach a class, to write a paper. Without those structures, it would not be possible to accomplish anything of social or personal value. If she did not want to do any of those things, the availability of structure within which to perform them would provide the conditions for freedom, and her action to *not* do would be freedom.

We go a bit further: Being *able to do* must entail *choosing to do* or choosing *to not do*. If one is not able, one cannot even choose *to do* or *to not do*. In such a case, there is no choice involved, only incapacity, which is clearly not freedom. Within any society or any structure, one must have accomplished the relevant socialization or acquired the requisite skills so that one is in a position to choose to do or to not do.

Illustrations from various cultures flesh this out: In order to act freely and effectively within a culture made up of enabling structures, one must appreciate these structures and have the requisite skills to interact with them. The adversarial relation between the individual and the culture, she lays to language conventions which treat the person and the environment as separate, but interacting, closed systems. She contrasts this separate but equal notion with the views embedded in Eskimo and American Indian languages in which neither the person nor the environment exist without the other. They co-constitute the world. Without the environmental and cultural context, the person *is not*, and without the engaged and experiencing person, the environment *is not*. It is not a question of the person adapting to the environment or the environment impinging on the person, it is a case of the two creating each other. Full participation in this creation is freedom.

Perhaps at a less esoteric level, she speaks of the creation of a game of tennis: two persons (or four) within a set of personal skills and a set of rules or constraints, create tennis. A game of tennis does not exist separate from the persons, nor separate from the rules, nor do the persons exist as tennis players separate from the rules and the court, nor the rules and court exist as a tennis venue without the players. So the emphasis is on human action in a context. Neither exists alone with respect to freedom.

## Some personal observations

At this point, I will add some of my own observations which complement, and in some ways contrast with, Lee's observations on her own state of affairs. As I write these lines (for the first time) I am sitting in a small flat which I have at the University of Reading. I am on Sabbatical Leave from York University. My family are in Toronto. I have a sabbatical salary, a fellowship which supplements that, and a research support grant. I have been appointed as Senior Resident of Wells Hall, where my flat is located, and my only responsibility in connection with that appointment is that I am expected to eat three evening meals a week in Hall. That is a low-order obligation, and is enforced only by the fact that the cost of those meals is included in my rent. As a matter of fact, eating meals in hall is very convenient, and while I have a kitchen of my own, it is small, dark, and ill-equipped. While I enjoy cooking at home, I have no desire to extend myself beyond tea and toast at present. I am also Visiting Professor in the Department of Psychology. In connection with that appointment, I also have no responsibilities – only the privilege of a faculty library card, and a room in the Department. I am here and have these amenities because I proposed to write a book about human freedom. I have no commitments to give a lecture or a seminar, and I need not make any; I am free to go to bed whenever I feel like it and get up whenever I feel like it. I can go out or not go out, I can write this morning, or I can read the *Times* or a heavy or light book; I can make another cup of tea or go back to bed. If I decide to stay at my typewriter, I can work on a chapter or write a letter or clean the keys. With respect to all of the conditions I have described, any outside observer would say I am maximally free: Indeed, many observers have said just that, glowing with either admiration or envy.

Then what constraints are there on my behaviour which, as Lee puts it, make human life possible? It is true that if I go to Hall for a meal, I cannot go at three o'clock in the morning. However, I do honestly believe that if I did drop into the kitchen at ten thirty in the morning or at three in the afternoon, I could get something to eat. If I do make an appearance at Hall during meal hours, there is no special dress code: I can show up in a three piece suit with collar and tie or in a two piece sweat suit with a hole in the knee. But I do feel a constraint to wear something. I cannot order the lobster thermidor and a split of champagne, because there isn't any: I take what is put on my plate. I sit on a chair, not on the table, I eat from my own plate and not from someone else's; I carry my dishes to the appropriate depository when I have finished.

If I decide to write, I must use a reasonable approximation of English syntax and grammar; if I go to the library for a book, I must have my card available; if I go for a walk, I must wear some clothes. These constraints are really minimal, some of them coming close to being the "natural" constraints which are crucial to simple survival. Some are "common curtesy" or norms of conduct, while others are the constraints inherent in carrying out whatever activity I choose.

While Lee described the apparent high degree of constraint on her life as the enabling conditions to do socially and personally valuable things, I describe the lack of constraint on my life as what makes it possible for me to do the same. But I've left something out, for I *must* make active choices all the time: there are very few outside forces, or pressures, or structures indicating what I should do, what commitments I should meet, what activities I would be wise to avoid. So whatever constraints there are on my activities are mostly self-initiated short term constraints in the service of a long-term goal. I see my principal mission as writing this book—a mission which I took on without coercion.

So on any given morning I can decide to write, and can turn that decision into action, employing the constraints of the commitment to a subject matter and the constraints of the English language. Am I able to write? That is, do I know how? Past evidence indicates that I do, so the choice to write or to not write is a meaningful one. Have I the requisite instruments, in this case a typewriter and paper, both in working order? Yes, again. Do I know the constraints of English? Apparently. So I seat myself at the desk, crank in some paper, and place hands on the keys. And nothing happens.

Am I free to write today? All appearances are that I am free—the desire, the skill, the decision, the materials. But no action. The translation from *the being able to* to *the doing* does not occur. Clearly, writing a chapter of a book is quite a different enterprise from creating a game of tennis. The difference seems to be that the writing of a chapter requires internal resources as well as external structures. The external sets of notes and references, the external constraints and supports of the machinery and the language are not enough to set guidelines for action. There is no opponent to serve the ball. It is always in my court. I have Dorothy Lee on one shoulder and Jean-Paul Sartre on the other.

Perhaps one might say that the situation is still too unconstrained, that the framework of what I want to write is not sufficiently set, that the limitations on what I can write are not clear enough to make action possible. Without further specification of the task, I am not free to act. This is a reasonable but paradoxical state of affairs: The situation does not yet have enough constraint so that I can be free. My circumstances are too unconstrained to support freedom which can result in coherent action.

Am I free to write on that Tuesday morning or am I not? It should be clear by now that a yes-no answer to such a question is quite impossible. We have already seen that there are probably no questions in this realm which can yield to such simplistic answers. Maybe we can agree fully on how to spell the word freedom, but we can't even agree on whether the terms freedom and liberty should be equivalent. Contradictions, paradoxes, complexities abound.

## Some generalizations from anthropology


Von Mering (1963) attempts to generalize an anthropological approach from the individual to culture, with the possibility of developing a scale upon which different cultures might be compared with respect to freedom. He describes a continuous dialectic between the negative (freedom from) and the positive (freedom to) aspects of freedom. There is a continuous cycle of "freeing-binding" — freeing oneself from one constraint and binding oneself by another which is repeated over and over again. This is the process of "...active individual existence..." (p. 115) of which risk-taking in preferential choices is the hallmark, and requires the anticipation of change and a future orientation.

For this dialectical process to occur, there must be:

1. some external as well as internal strife, contention or dissatisfaction;
2. a perception of incompleteness and some effort to cope with it;
3. opportunities for risk taking;
4. anticipation of change;
5. aloneness within a matrix of relationships. (p. 117)

Von Mering considers operating within this framework as the active practice of freedom, and without these components, freedom is fractional at best.

He then identifies ten value orientations which articulate with the above conditions. These orientations may be represented in individuals, groups of individuals, or may be institutionalized as cultural values. The most primitive orientation is the Emotional, Paleologic, characterized by exclusive reference to the immediate gratification of impulses. This orientation, he argues, is characteristic of psychotic states. Another is the Impulsive and Symbiotic, in which acts of all kinds are tolerable, as long as one is not caught. This is characteristic of psychopaths and sociopaths. The value orientations range through adherence to various kinds of codes of means and ends, including rigid conformity and act-repetition, and on to ethically-based value systems where the possibilities of meeting and acknowledging progressively more of the previously cited criteria for active individual existence increase.

Von Mering has described a dynamic of human freedom — a cyclic process which is never complete, which cannot be bestowed nor received, but which must be practiced. He does not make explicit, but he does imply, that the ethic-based value systems rely on principles such as perfectibility and dignity or equality, although this need not necessarily be the case. An ethic does not have to be a positive one, and organizing principles such as corruptibility, stupidity, and exploitability would serve just as well for either an individual or a culture to foster active individual existence organized around these principles.

This formulation, further, espouses a value of individualism. This is characteristic of most of the sources cited here because they arise from

Western traditions which emphasize individualism. Quite to the contrary, freedom through collectivism might well be preached, and arguments made that the power of the individual is so limited that only collective action can serve to formulate plans, carry out projects, and reap benefits. There is nothing in any of the formulations offered which could be said to require persons to act individually — indeed Von Mering's notion of aloneness, itself, is within a matrix of relationships.

It is only the existentialist position which argues that human beings are alone, inevitably and irretrievably, and that whatever they do, they do alone, regardless of the matrix within which it may be done. Malinowski's planning, executing, can just as well be collective; Lee's constraints which make life possible are, in general, collective constraints. Is freedom in individual life or in collective life or in both? These questions, as so many others, are not answerable in any simple way. To make a simple answer would be to imply that there is one useful definition of freedom; we have seen that this cannot be so.


## Summary of the anthropologists' morass


The anthropologists have made abundantly clear that for them, freedom must be considered in a concrete context, and that there are many concrete contexts in which the term is used. Anthropologists have tried, without noticeable success, to provide a single sweeping definition or concept of freedom which will encompass the phenomena arising in this great variety of contexts. They have tended to consider freedom a human social good, one which leads to both suitable stability and suitable change, all contributing to the utilization of the finest human powers. They have surely added to the positive connotations of the term. Further, there appears to be a universal agreement that freedom — to whatever extent it represents a release from or absence of constraint — must also include constraint in the form of custom or law. Simple negative freedom — freedom from — is quite insufficient for the consideration of freedom in any human society. A balance of some kind, struck by some mechanism, between restraint and lack of restraint is critical if one is going to talk about freedom among human beings.

So the anthropologists have provided a bridge from the pure abstract analyses provided by the philosophers. They have taken the notions offered in the philosophical analyses and have placed them in human action in the context of human society, and have looked at the consequences, empirically or speculatively.

While being aware of the variants of freedom one might encounter in different societies, and of the fact that some languages do not credit the western difference between causing and being caused, and that words rendered as "free" and "not free" in translation may not have anything like the same connotations in the original, they have still tried to offer broad generalizations, particulars of which might encompass the concept for all cultures. This has not been successful, so far, but our attention has been drawn to further complexities in any simple aspiration or call for freedom. We cannot even be sure what the term means when used by different members of the same culture, let alone what it means when used by members of different cultures. Indeed, it seems that the users of the term often do not even know with certainty what *they* mean when they use it.

The anthropologists have provided a variety of quite explicit definitions or descriptions of human freedom, but it is very unlikely that anyone using the term "free" in ordinary discourse would have anything so elaborate in mind. And we must be aware that the term is used in ordinary discourse, often of a very fiery kind.


### Some psychological universals


It may seem inappropriate to include the work of Eric Fromm in this chapter focussing on anthropological conceptions of freedom. Indeed, Fromm considers his work social psychology, but it is rooted in historical and cultural context, in precisely the way that the anthropologists insist any conception of freedom must be. Further, it seems to form a further bridge between the strictly anthropological treatments we have been discussing and the psychological treatments we will address subsequently.

Perhaps Fromm's *Escape from Freedom* (1941) has never been taken quite seriously. We have already found that freedom is seen by almost every writer, of whatever stripe, to be a social good, even the good upon which all other social goods arise. Freedom has been noted as a sacred and profound goal of all humankind; Gibbs (1976) asserts that "all men yearn to be free" (p. 9); Cranston (1967) tells us that Lord Acton proposed to write a history of mankind in terms of its struggle toward freedom (p. 6); Malinowski (1944) says "Freedom is an ideal which throughout human evolution has inspired the most sublime philosophies and creeds" (p. 43).

But Fromm's thesis is that humankind is torn between two conflicting needs — the need to belong, to be part of something, part of the mother, the group, the movement — and the need to be an individual. The former is historically and psychologically primary, and the second is a cultural product, quite recent in cultural evolution. Further, the first need aspires to comfort, security, certainty, while the second need may result in great individual satisfaction, but bears the seeds of nearly intolerable anxiety, uncertainty and error.

Fromm argues that prior to the decline of medieval civilization, life was, for most, however brutish and short, at least secure. There were the certainties of one's social position, however mean, the certainties of obligation to the

Church, however tyrannical, the certainties that one was what one was. The emergence of the Renaissance eroded the firm solidarity of social, economic, political and religious structure, and while providing for the appearance of the individual as a relatively free agent, cast that same free agent into a world of uncertainties. Instead of an identity which was rooted in connectedness with an existing order, each was free from prior constraints and was alone to find what opportunities there were to engage in rewarding activity. Fromm argues that there has always been, since that time, a lag between the loosing of constraints and the availability of prospects. In such a gap, the terrors of a lack of solidarity and certainty become dominant, and the possibility of a rapid retreat from freedom emerges. We have here at the cultural or societal level the kind of dialectic of freeing-bonding which Von Mering spoke of at the individual level.

Some of the doctrines which filled the gap of aloneness and uncertainty were those of the Reformation — the doctrines of Luther and Calvin. The dominance and certainties of the Catholic Church, the infallibility of Rome, the high commercialism of the indulgence were gone, and those who listened to, understood, and followed Luther received magnificently mixed messages. They could think freely, but at the same time, according to Luther, salvation was to be gained only by an act of faith, a blind reunion with God whereupon one had not only this union but a union with the others who were saved. Through the doctrines of Calvin one was predestined to be saved or not saved, and not only could one do nothing about it, one could not know to which class one belonged. However, there were some signs of being in the favoured group: success and good works which flourished. That is, if one tried good works in this world and tried to accumulate the best of this world, and were successful, it could be taken as a sign of one's impending salvation. One had little choice but to labour tirelessly with the hope that the sign would come. In this, of course is the seed of the protestant ethic and the rise of capitalism, as Weber explored in detail. Also, in this is the doctrine of the inherent and immutable inequality of men — which Fromm reminds us became a fundamental tenet of Nazism.

So the freedom bequeathed to people through the Renaissance and the Reformation provided the possibility for individuality and all of its attendant terrors. The fretful nature of this freedom gave rise to new religious formats which provided the reassurances which were lost. The cycle was repeated in the enlightenment, where the rise of scientific thinking fostered doubt of all things not scientifically provable. Faith in authority and solidarity were again lost: "Truths" became "myths", "beliefs" became "superstitions", and as humans were freed from authority, from myth, from superstition, they were faced with uncertainty and anxiety, which again must be relieved. The possibility for the endless cycle of escapes from freedom is evident, and the source of the loss of freedom resides in the individual, not in economic or political forces. There are psychological characteristics of human beings which contribute to an escape from freedom as much as other characteristics contribute to a pursuit of freedom.

Other anthropological views have stressed the necessity of a balance between freedom and control, between liberty and law, and argue that the former cannot exist without the latter: law and control are the necessary conditions for freedom in a society, just as structure and obligation are necessary conditions for freedom in an individual life. The implication is that without law, structure, custom, people would be inclined to demand and exercise untrammeled unconstraint, with the negative consequence being anarchy. Fromm's argument would say that there is a built-in, though faulty, control mechanism: that humans become terrified of the uncertainty and aloneness of excess freedom and can readily fall prey to authoritarian political, religious, economic, or social doctrines if such doctrines will provide some of the solidarity and certainty which freedom has taken from them. So the balance demanded may be built in. But the balance may be one of mindless authoritarianism which obliterates freedom.

## Some literary observations

In "Misalliance", G. B. Shaw sets the notion of freedom very neatly in the cultural context of complacent England of 1910, beginning to writhe in the presence of the emerging "new woman". At a very proper country house weekend, the following interchange between a sparkling Hypatia and an insufferably stuffy Percival takes place:

HYPATIA. Aha! Arnt you glad Ive caught you?

PERCIVAL. (illhumoredly turning away from her and coming towards the writing table) No I'm not. Confound it, what sort of girl are you? What sort of house is this? Must I throw all good manners to the winds?

HYPATIA. (following him) Do, do, do, do, do. This is the house of a respectable shopkeeper, enormously rich. This is the respectable shopkeeper's daughter, tired of good manners. (Slipping her left hand into his right) Come, handsome young man, and play with the respectable shopkeeper's daughter.

PERCIVAL. (withdrawing quickly from her touch) No, no: dont you know you mustnt go on like this with a perfect stranger?

HYPATIA. Dropped down from the sky. Dont you know that you must always go on like this when you get the chance? You must come to the top of the hill and chase me through the bracken. You may kiss me if you catch me.

PERCIVAL. I shall do nothing of the sort.

HYPATIA. Yes, you will: you cant help yourself. Come along. [She seizes his sleeve]. Fool, fool: come along. Dont you want to?

PERCIVAL. No: certainly not. I should never be forgiven if I did it.

HYPATIA. Youll never forgive yourself if you dont.

PERCIVAL. Nonsense. Youre engaged to Ben. Ben's my friend. What do you take me for?

HYPATIA. Ben's old. Ben was born old. Theyre all old here, except you and me and the man-woman or woman-man or whatever you call her that came with you. They never do anything: they only discuss whether what other people do is right. Come and give them something to discuss.

PERCIVAL. I will do nothing incorrect.

HYPATIA. Oh, dont be afraid, little boy youll get nothing but a kiss; and I'll fight like the devil to keep you from getting that. But we must play on the hill and race through the heather.

PERCIVAL. Why?

HYPATIA. Because we want to, handsome young man.

PERCIVAL. But if everybody went on in this way—

HYPATIA. How happy! oh how happy the world would be!

PERCIVAL. But the consequences may be serious.

HYPATIA. Nothing is worth doing unless the consequences may be serious. My father says so; and I'm my father's daughter.

\* \* \* \*

PERCIVAL. Look here: this is no good. You want to do what you like?

HYPATIA. Dont you!

PERCIVAL. No. Ive been too well brought up. Ive argued all through this thing; and I tell you I'm not prepared to cast off the social bond. It's like a corset: it's a support to the figure even if it does squeeze and deform it a bit. I want to be free.

HYPATIA. Well, I'm tempting you to be free.

PERCIVAL. Not at all. Freedom, my good girl, means being able to count on how other people will behave. If every man who dislikes me is to throw a handful of mud in my face, and every woman who likes me is to behave like Potiphar's wife, then I shall be a slave; the slave of uncertainty: the slave of fear: the worst of all slaveries. How would you like it if every laborer you met in the road were to make love to you? No. Give me the blessed protection of a good stiff conventionality among thoroughly well-brought up ladies and gentlemen (Shaw, 1931, pp. 626-627).*

Apparently one need not seek out exotic climes or cultures to make important anthropological observations. But to Shaw, every clime and culture was exotic.

### Retrospect and prospect

In this chapter we have considered some views of human freedom which are perhaps more problematic than those of the preceding chapter. They are more problematic because they try to take account of the human context of freedom and the conflicts and complexities which are introduced. We have looked more closely at the problems of freedom and constraint, and the argument that constraint is necessary so that freedom may be exercised. Frankly, I don't know if the matter becomes more clear or more murky, but I am sure that the matter becomes more realistic, in the sense that attempting to gain an understanding of human freedom must take into account the ways in which human persons understand freedom.

From all of this, we have seen that the issue of human freedom is complex, convoluted, even confused, in the philosophical and anthropological literature. Alternative visions abound, and they don't seem to move in a progres-

---

*spelling and punctuation as in the original.

sive fashion. Perhaps it is the case that clear thinking psychologists, with laboratory methods, can cast a clear light on the issue, and it is to these that we turn next. In Chapters 3 and 4 we will be concerned with two well-established psychological traditions of study concerning human freedom: reactance theory and attribution theory. The former addresses the robust phenomenon of individuals acting so as to reinstate options or courses of actions which they believed to be available to them when such courses of action are thwarted; the latter is concerned with the conditions under which observers and actors (in that order) perceive human behaviour to be free, and the consequences of such perceptions or attributions. Both of these research traditions are firmly rooted in traditional experimental social psychological assumptions and methodologies deriving from the natural sciences. Hence I refer to these next two chapters as the Nat Sci Variations. They contrast with the Hum Sci Variations, derived from human science assumptions and methodologies, which we will take up subsequently (cf. Westcott, 1984).

# PART II: PSYCHOLOGICAL STUDIES: The Nat Sci Variations

# 3 Reacting to Reactance

## The plan

Surely the study of psychological reactance is the longest continuous line of psychological research said to be concerned with human freedom. Originally, my plan for this chapter was simply to present an outline of this theory and a summary of the research findings within this tradition, as described in the three books which have been published on the topic. However, the more I read, the more perplexed I became about the relationships among the theory, the hypotheses, the research findings, and the concept of human freedom. More and more recourse to original sources was required in order to clarify obscurities and contradictions, and ultimately, the result is a sustained critique.

## Concept and theory: clarity and confusion

The concept of psychological reactance and experimental research based on it was introduced by

Brehm, in *A theory of psychological reactance* (1966), elaborated by Wicklund, in *Freedom and reactance* (1974), and has received its most complete statement so far by Brehm and Brehm, in *Psychological reactance: a theory of freedom and control* (1981). Brehm's initial presentation was in a relatively short monograph of some 130 pages, with 28 references, two of which had the term "freedom" in their titles, and none of which had the term "reactance". Wicklund's work is more extensive — more than 180 pages and 113 references, in which "freedom" appears 13 times and "reactance", 5 times. The most recent work has nearly 400 pages, has 445 references, of which 37 contain the word "freedom" and 34 the term "reactance".

These descriptive features give some idea of the growth and development of what is certainly the most systematic contemporary psychological research programme said to be concerned with human freedom. The work, throughout, is rooted in the methodologies of experimental social psychology, with principal emphasis on laboratory studies, although in its later phases, field studies and applications to a wide variety of daily human problems have become plentiful.

The theory addresses a robust common observation: Everyone knows that people often show resistance when efforts are made to influence their behaviour; prohibited actions or goals become more intensely sought, while goals and activities actively promoted by someone else are often rejected. This observation gives rise to the notion that people have, in their daily lives, free behaviours — behaviours that they believe they can choose among and have the requisite capacities to carry out. When the freedom to pursue any of these free behaviours is interfered with by either elimination or threat of elimination, a motivational condition, called *reactance*, develops and guides behaviour in the direction of reinstating the eliminated or threatened options. The options threatened or eliminated may be either *to do* or *not to do*: the pushy salesman threatening one's freedom to *not buy* induces reactance in the same way as the authority who prohibits an action induces reactance.

Many variables are said to influence the development of reactance: for example, the extent to which the elimination or threatened elimination appears to be personal, (as in, "you may not go on that picnic"; "you've gotta buy this car") compared with an impersonal elimination or threat, (e.g., a rainy day). Other influential variables are the importance of the freedom to the individual, the proportion of freedoms which are threatened or eliminated, and so on. A set of fairly straightforward hypotheses can be derived from the basic theory, and can be subjected to laboratory test. A very large proportion of those studies which have been published have yielded support for the hypotheses posed.[1]

The bare skeleton of a laboratory study of reactance includes assessing $S$s reactions (usually preference) toward two or more objects or activities, and

---

[1]It is important to distinguish between statistical hypotheses and psychological hypotheses (cf. Bakan, 1967). The vast bulk of hypotheses posed in reactance research are of the statistical sort, e.g., that one set of numbers will be different from another set of numbers.

telling $S$s that they will be able to choose among them. Then the opportunity for choice is threatened or eliminated by one means or another, and following this manipulation $S$s reactions to the objects or activities are assessed again. The differences between the pre-manipulation assessment and the post-manipulation assessment is the measure of reactance. As will become evident, this skeleton can be fleshed out in many ways.

Within reactance theory, the complex issue of human freedom, as it has been explored in the preceding chapters simply does not arise. Instead, the fundamental assumption is made that people frequently believe that they have options for various actions, and if they believe that they have the competence to carry out any or all of the options, they have behavioural freedom. The underlying issue of human freedom which has preoccupied the philosophers and the anthropologists is not of concern: "Whether or not a person 'really' has freedom, he can and almost certainly will believe that he has" (Brehm, 1966, p. 1). Wicklund (1974, p. 1) puts it this way: "The point of view adopted here assumes that humans often believe and act as if they are their own masters — that they can control and master their own fate. Whether or not people do in fact control their own destinies is not an immediate issue." With respect to free will, "The issue is not vital in the context of reactance theory..." (Wicklund, 1974, p. 181). Most recently, Brehm and Brehm (1981, p. 12) quote the original statement from the 1966 work, and go on to point out that behavioural freedoms addressed by reactance theory are not abstractions, but are concrete behavioural realities: If one believes that an option exists and one has the competence to pursue it, concrete behavioural freedom exists. The theory is not about the acquisition of freedom or the enhancement of freedom or the expression of freedom. It is about the defense of specific behavioural freedoms in everyday life: to do, to think, to feel, or to believe, or to refuse to do these things.

Reactance theory holds that behavioural freedoms are defined internally and subjectively (Brehm and Brehm, 1981, p. 23). They are based on knowledge or belief that options are available and that one has the competence to pursue them — again, not in general, but in the specific. Whether there is any general propensity to pursue freedom or to escape from freedom — and if there are such propensities, where they come from — are all matters that lie outside reactance theory. Reactance theory is concerned with how people react when an existing behavioural freedom is eliminated or threatened with elimination by whatever means.

There are already some conceptual difficulties which should be pointed out: Behavioural freedom is said to be based on knowledge or belief that one has options and requisite capabilities. It is also said that the beliefs must be realistic (Brehm, 1966, p. 3); but the realism of a belief is quite an indeterminate notion. In most of the studies carried out, the "realism" of a belief depends on subjects believing that an experimenter has told them the truth about what choices are available in an experimental setting. In addition, the elimination of freedoms, and more especially the threats of elimination of freedoms must be part of a belief structure, as must be the perception (belief) that an individual eliminating or threatening to eliminate a freedom has greater or lesser power to do exactly that. The concept of "belief" is often cast as "perception" — that is, an individual is "perceived" as having the intent to persuade, or the elimination of a freedom is "perceived" to be personal or impersonal. The implication of the use of "perceive" is that this perception is fairly simple, straightforward, and not unlike perceiving a flash of light. Quite to the contrary — any of these "perceptions" are complex judgments, and must be seen as complex cognitive constructions, not as simple perceptions.

For example, Brehm (1966) describes one experimental situation in which a confederate "...was a freshman with a relatively naive appearance" (p. 55). Another experimental manipulation presented a personality description, said to be written by another person as a self-description, and is described by Brehm as follows: "The self-description portrayed a typical teenager" (p. 59). It is one thing to describe a stimulus or an experimental manipulation as a 5 msec. flash of light at $x$ wave length and $y$ energy. It is quite another to describe a "stimulus" as having a "naive appearance" or being a "typical teenager", as if all respondents would conceptualize the same physical appearance or description in the same way. This is one of the problems of calling beliefs perceptions — they seem to be so simple.

We have already pointed out that behavioural freedoms are determined subjectively and internally, on the basis of knowledge, perception, or belief that options are available and that the individual has the capacities to carry out any of the available courses of action. In effect, what is said to mediate between an experimental manipulation and a behavioural outcome is *explicitly* a set of cognitions. Brehm devotes a section of his book to the phenomenology of reactance (1966, pp. 9-10) although it does not appear in the index. Here he says "While there is no assumption that a person will necessarily be aware of reactance, it should be true that when he is, he will feel an increased amount of self-direction in regard to his own behaviour" and that "If the magnitude of reactance is relatively great, the individual may be aware of hostile or aggressive feelings as well" (p. 9). Presumably, the hostility or aggressiveness would be directed toward the source of the threat or elimination of behavioural freedom. But, he further states that "...it would not be surprising to find that a person in whom reactance has been aroused would tend to deny that he was either motivated to restore freedom or upset, and he might even convince himself of this" (p. 19). But there is no indication of why one would deny the importance of an intrusion on his freedom.

While it appears that this phenomenology mediates between the S and R in question, at no point does any of the phenomenology described appear to be central, or even relevant to the experimental studies carried out. On one or two occasions (p. 46, p. 89), Brehm does report the results of some inquiry conducted with some subjects, but nowhere is this done systematically nor is it related to the formulation of reactance.

But, interestingly, *speculations* about what subjects *might have* thought or believed or perceived or felt in a particular situation abound. For example:

"Thus, it seemed possible that for some reason there was a general tendency in this experiment to see the eliminated movie as less desirable, and that this tendency overwhelmed the slight amount of reactance..." (p. 30);

"The child presumably thought that he had been victimized by an assistant ... What the child may have thought ... we do not know" (p. 49);

"There is the additional possibility that the subject thought the confederate a witless blabbermouth..." (p. 57);

"Males, we may assume, are less knowledgeable and discriminating about products in a grocery store" (p. 89).

Repeatedly there is reference to subjects *experiencing* reactance. There is consistent reference to the fact that all the important conditions giving rise to reactance are subjective: the subjective nature of behavioural freedom, the perception that a threat of elimination is present, the subjective evaluation of the importance of the particular freedom threatened or eliminated, the assessment of the relative power of the subject and the threatener, etc. In each case, it is the experimenter who establishes a set of conditions, assumes that some or all of the above subjective judgments are being made, and systematically ignores any possibility of a direct inquiry into these important conditions.

The reasons for this become clear, when we read that "...there is no necessary connection between thought and overt behaviour" (p. 91). This, despite the fact that the entire theory depends on such a connection!

Thus, we have a theory which is rooted explicitly in subjective assessment of a situation, couched in terms of beliefs, perceptions, expectations, knowledge, value, yet at no point is there assessment of any of these as central to the process of reactance. There is *speculation* about them, but no inquiry concerning them. And then we find that the elaborate set of beliefs, expectations, perceptions, and thoughts which (presumably) have been generated by experimental manipulation have no necessary connection with overt behaviours, which are the dependent variables. But surely these internal subjective elements are important. They are *said* to be important, and a lot of *speculation* about them goes on, in the form of *possible explanation*. One wonders why some direct inquiry is so consistently eschewed.

Some of these difficulties persist in the Wicklund (1974) volume, and some new ones are introduced. In his introductory description of a concrete situation involving reactance, where a boy exhibits a more radical attitude as a consequence of censorship, he includes the following central constructs: "...learns, anticipates...attitude...perceives... From the boy's standpoint...intends...feels free...feels pressure..." (p. 3). At no point in the experiments subsequently reported do we find out anything about any of these states in Ss who participate in experiments about reactance. Subsequently, Wicklund describes the occurrence of reactance as inevitable. In response to an anticipated query, he says,

"Why can't reactance lead the person not to react at all? That is, why didn't the boy freeze in his pre-existing attitude when confronted by pressure to change? Was a negativistic response necessary? The answer is quite simple. Being free means that a person can go in any of several directions (we will limit this to two directions for the present discussion), and a threat to freedom will inevitably force the individual toward one of those potential directions. But the motivational state of reactance is also directional... It impels the person to reassert the freedom, and because of this directionality the individual does not "sit still" when freedom is threatened. The rational observer, musing over the young man whose freedom has just been threatened, might think the rational response to censorship would be to maintain the original attitude — to show zero change. But the forces of reactance do not allow for this. There will always be forces moving the person in a direction opposite to the one implied by the threat" (p. 4).

From this formulation, once a threat to behavioural freedom has been made, the person so threatened is trapped. One is no longer free to hold an attitude that one formerly held or to carry out an activity in which one was about to engage. One is compelled by reactance to behave contrary to the direction of attempted influence. In effect, it appears that there is a self-contradiction, or a paradox: reactance, as the motivating force toward the re-establishment of threatened or eliminated freedom, makes it impossible for an individual to hold the evaluations or attitudes or preferences held before. One is no longer free to be, to do, or to think what one was, did, or thought before. In effect, one is enslaved by reactance — the motivating force to re-establish behavioural freedom. Neither the research nor the reasoning at this point go so far as to take the subject back to the point of earlier freedom, or forward to where, perhaps, reactance dissipates, and prior *status quo* returns.[2] It may be that one's behavioural freedom is lost forever, once threat and reactance have worked their wiles.

Wicklund goes on to describe another imagined boy who has several girls he can call up for dates, and on one occasion, when he calls one, she turns him down, saying that her social calendar is full for the next several weeks. Wicklund says, "...there is one notable effect soon after his phone call: he becomes increasingly attracted to the girl" (pp. 6-7). Wicklund goes on to describe the extent to which the young man must now pursue the girl with ever increasing fervour, in order to re-establish his behavioural freedom.

In 1974, at the time of Wicklund's writing, I was no longer part of the dating scene, but when I was, some twenty five years previous, one did not necessarily feel this compulsion. "Go whistle for it, Janie" or some more pungent instruction might well follow the telephone interchange — whether Janie ever heard it directly or not. If a friendly interrogator were to have asked me why I did not pursue Janie with ever-increasing vigour, I might well have replied with some simple notion such as, "I've got my self-respect to think of...", or I might have been more subtle, and said that "Spending my time trying to figure out how to get a date with her erodes a lot of other important behavioural freedoms — such as when to decide about going somewhere, deciding where to go, and so on. I like to have things my way, and she won't go along with that. I figure she can whistle for it. Besides, Marie is available, and she doesn't threaten any of my freedoms. As a matter of fact, she has increased them significantly ($p < .001$)."

---

[2]This issue is taken up later, and an attempt at resolution is made.

The scenario I have provided is every bit as reasonable as Wicklund's, and most readers will be able to call up their own examples of either route. The major difference between the two is that mine is based on common direct experience and reports of experience, while Wicklund's is based on a theory which claims inevitability.[3] There is an entire literature on the "playing hard to get" phenomenon and its consequences.[4]

In Wicklund's reports of research, there is a good bit less in the way of speculation about the mental events comprising reactance than in Brehm's (1966). Rather, the necessary cognitions are simply assumed to occur.

## The principal consequences of reactance

Throughout the literature, it is asserted repeatedly that the principal consequence of reactance and the major concern of the theory involves attempts at direct re-establishment of lost or threatened behavioural freedoms: "Psychological reactance is conceived as a motivational state directed toward the re-establishment of the free behaviours which have been eliminated or threatened with elimination" (Brehm, 1966, p. 9); "The central focus of reactance theory is the motivation to directly reinstate the threatened or eliminated free behaviour" (Wicklund, 1974, p. 11); "...the direct manifestation of reactance is behaviour directed toward restoring the freedom in question" (Brehm and Brehm, 1981, p. 4).

However, in addition to efforts or success in reinstating threatened or eliminated behavioural freedoms through direct action, such activities can be pursued through implication. This can be done, for example, by engaging directly in behaviours related to those prohibited or thwarted, or by encouraging or facilitating others in the practice of the prohibited behaviours or related behaviours (Brehm, 1966, pp. 10-11; Brehm and Brehm, 1981, pp. 105-107; Wicklund, 1974, pp. 76-78). Associated with a high level of reactance, we have been told, there might well be feelings of hostility and aggression against the agent who threatens or eliminates freedoms. And associated with a motivation to reinstate lost or threatened free behaviours there should be an increase in attractiveness of those behaviours (Brehm, 1966, p. 10; Brehm and Brehm, 1981, p. 4; Wicklund, 1974, p. 11).

---

[3]Remember that one experiencing reactance may very well deny it. This makes the declaration of its inevitability a tough act to follow in disputing its occurrence through reports of experience. However, since $S$s are rarely asked about their experience, acknowledgement or denial is mere speculation.
[4]Other research (Walster, Walster, Piliavin and Schmidt, 1973) indicates that reactance occurs in the "hard to get" situation only if the pursuer believes he has a prior right to a date with the "hard to get" other. But then, there are males who believe they have all kinds of prior rights with respect to females. And vice versa?

55

Here we run into another paradox: If an alternative is *in fact eliminated*, an increase in attractiveness of that option cannot but make an unpleasant or disappointing situation worse. As such, reactance motivation is clearly maladaptive. On the other hand, if a behavioural freedom is threatened, and realistic attempts can be made to reinstate it, then increased attractiveness of the option might well be supportive of efforts to reinstate freedom. There are two quite different situations here—threatened elimination and actual elimination, although Wicklund considers them to be the same, different only as a matter of degree: "The limiting case of a threat is an actual elimination of freedom, which has the greatest power to create reactance" (1974, p. 10). Thus, the paradox: When a freedom is genuinely eliminated, reactance is the highest, and we should see the greatest attraction, the most persistent efforts to accomplish the impossible re-establishment of the freedom, and the greatest aggression and hostility toward the agent which eliminated the freedom. This is a tragic state of affairs, if it persists very long, and certainly it appears maximally maladaptive.

But there are several kinds of resolutions of this paradox. First, Wicklund says (1974, p. 11) "Attraction to behaviours threatened with elimination is not conceptually different from engaging in them...". Since he has just said that true elimination is simply the limiting case of threatened elimination, and almost every theoretical statement includes "...eliminated or threatened with elimination..." we must include eliminated behaviours in the assertion. In this simple statement, he is simply wrong. *Engaging in* a behaviour and *finding it attractive* are conceptually quite different: anyone who has (and who has not?) had a fantasy about an unattainable goal knows the difference intimately. But Wicklund completes his sentence by saying, "... attraction is listed separately (from direct reassertion of freedom through behaviour) because it is a common method of ascertaining the presence of reactance, and because it is the only form of reassertion possible when events make performing the threatened behaviour impossible" (p. 11).

It would seem that if performance of the threatened behaviour is made impossible, the option is effectively eliminated, not simply threatened. It also appears that a simple increase in attractiveness cannot possibly be a method for reasserting a behavioural freedom, unless one cares to blur the distinction between availability and attractiveness. There are other realms of psychological investigation where availability and desirability are inversely correlated (e.g., decision making, risk-taking) but I believe there are none that consider an increase in desirability as a method for producing availability, nor which confuse these two so fully. Unless increases in attractiveness are so great as to drive experimental subjects into crazed primary process hallucinations of fulfillment, increases in attractiveness of eliminated behavioural freedoms simply cannot serve as an equivalent to re-establishing them by engaging in them.

But Wicklund provides further justification, in that "...it (attraction) is a common method of ascertaining the presence of reactance..." (p. 11) and in this he certainly is correct. Whether justified or not, increases in the attractiveness of threatened or eliminated options are the *principal measure* of reactance in the studies reported, *however different they may be* from the repeatedly asserted focus of the theory and from the asserted principal consequence of reactance: re-establishment of the eliminated or threatened freedom.

The justification for the use of a measure of attractiveness rather than a more direct measure of reactance goes further: Brehm has pointed out that "If the magnitude of reactance is relatively great, the individual may be aware of hostile and aggressive feelings as well" (p. 9), and he says further, and surprisingly, that reactance, i.e., motivation toward the re-establishment of one's behavioural freedoms, can be an "uncivilized" motivational state (p. 9). I say *surprisingly*, because this theory is developed in a western society, fully devoted to the support of freedoms and rights (however conceptualized), and the belief that having freedoms and defending them is one of the highest ideals of the western world. Many would argue that when a state of affairs exists in which one's freedoms can be capriciously threatened or eliminated and one can do nothing to defend or reinstate them, civilization has deteriorated.[5] However, it is due to this characterization of reactance as "uncivilized", that Brehm argues further "...it would not be surprising to find that a person in whom reactance as been aroused would tend to deny that he was either motivated to restore freedom or upset, and he might even convince himself of this" (p. 9). The implication is, alternatively, that an individual might *not* be able to convince himself of the absence of reactance, and this "...should tend to result in some awareness of one's increased motivation to have what was lost or threatened" (p. 10). He then points out that "...the studies in support of reactance theory have tended to use measures which do not require people to be uncivilized, or they have measured relatively subtle uncivilized responses" (p. 9).

At this point, I feel that my arm has been rather badly twisted and my freedom to think straight is under severe threat. I must admit that I feel somewhat uneasy while writing this: I would rather not be engaged in what is clearly an attack on the conceptual base and clarity of reactance theory. But my criticism serves me as a behavioural attempt to restore my freedom to think. I do not admit to feeling genuinely threatened, however, since I claim that I could easily ignore the above reasoning altogether. I deny any hostility directed toward the persons who have written about reactance theory, but nonetheless, I am obliged to write this many pages of negative critique when I would prefer to be writing something else. That is the nature of reactance. It occurs, I cannot be free of it, and I am not free to do what I would prefer: Inevitably, I am obliged to occupy myself with the reassertion of my freedom or with fantasies of the reassertion of freedom. And in justification I can only quote Martin Luther once again: "Here I stand... I cannot do otherwise. God help me. Amen."

---

[5]It may be that this is one example of how very special, unusual, and divorced from human life the psychological laboratory actually is. Or how dehumanizing it can be.

Further to the paradox of the increased attractiveness of threatened or eliminated options—which is certainly a well-demonstrated phenomenon—Wortman and Brehm (1975) have argued that "giving up" with respect to an eliminated option can occur, and does not result in reactance, but "...only when the individual becomes absolutely convinced that there is no way to restore the freedom" (Brehm and Brehm, 1981, p. 4). But we have already been told that maximal reactance is aroused when a freedom is eliminated altogether. It would seem that the contradiction remains: Complete elimination of a freedom arouses the greatest reactance; but when a freedom is completely eliminated there is, by definition, no possible way to restore the freedom; when an individual is convinced there is no way to restore the freedom reactance does not occur. So it appears that reactance, when greatest, does not occur.

It is possible to resolve the contradiction if one is willing to be quite convoluted and hypothesize that an experimental manipulation ("$E$'s elimination of a freedom") is not equivalent to $S$'s being convinced that a freedom has been eliminated ("$S$'s elimination of a freedom"). In effect, the elimination of freedom is suspect (to $S$), if reactance is found; or reactance is suspect if it occurs when $S$ is convinced that a freedom has been eliminated. One can easily imagine a situation where an option is gone, acknowledged to be gone, but becomes progressively more attractive.

The convoluted state of affairs I have described seems to be a situation in which the phenomenology of reactance might be of central importance. Just what do $S$s believe about the situation in which they find themselves? Since the theory initially hinges on the experience of reactance, and the resolution of the "attractiveness paradox" involves a conviction—or lack of conviction—that a freedom has indeed been eliminated, the phenomenology of $S$ seems crucial. Yet phenomenology is not even indexed in any of the three major works cited. Nor are any studies reported in which experience or phenomenology are *central* data.

Thus, as I have described it, the theoretical presentation begins with the centrality of the experience of reactance as a consequence of the perceived elimination or threatened elimination of behavioural freedoms. The existence of, the value of, the nature of the freedoms and their elimination or threat of elimination are internally or subjectively determined. But $S$s may or may not be aware of reactance, and if they are aware, they may deny its presence. But they are inevitably compelled by it, and will pursue with increased vigor the eliminated or threatened behavioural option or hold it in enhanced esteem until they finally believe the option is truly gone. Then reactance evaporates and "giving up" occurs. The central concern of the theory is attempted direct or implied restoration of behavioural freedom, and secondarily, the associated increase in attractiveness of threatened or eliminated options. This seems a fair integration of the theoretical statements made by Brehm (1966), Wicklund (1974), Wortman and Brehm (1975) and Brehm and Brehm (1981). And I have pointed out more than a few conceptual problems.

But there is more unclarity with respect to this paradoxical enhancement of attractiveness. Reactance theory is phrased in terms of behavioural freedoms — the option to engage in *various forms of behaviour*, their elimination, threatened elimination and reinstatement. Yet a great many of the studies are directed at enhanced attractiveness, *not of behaviours, but of goal objects*. It is not clear whether the *having* or *gaining* of a goal object is properly to be considered as a *behaviour*. The having of a goal object is often treated as a behaviour, but in experimental studies is often referred to as a *gift* or a *reward* or an *incentive* — hardly behaviours. These gifts or rewards are often provided as a consequence of being allowed to choose or not being allowed to choose — the latter being the removal of a behavioural freedom. But it is the attractiveness of the goal object which is enhanced, or not enhanced, rather than the method of acquiring it, namely by choice or by no-choice.

In fact, in one study, to be described below, one of the principal manipulations, said to be frustration, is not focussed on the interruption of an ongoing behavioural sequence at all. The behaviour sequence is over, and "frustration" is in the form of receiving a reward different from the one expected. So the logical status of "receiving a reward" with respect to behaviour is somewhat obscure as well. Are receiving a reward or gaining a goal object "behaviours" or "consequences of behaviours"? In what respect does the term "behavioural freedom" refer to them?

## Some illustrative studies

Now I would like to describe two studies in the reactance paradigm, both of which are said to support reactance theory, both of which have results in reasonable conformity with predictions, both of which illustrate many of the problems I have tried to illuminate above.

The first study has an interesting history. First, it was a Ph.D. dissertation (Worchel, 1971), second it was given a detailed treatment by Wicklund (1974, pp. 142-146) because it was not yet published at the time Wicklund's book went to press. Third, it was published by Worchel (1974) and subsequently was described again by Brehm and Brehm (1981, pp. 110-111). The study is reported as a comparison of the consequences of several conditions of thwarting. One of the conditions of thwarting is denial of a promised freedom to make a choice, hence the particular interest to reactance theory.

I will eventually describe the study, but first, it is worth pointing out that the author (Worchel, 1971, pp. 46-47; 1974, pp. 307-308) calls the most relevant dependent measure *aggression*, while both Wicklund (1974, p. 145), and Brehm and Brehm (1981, p. 110), call the same measure *hostility*. In all four presentations the data are the same and are from the same source. This is of some importance because Wicklund (1974) makes a considerable matter of the distinction between the two, as follows: He asserts that aggression can result from reactance, "...even though it does not serve restoration of the freedom" (1974, pp. 11-12), and he notes that this matter receives further attention later in that volume. Later in the volume (Chapter 15) he discusses aggression and hostility, and points out that *instrumental aggression* can serve the end of renewed freedom, but that one should also be aware of *angry aggression* which inflicts more injury on the target than is necessary for the accomplishment of an end, and *hostility*, which is an attitude which corresponds to aggression, but is not aggression itself. Hostility is unlikely ever to serve the end of renewed freedom. We have, then, clear conceptual distinction between instrumental aggression which may renew freedom, angry aggression, which may do the same but is also excessive, and hostility, which is an attitude which accomplishes nothing (p. 141). That this is a direct contradiction of his assertion cited above (p. 12) is only the start of a roller coaster of contradictions. But on to the study.

As described by Worchel (1974), the study was designed "...to investigate the amount of aggression resulting from three types of arbitrary thwarting: one that is seemingly random but not violating any strong expectations, one that involves a violation of expectation, one that involves an elimination of behavioural freedom " (p. 303). Male subjects were recruited for an experiment in "Motivation and Performance" and in the recruiting bulletin they were told that "One hour experimental credit — money — or a gift will be given for participation in this experiment" (p. 303).

When each subject arrived for the experiment, he (they were all male Ss) was met by E and informed that while E would not be conducting the experiment itself, he would explain what it was about. Two laboratory tasks were described, S was told that there were three different incentives being employed, and that S would receive only one of them — one hour experimental credit, five dollars cash, or a bottle of men's cologne. The subject then was asked to rate how attractive each of these three incentives was to him on an 18-point scale. As the subject was making the ratings, E looked over his shoulder to see what was being rated most attractive. Following this rating, and E's knowledge of it, S was assigned to one of three conditions:

*No Expectancy Condition*: After completing the rating form Ss were told that the assistant who would actually perform the experiment would be responsible for assigning the incentive, would explain the experimental tasks, and would then decide which object S would receive. S was apparently not told when he would know the exact nature of the incentive.

*Expectancy Condition*: After completing the rating form, Ss were told that the incentives were being assigned randomly, and that he (E) would draw from a box of envelopes to find out which incentive this particular S would receive. The "random" draw was rigged so that for each S, the incentive highest on his list was "drawn", although it was represented to be at random. S was then told twice which incentive he would receive, namely, his most preferred.

*Choice Condition*: After completing the rating form Ss were told that they were to have a free choice of whichever reward they would like. (Note that sometimes they are called incentives, sometimes rewards). They were told that they had merely to indicate to the assistant at the proper time the one they would like to have.

Following these instructions, Ss were also informed that there were three people who wanted to be research assistant for this project and that after completion of the experiment, E would like to have S fill out another form concerning S's impressions of the assistant, as an aid to E in deciding which person to hire for the position.

Then E "...penciled the subject's name on a code slip which read: Mr. ____ has been briefed as to the purpose of the experiment on Motivation and Performance." (Worchel, 1974, p. 305). However the purpose of the code slip was to inform the assistant which incentive/reward was actually to be given to S. The instructions to the assistant were not the same as the information given to the Ss. In fact, each S was *assigned* a reward by E as part of the experimental design, and each S was unilaterally given either his first, second or third preference, on a predetermined schedule, regardless of whether he had been told he could choose, told what he would receive as a result of the "random" draw, or told that it was to be decided by the assistant. This manipulation was to provide varying degrees of deviation from preference or choice of incentive for Ss in the *Choice* and *Expectancy* conditions. For the *No Choice Condition*, it was, on the face of it, exactly what (presumably) Ss expected. Once again, Ss were reminded of what they had been told about the giving of incentives or rewards: either to be assigned by the assistant, to receive his first choice as determined by the draw, or to be free to choose at the appropriate time. The assistant received the code slip, but did not look at it so as to remain uninformed of the experimental condition of the S.

A motor and verbal task were explained and carried out. At this time the assistant read the code slip and saw which incentive (reward) was to be given. When the second task was completed, the assistant said: "This completes the experiment. You will get the ___ (incentive named in the code slip). I've decided to try and (sic!) give out equal numbers of each incentive, so you'll get this one" (Worchel, 1974, p. 306).

Each subject was then given either his first, second, or third most attractive item, as dictated by the code slip, and was thanked for his participation. If the subject protested, the assistant told him this was the way he (the assistant) had decided to run the experiment, and then ushered S out of the office. We are told nothing about how many Ss protested, or to what extent. Thus the principal index of reactance is clearly ignored from the outset.

Following this possibly contentious interchange, S returned to E's office to fill out the evaluation form concerning the assistant, as well as another questionnaire concerning how enjoyable he had found the two experimental tasks. The principal dependent measure in the experiment was the Assistant Evaluation Form, on which S rated the assistant on five dimensions: (1) efficient, (2) conducts experiment smoothly, (3) pleasant manner, (4) likeable, (5) should be considered for the job. Each was rated on a 31-point scale from "very definitely yes" to "very definitely no". Question 5 was the principal focus of analysis since responses to it were considered to be a measure of aggression, *not* just hostility, since subjects believed (presumably) that they could "injure" the assistant by keeping him from being hired for a very attractive job.[6] The specific question was: "Everything considered, do you think this person would make a good experimenter and should be considered for the job?" (Worchel, 1974, p. 307). "Considered", of course, doesn't mean "Hired". The assistant was obviously being "considered", or he wouldn't have been there.

The major hypothesis was that there would be aggression (negative ratings of the assistant) shown by $S$s in the Choice Condition, inasmuch as the promise that these $S$s could choose their own reward was violated, and within that group, the most aggression would be shown by the $S$s who received their least attractive reward by the arbitrary procedure employed. Hypothesis confirmed.

The second most aggressive (negative toward assistant) group was hypothesized to be the *Expectancy Condition*, who, by "random draw" expected to receive their favored incentive, but did not necessarily receive it. Again, hypothesis confirmed, particularly when instead of the *most* favoured alternative they received the *least* favoured. Finally, the least aggressiveness (negative toward the assistant) was hypothesized to occur in the *No Expectancy Condition*, in which the conditions, as described by $E$ were essentially carried out as expected. Again, hypothesis confirmed.

But severe problems arise in the psychological interpretation of the statistical results as related to the experimental manipulations and the concepts of reactance theory. First, there is clearly a dispute as to whether the negative recommendations concerning the hiring of the assistant are to be construed as "aggression" or "hostility". Wicklund makes much of the distinction between the two, as we have pointed out, and while Worchel (1974) clearly labels his results "aggression", both Wicklund (1974, p. 145) and Brehm and Brehm (1981, p. 110) label the same data "hostility". As we have seen, hostility can do nothing to re-establish behavioural freedom, according to Wicklund, and aggression (which might do this, according to Wicklund) is seen by Worchel primarily as an opportunity to "injure" the assistant by denying a cushy job. We seem to have lost track of the central focus of reactance theory—the restablishment of behavioural freedom. Here we have data which are interpreted only as spiteful grumbling or attempts to injure.

Let it be pointed out here—and this is my own reasoning—that from the point of view of reactance theory, a negative rating of the assistant could provide far more than grumbling or an opportunity to "injure" the assistant as

---

[6]Keep in mind that aggression is supposed to be directed toward reinstating a lost freedom—clearly impossible by now. Angry aggression is supposed to do the same, with excessive vigour. Hostility is an attitude. We have no category for simple injury which is supposed to be the purpose of a negative rating.

a candidate for the job. To make a negative recommendation on this person's appointment could serve a very important function of reactance: to *reinstate behavioural freedoms through implication*. Specifically, if the assistant is seen to be a capricious eliminator of behavioural freedoms (which was the design) bucking him off to the unemployment line may very well be a way of insuring that others' behavioural freedoms are not interfered with. This possibility has not seemed to occur to reactance theorists, as it is not mentioned by Worchel, Wicklund, or Brehm and Brehm, despite the fact that it makes use of an important element of the theory.

There is another very straightforward interpretation of why $S$s thought the assistant might not be very good for the job. He simply fouled up the experiment with respect to the information $E$ had given $S$, and the more the assistant deviated from what $S$ had been led to believe — both in terms of the manner of choosing or assigning the reward and in terms of the attractiveness of the reward — the greater the foul-up. The greater the foul-up, the less should the assistant be considered for the job. This could be the reasoning of a conscientious subject who had been asked to assist the experimenter in evaluating the assistant, reactance notwithstanding. But here I go, speculating — just the way reactance experimenters speculate! They could have inquired of their $S$s, and I cannot.

There is one more feature of this study which deserves comment. Worchel says (1974, p. 303) that the subjects were 123 undergraduate males, but that the data from 9 $S$s had to be eliminated from the analyses. To find out why the nine $S$s had to be eliminated we must go back to the original (Worchel, 1971) and we find the following description: "...five subjects were suspicious... one subject failed to return to fill out the assistant rating... two subjects refused to take the incentive offered by the assistant...and one subject had been told of the experimental manipulations beforehand" (Worchel, 1971, pp. 29-30). We are not told what the five $S$s were suspicious of, but surely their suspicions were a significant part of their belief systems with regard to what was going on in the experiment — significant enough to eliminate them from the analyses. Recall that the entire existence of behavioural freedom is internally and subjectively determined, and these suspicions may be very important. Of perhaps greater importance are the other three — one who didn't return to fill out the questionnaire after the assistant had violated his expectations, and two who refused to be manipulated by the assistant's arbitrary assignment of an incentive. These $S$s, in my view, exhibited the greatest degree of reactance and the most definitive response: They re-asserted their behavioural freedom by refusing to participate further in the study. But they were eliminated from the analyses. What could be a more striking example of the method dictating the question, or the design having to reject the strongest evidence. We are also told that some subjects protested (Worchel, 1974, p. 306), but their protests were immediately dismissed, and we might well speculate that these subjects also showed great reactance — which is what they were supposed to show. We are told that the greatest number of them came from the condition which was supposed to produce the greatest reactance —

where the promised free choice was denied and they also received the least attractive "reward". One might reasonably expect, if one takes reactance theory seriously, that these *S*s would attempt to directly re-establish their opportunity to choose.

\* \* \* \* \*

Here is my speculative scenario:

*S*: "Hey! What's this, you twit? The guy downstairs said I'd get my choice!"
*E*: "This is the way I have decided to run the experiment."
*S*: "I don't want that bloody perfume. I want the five bucks!"
*E*: "Thank you for your participation."
*S*: "Where do you get off with this kind of a rip? You'll thank me for a fat lip!"

*S* stops short of violence and leaves the building providing no data on The Assistant Evaluation Form.

\* \* \* \* \*

This high reactance subject has not re-established his free choice behaviour with respect to the "reward", but he has re-established the principle of who is in charge of what he does. He certainly has reasserted his freedom to participate or not to participate. This is entirely in keeping with a reactance interpretation, because he is reasserting self direction by implication, just as those who think the assistant should not be hired are doing—only in this case he is reasserting a related behavioural freedom, that of non-participation. Data from the subjects who show the behaviour which is the *focus of interest* for reactance theory are excluded because their behaviour is a bit too heavyweight for the lightweight experimental design.

Worchel (1974) explores some alternative interpretations of the findings through speculation about the mental events possibly associated with the different groups. He describes the possible mentations of two groups of subjects—each of which had rated three alternative incentives in order of preference. The *Choice Condition S*s had been told, at length, that they would be allowed to choose whichever they wanted as a reward for their experimental participation. The *No Choice Condition S*s had been told that the experimental assistant would select which reward would be given. He says, "...subjects in the Choice condition may have given more thought to the alternatives since they *did not know* (my emphasis) which alternative they would receive" and immediately thereafter, "...it should be pointed out that subjects in the No Expectancy condition also did not know which alternative they would receive..." (p. 317). Some of the speculations about what subjects may have been thinking are reasonable, but the above is sheer nonsense. The subjects in the *Choice Condition* had already identified what they preferred, and were repeatedly told they would have a choice. That comes as close to knowing (believing) what you're going to receive as one can reasonably get. We do come to a sad state of affairs, it seems to me, when psychologists attempt to explain their findings by speculation about mental events of their subjects and will not even admit that the self-reports of subjects might be as worthwhile as their own speculations.

Despite my criticisms, it remains true that the main hypotheses of Worchel's study were "confirmed", as were several other hypotheses in the same study. But it certainly is not clear what relation the data have to the theory.

### Reactance in the market place

The second line of research to be described here in some detail is a series of field studies of consumer behaviour, first presented as a single study by Brehm (1966). The study "...was designed to threaten a shopper's freedom with both verbal and monetary inducements to buy a specific product. Whereas relatively high freedom was left to a shopper by giving him a polite request to buy the product, the freedom was threatened by instructing him that he was going to purchase the product whether he had intended to or not" (pp. 82-83). In addition to the verbal request/instruction, the shoppers were all given enough money to pay for the specific product, and in one condition, given more than enough. This last was to serve as an additional monetary threat to freedom of choice.

We have here something of a departure from the majority of reactance studies: first, it is a field study rather than a laboratory study; second, the freedom threatened is not the freedom *to do*, but rather the freedom to *forbear from doing*.

Recall that the central interest of reactance theory is the matter of free behaviours, and the consequences of their elimination or threats of elimination. Free behaviours are acts that a person could engage in realistically at a given time, but all elaboration of the theory is in the direction of taking action, i.e. *doing something* as contrasted with *refusing to do something*. No mention of forbearing or "not doing" is made at the theoretical level. *Doing* and *not doing* may be the same, psychologically, or they may not.

The specific inducements to purchase were in the form of cards passed out to shoppers in a supermarket which said: "Today, regardless of whether or not you planned to buy bread or what kind you planned to buy, please try ___ (brand name) sandwich bread, king size loaf, 25¢." Alternatively, for the high pressure condition, "please try" was replaced by "you are going to buy". In addition, on Monday each card contained a quarter, which was the price of the bread (Those were the days!), while on Tuesday, there was a quarter and a dime attached.

Elaborate care was taken to assign the cards randomly and to record the purchases made and to record comments made by customers both who accepted cards and those who rejected cards. In addition, an interviewer rotated among the check-out lines, interviewing from each line the first one whose total sales (purchases?) he could identify. We are not told why this was the selection basis, but it may have been because of hypotheses about the relationship of total buying to the compliance/reactance dimension. Approximately one-fourth of the shoppers were interviewed. The total N was approximately 199.[7]

The general results were as follows: Compared to the control (normal buying) determined in the premeasure on two days of the previous week, all groups of subjects who received inducements bought more bread of the specified brand than those in the premeasures. However, this general increase varied in magnitude from group to group. For female shoppers, the low pressure condition ("please try") with 25 cents attached produced the largest increase in bread buying, the high pressure condition ("You will buy") with 25 cents was next, and the two conditions with 35 cents the least. Some of these differences are significant and others are not, but Brehm has it both ways when he says "While the difference between the Low and High Pressure conditions might fairly easily have occurred by chance ($p > .10 < .15$), it nevertheless lends some support to our expectations that the stronger verbal inducement would arouse reactance and result in less compliance" (p. 88). It seems a bit much to conduct research with this kind of a design, making much of small differences if they are statistically significant, and then to simply state that an inability to reject the null hypothesis lends some support to our "expectations" in favour of its rejection.

However, the results were quite different for male shoppers: Men bought the most bread under the high pressure message with 35 cents appended, next most under the conditions of high pressure plus 25 cents, next was low pressure and 35 cents, lowest under the conditions of low pressure and 25 cents. These results are the *exact inverse* of what is expected from reactance theory: That as pressure mounts, reactance mounts, and erodes compliance. However the results are said to be entirely "...understandable in terms of our previous analysis" (p. 89). To make these completely contrary results understandable, it is necessary only to assume that males "...are less knowledgeable and discriminating about the products in a grocery store. It should be true, then, that the importance of the freedom to select one item rather than another would be less for males than for females. Thus, inducements to buy a given item would be less likely to threaten an important freedom for males, and males would therefore experience less reactance and would be more likely to comply" (p. 89).

In contrast, I am prepared to speculate, for example, that men might be more in the habit of being told what to buy, by their wives; or that they might be more adventuresome; or that they might recognize the good deal of having a dime left over for a beer (if bread is only a quarter, beer must be only a

---

[7]I say "approximately" because there is quite a number of discrepancies between the numbers of usable subjects in each condition listed in Table XVI (p. 87) and the Ns entered for those same conditions in the data tables XVII and XVIII (pp. 88-89).

dime) or being able to get the bread and pocket the extra money given for it in the little purses they carry. Some of these alternative interpretations are subsumable under the rubric of reactance, or the lack of it, since they all address the fact that the "reactance" manipulation was ineffective, or that the whole exercise just didn't make much difference to the male subjects.

Brehm goes on to say that the interview data add some support to the reactance interpretation. The interviewer "...used an interview schedule, but allowed himself some flexibility in order to glean maximum information" (p. 86). The interview data from the approximately 50 interviews conducted so as to glean "maximum" information take one short paragraph to present. While few interviewees expressed strong annoyance at the various inducements, there was a tendency for those who were in the high pressure conditions and did not buy the bread to report more annoyance than did those who were in the low pressure conditions and did not buy bread. Here, those who were supposed to experience reactance and respond by refusal to buy, expressed their awareness of it directly; this is neither unawareness nor denial. The most frequent view was that it was "just another advertising scheme", but three shoppers said outright that they did not like to be told what to buy. These data are not presented systematically, and it is very difficult to see how the interview data which show that only a few people took the presumed matter of threatened freedom seriously enough to express strong annoyance can be subjective evidence for the occurrence of the experience of reactance in the aggregate. But we have already pointed out repeatedly that people are not necessarily aware of the reactance experience, and if they are, they may very well deny it. While very few subjects directly reported experiencing reactance, at least they came from the right group. Overall, I have made more of the interview data than the authors have.

But finally, Brehm does acknowledge that "...while it is undoubtedly possible to construct alternative interpretations for the obtained results, it must not be forgotten that the obtained negative effects on compliance were predicted" (p. 90). This is true, of course, only if we completely discount the positive effects of pressure on compliance shown by the men, and the overall effects that *all* pressured groups bought more bread than the control.[8]

The last portion of the above quotation is of some importance to this critique. Specifically it reinforces the notion that I have put forward in various forms: that the theory of reactance is not of much importance for the experiments performed; nor are the data generated of much importance to the theory. What is important is the consistent relationship between predictions and findings, regardless of explanation.

This infatuation with covariation is described in detail by Harré (1981) as the exemplification of the positivist position, in which understanding is ex-

---

[8]An attempt to replicate this study (Gilbert, L., 1970) yielded results quite different from the original. Specifically, compliance was highest in the strong message +25¢, next highest in the mild message +35¢, next was mild message +25¢, and strong message +35¢ was lowest. No differences between males and females was found. The lowest compliance was in the condition predicted, but none of the other conditions fall into line.

hausted by two processes: description of regularities and ordering these regularities into so-called "laws". Reactance theory has exploited the former of these, but has by no means formulated "laws" in the regularization of these relationships. Experiments in reactance production do not quantify, beyond the form of "more or "less", after more than 20 years of research; when the predicted results are not obtained, as in the above study, they are then explained by speculation about variables which play no part in the original explanation of the phenomena.

The form of the theory, and the use of it, is entirely in the operationist-positivist framework: antecedents are said to give rise to consequences and the intervening variables are statements of relationships. But the canons of this kind of theory require that the intervening variables and hypothetical constructs which mediate between the antecedents and consequents are to be strictly anchored at both ends, and the concepts are to be defined by their operations. None of these criteria for theories in this format are met by reactance theory. Rather, there is a commonsense relationship between some kind of threat, thwarting, or deprivation, with the bridging described in equally commonsense experiential terms, and the outcomes predicted with greater or lesser accuracy, in terms of more or less. There is a kind of formalistic precision implied which is misleading.


### Self-generated reactance


In almost all discussions of freedom which place freedom in a context of concrete human behaviour, there is a fundamental paradox: The only way to realize or exercise freedom is to give up that very freedom. More specifically, when one has the freedom to do or to forbear from doing, one can display or exercise this freedom only by either doing or forbearing from doing. Once this is done, the freedom to do the other is gone. This is true at the decision point, of course, but one can forbear for a period of time, reserving the freedom to act in the future. Indeed, one can only preserve one's freedom by *not* making an unequivocal commitment to one option or the other. Recall that such a notion was proposed by Fosdick—that freedom consisted in retaining options, and entailed the possibility of changing one's mind repeatedly, picking things up and laying them down. Recall that Lee considered this infantile. That's as may be, but it is the only way to retain freedom, while it may be an infantile way of exercising freedom. Lee argued that freedom is in the *doing*—essentially committing oneself and abandoning options.

Reactance theory deals with this paradox by reference to the changing valuation of options as one approaches a choice among them. While it is clearly the case that the explicit choosing between options eliminates freedom—if I choose A, I eliminate my freedom to choose B—the process of deciding is one in which preferences shift progressively out of balance until one alternative is selected over another. But as preferences begin to develop, an increasing preference for alternative A begins to threaten the freedom to select alternative B. When this occurs, reactance theory predicts that the motivation to restore the behavioural freedom will become active, and efforts to restore a balance will be taken: B will become more attractive.

It should be noted, that by the time we have arrived at the study of self-imposed threats to freedom, the principal measure of reactance is change of evaluation of the alternatives. The prospect of studying the central dependent variable of reactance theory – concrete behavioural steps taken to restore the availability of threatened or lost options – has long since gone by the board. The fundamental error in equating an increase of attractiveness of an option with restoring its availability has never been questioned in reactance theory, despite its patent absurdity: wanting something is not the same as having or doing it, as has been pointed out. It is interesting that in much of decision theory (e.g., Atkinson, 1957 – a theory of decision making which reactance theorists do not entertain) the availability and desirability of options are negatively correlated – that is, as options become less available they become more desirable, and desirability does not, in that theory, affect availability, any more than changes in attractiveness can be conceived of as efforts to restore availability.

That, too, is as may be, and the reactance beat goes on. Quite a variety of studies within the reactance paradigm do, in fact, show that as one approaches a decision between alternatives, the attractiveness of the less favoured ones tends to increase. This is, of course, in conformity with the theory, although the interpretation is somewhat loose. Brehm and Brehm (1981) point out, "...in no case has there been a reliable decrease in the attractiveness of the preferred alternative..." (p. 211). They point out that the freedom to reject this favored alternative is of low importance, while assuming that the freedom to pursue the less favored alternatives is of higher importance. But again, the increase in valuation is not tantamount to restoration of availability.

Brehm and Rozen (1971) is frequently cited as a study of the effect of a high valuation of one option as a threat to freedom to select other options. It is cited three times by Wicklund (1974) and four times by Brehm and Brehm (1981). In this study, subjects were recruited for what was called a consumer research project. The importance of the accuracy of ratings was stressed, but Ss were also told that the products evaluated were not to be marketed, and the ratings would have no bearing on marketing (Brehm and Rozen, 1971, p. 263). Apparently no Ss inquired as to the point of running the study, but it seems reasonable that there may have been some doubts about the genuineness of what was going on. We are told that no such suspicions were unearthed in interviews; nor are we told anything that was unearthed.

Ss were asked to rate the *appearance* of three exotic desserts of Argentinian origin, namely quince paste, sweet potato paste with chocolate, and sweet potato paste with candied fruit. In the first session, Ss also tasted all three and then rated them on taste as well. In subsequent sessions (sessions 2-5) they again rated the appearance of the desserts, and in each session tasted one only. One group of Ss was allowed to choose which they would taste, and one group of Ss was assigned one to taste. The assignments were based on each S in the no-choice condition being yoked to an S in the choice condition; the no-choice tasters were told that the tasting assignment was determined by a pre-determined pattern.

Then, in the sixth session, the three original desserts were presented, but in addition, a fourth was also presented: either a piece of pound cake or a piece of cherry cheese cake.[9] (All of these were in one-inch cubes, which must have been pretty harrowing for a real dessert eater.) The four items were rated for attractiveness, the choice group was allowed to taste any one of the four, and the no-choice group was assigned one of the four (always the new item). Brehm and Rozen state "...our major interest was in the rating of attractiveness of the old items in the presence of the new alternative..." (p. 263), but as noted above, all were given a taste of some dessert. The no-choice Ss were all assigned the new alternative, and of the choice group (n = 27) only three selected something other than the pound cake or the cheese cake. It is interesting that these three Ss do not become special data, inasmuch as they might be the ones who exhibit what reactance theory predicts most centrally — engagement in the behaviour which is threatened with elimination, as a means of re-establishing one's behavioural freedom. Brehm and Rozen state that the data of these three Ss did not appear different from those of other subjects in the choice condition; however, it is evident that their behaviour *did differ* in important ways. The point is that the selection of an item to taste *are not data* in this study in spite of the centrality of precisely such data for the theory: the exercise of behaviour which re-establishes the behavioural freedom. This oversight is parallel to the omission of data concerning Ss who walked out of the experiment discussed earlier (Worchel, 1971, 1974): Those who *really* exhibit the central behaviour associated with reactance are ignored.

We do not know if the Ss who selected to taste something other than the new (and generally highly preferred) dessert individually actually rated the new dessert higher or not. We know only that the group, on the average, rated it higher. If this maverick group of three Ss did not rate the new dessert higher, then, of course, its presence was no threat to behavioural freedom and is irrelevant to reactance.

In any case, it is obviously central to examine the relationship between a *specific S*'s evaluations of attractiveness of the new item as related to any changes in attractiveness of the old items. Reactance is reported to be shown only in the choice condition and only for an increase in attractiveness of the most attractive old item — an increase of +.33 on a 31-point scale, which when treated statistically turns out to be significant. A change of just over 1%

---

[9]These were both found to be very attractive, by pretest, and in the experiment were found to be significantly more attractive than any of the Argentinian delicacies. So much for the gustatory adventuresomeness of experimental subjects.

in the attractiveness of an Argentinean dessert which was only moderately attractive to begin with (12.70 on a 31-point scale) can hardly be seen as a heavyweight finding regarding human freedom.

Ultimately, Ss were "...interviewed and then fully informed about the deceptions and true purpose of the study. No evidence of suspicion was uncovered in the interviews" (Brehm and Rozen, 1971, p. 263). It would also appear that no evidence of reactance was sought or uncovered either.

Finally, in the abstract of the article (Brehm and Rozen, 1971, p. 261) the authors say, with respect to their hypothesis "...old alternatives will tend to become more attractive to the extent that the individual had previously felt free to choose the old alternatives..." and "The experimental test manipulated the amount of freedom that subjects felt..." The study itself yields no evidence whatever on either of these points. There are no individual data reported (although, as I have pointed out, some might have been particularly interesting and germane); there are no direct assessments of how free anyone felt to choose anything. There are only group data and manipulations assessed by the experimenters, not by the subjects.

In addition, they conclude the abstract by saying "...changes in attraction (sic) of the old alternatives supported the idea that when an attractive, new alternative is introduced, the increase in attractiveness of old alternatives in a condition of high freedom is greater than that in a condition of low freedom in proportion to the initial attractiveness of the old alternative" (p. 261). This simply isn't so, as indicated by Table 1, p. 264. In fact, there is only *one* condition in which an old alternative becomes more attractive, and it is only the most attractive of the old alternatives under the high freedom condition which enjoys this fate. In all other conditions, the old alternatives become *less* attractive, and the greatest decrease in attractiveness occurs for the least attractive old alternative in the high freedom condition.

## Overview

In this discussion of reactance theory, I have raised what I consider very serious questions about the conceptualization of the phenomenon, about the relationship of the conceptualization to both the independent and dependent variables in the experiments, and finally about whether the entire realm of research has much to do with human freedom in any important way. More specifically, while the notion of reactance arises from very common experience of which almost anyone can give multiple examples, the severe limitations imposed by bringing the phenomenon into the laboratory, by mistakenly equating "wanting" with "doing" and the need to rule out so-called "uncivilized" behaviour have all tended to trivialize the findings. It appears that when the central predictions of the theory come to pass, the data pertaining

71

to them are ignored, unless the predictions have been explicitly made for that experiment.

In addition, while it is perfectly explicit that behavioural freedom itself, as well as all of the other theoretical concepts, are said to be subjectively determined, almost no systematic effort is made to assess the subjective state of $S$s with respect to any of them. The exceptions to this are the assessment of attractiveness of various items which become baselines for assessing change in attractiveness, which are the most common dependent variables. So the central variables of the theory are never assessed, and indeed the central dependent variable — overt efforts to restore behavioural freedom — has been displaced by changes in attractiveness, misconstrued as an equivalent.

Inasmuch as almost all human behaviour involves daily choices, some trivial, some important — most of them far more important than those provided in the laboratory — it would seem that a vast array of human activity would be affected by reactance. It would appear that the oppositional forces involved in decision making and choosing might be better dealt with through a more broadly based general theory of motivation, such as Solomon's opponent process theory (Solomon, 1980).

Finally, does the study of reactance have much bearing on human freedom in a meaningful human context? Certainly the formulation does, rooted as it is in very common observation, but the research findings have been degraded so that they have become repeated demonstrations of a different common observation, tightly controlled and trivial changes in attractiveness. As Gergen (1978) puts it, rigour is substituted for realism and statistical significance is mistaken for psychological significance.

With the strength and reasonableness of the initial formulation, it seems entirely possible that evidence could be gathered which would support the formulation. But it does not seem possible as long as the research is limited to the positivist-experimental-laboratory mode. Investigation of what people ($S$s, if you prefer) actually think and feel in reasonably important situations and how they respond to these thinkings and feelings is necessary if the studies are to have any noticeable relation to the common real-life observations which give rise to the questions in the first place.

The purpose of this detailed reporting on reactance theory has been threefold: first, to present what I have described as the longest single tradition of systematic research in the psychological literature, said to be concerned with human freedom; second, to illuminate and comment on some fundamental conceptual unclarities and confusions; third, to point out the elaborate accumulations of both laboratory and field findings which have been generated by this research.

In particular, I found fault with the stated contents of the theory and the relationship of these contents to both manipulations and outcome variables, and the fact that the theory hinges on a great many subjective variables which show up as explanatory only in the speculative sense, and never show up as central data. It must be noted that subjective outcomes in the sense of changed valuation of goal objects are *outcomes*, not *processes*, and we have no direct evidence whatsoever that freedom or threats to freedom, in any meaningful human sense, played any part in the findings. We have only the experimenters' surmise that this is what the manipulations represented to the subjects.

It may be that direct inquiry could be carried out. There is every reason to think so, except for the theoretical statement that subjects may not be aware of any of the processes of reactance, and if they are aware, they are likely to deny it. This, perhaps makes it quite impossible for the theory, as such, to be put to test. On the other hand, if the purely positivist stance is maintained — and there are many who argue that it has failed utterly in psychology — then the hollow shell of disembodied antecedents and consequents remains to be explained.

There is a further possibility. Almost all the studies reported have been carried out in the United States, and mostly with university students; the manipulations have been handled so that "uncivilized" behaviour was not demanded of subjects, nor even allowed. As we noted in one of the studies earlier, subjects who did actively reassert their independence of being manipulated by experimenters did not complete the experiments, and were eliminated from the data. We also noted that in a field study using ordinary citizens, most of them hardly noticed that anything was going on. Thus, the social and cultural context of general freedom, as represented by the United States, may allow for tiny erosions of trivial freedoms to pass unnoticed without producing anything like the kind of direct re-establishment of behavioural freedom predicted by the theory, and much more genuine threats to freedom must be utilized if the phenomenology of reactance, so important to the theory, can be observed. However, the failure to explore *any* phenomenology systematically, or to even attend to it, does not lead the reader to believe the theory is taken very seriously as explanatory in any sense.

# 4 Attributed Freedom, Perceived Freedom, Choice, and Self Control

## The plan

In this chapter I will describe some of the conditions under which observers attribute freedom to others, or perceive freedom in the actions of others. This is important for the general attribution process, inasmuch as when actors are perceived as free in their actions, the origins of those actions are seen to be personal dispositions, rather than particular consequences of environmental pressures. I will describe how this line of research has evolved into the study of perceived choice, which may be quite a different issue. The conditions under which people attribute freedom to their own actions will be considered, and we will see that there is some, but not a great deal, of study of people's experiences of themselves as having choice and making decisions. Throughout, as you might imagine, I am critical of the extent to which theorizing refers to mental events such as perceptions and beliefs, while the research rarely addresses these processes directly.

## General issues

A second line of research concerning freedom within the mainstream of experimental social psychology was crystallized by Steiner (1970) in his paper "Perceived freedom" in Berkowitz's Volume X of *Advances in experimental social psychology*. This chapter was a signal event in the psychological study of freedom for two reasons: First, it brought together a great variety of research which could be conceptualized within the respectable framework of attribution theory, and second, it appeared in a very prestigious publication. In it, there was almost no reference at all to the research on freedom which had gone on under the aegis of reactance theory. This observation merely indicates that the two traditions are quite separate, and although Steiner (1970) referred to Brehm (1966), it was at a very general level.

Steiner's approach was to analyze the components of the conditions under which actors are perceived by observers to be free in their actions, and to explore the consequences of such perceptions for the attribution of attitudes and dispositions. This is quite a different enterprise from the study of the consequences of restricted choices—the focus of reactance theory. But before proceeding with a discussion of perceived or attributed freedom, a few words are required concerning the general concerns of attribution theory.

In my view, the best single review of attribution theory is by Harris and Harvey (1981). This particular review benefits from an historical orientation tracing the developments and distortions of the theory over a span of more than twenty years. Attribution theory has its origins in the work of Heider (1958), or even earlier in the work of Heider (1944) or Heider and Simmel (1944). The point of this early work was that naive observers attribute *motivations* and *causations* to events which they observe, and in effect, explain or make intelligible the behaviour of both animate and inanimate objects in these terms.

Heider's most cited examples are the showing of animated films of geometrical figures moving about: "...a large triangle, a small triangle, a circle, and the outline of a square with a moveable side (which opened and closed)" (Harris and Harvey, 1981, p. 61). These figures moved about in sequence and simultaneously, and human-like explanations of social situations were attributed to the patterns of interaction by observers. Complex patterns of movement were organized into conceptualized purposive behaviours—such as "looking for something", "chasing", "running away" and so on. In addition, there were causal sequences reported, so that individual persons (objects) were seen as the originators of actions. Thus, intentions, motivations, originations were attributed to what were actually merely moving geometric figures.

It is not difficult to extend this concern to the observation of actual human figures in fairly explicit or enigmatic social interaction, and to the study of attributed motivations, intentions, praise, blame, responsibility, dispositions, and coercion. When faced with a real human person, $A$, acting in a specific way, an observer typically will attempt to determine what caused $A$ to do as he or she did. The observer will often look for pressures from the environment, as the "cause" of the behaviour. If the observer finds nothing in the environment, the causes will be sought in the actor. Ultimately, some set of causes will be attributed to the event, and the causes will be partitioned between $A$ and the environment. The ways in which these attributed causes are partitioned will lead to beliefs about $A$'s dispositions as stable contributors to behaviour, beliefs about the forces in the environment as compelling, and beliefs about $A$'s susceptibility to environmental influence. Through this kind of a matrix of attributed causation, observers come to their understanding (accurate or inaccurate) about the causation of social interactions. In turn, an observer's understanding of the causation of another's behaviour is at least one important influence determining subsequent behaviour of the observer toward the observed. In effect, attribution theory is concerned with the ways in which observers explain, in a causal fashion, the behaviour of others whom they might be observing, or with whom they may be in actual interaction.

It is not our purpose here to delve deeply into attribution theory, but merely to set the stage for a discussion of the attribution of freedom. The question, simply put, is "under what conditions do observers attribute freedom to the actions of those they observe?" The question can easily be made more complicated, such as including "under what conditions do persons attribute freedom to their own actions?" and additionally, "what are the consequences of attributing freedom to one's own actions or to someone else's actions?"

### Perceived freedom

We now return to Steiner's analysis of these problems. Steiner's chapter was titled "Perceived freedom" and I have been talking about attribution. It appears that the terms "perceived" and "attributed" are essentially interchangeable in these discussions. There is a bit of a problem here, because we generally understand the perception of something to be pretty much veridical — that is, a reasonably accurate report of something "out there". Attribution, on the other hand, is much more of a judgmental, inferential, process, often based on complex chancy information. But the two are used interchangeably in spite of their quite different implications. deCharms (1968, 1979) has been consistently critical of the use of a "perceptual model" for these complex inferential and judgmental events, but the practice continues.

Steiner argued that there were two conceptually different notions of freedom to which observers might be sensitive: *decision freedom*, and *outcome freedom*. *Decision freedom* is the extent to which a choice between or among alternatives is not coerced by the characteristics of the alternatives. For example, low decision freedom is represented in a choice between a new Mercedes and a dish of rice pudding. This choice is coerced by the vast difference in value for most persons. The differential in favour of the Mercedes would be modified, of course, if the person choosing were starving and already had a garage full of Mercedes, Volvos, and Cadillacs. At the other extreme, a choice between two identical Mercedes or between two identical dishes of rice pudding would have maximum decision freedom because the negligible difference between the alternatives has no coercive power. A choice between them would depend entirely on the person choosing. While this distinction holds up logically, it is not entirely linear, since under the condition of identical alternatives, the action of the chooser may become essentially random (cf. Westcott, 1977, p. 256). Steiner, and subsequent writers have said that maximum decision freedom exists when alternatives are very similar, but not identical.

*Outcome freedom*, on the other hand, is concerned with the probability that the alternatives in question can actually be obtained. As the probabilities of attaining the various alternatives increases, outcome freedom increases; as the individual's perception of his or her resources and the costs of pursuing an outcome proceed toward a favorable balance—that is, the payoff is high and the cost low—outcome freedom rises.

In combination, high decision freedom where alternatives are approximately equal in value, and high outcome freedom—where alternatives are readily and about equally attainable—produces the highest levels of perceived freedom of action. This is the theoretical pure case, but there are a few constraints: First, when alternatives are seen as identical, decision is not at issue, and although this should be the highest decision freedom level if the relationship were linear, in fact decision freedom drops off to near zero with identical alternatives. Second, when the alternatives are very similar, but neither is attractive, decision freedom becomes trivial. Third, as in decision theory, there is an interaction between the attractiveness of an alternative and its availability: as the probability of attainment (outcome freedom) decreases, the attractiveness of an alternative increases.[1] The two major variables—outcome freedom and decision freedom are confounded. At the time of Steiner's (1970) writing he was perfectly explicit that the theory had plenty of bugs still in it, and that the data available were still quite sketchy, but he did add a considerable increment to the respectability of the study of human freedom within experimental social psychology.

The study of perceived freedom was related to general concerns of attribution theory in that when an individual engages in behaviour which is perceived

---

[1]This has been the repeated finding in reactance studies: threatened alternatives increase in value; in fact this has been one of the commonest research formats in reactance.

by an observer to be free, the observer is more likely to attribute some stable explanatory motivational disposition to the actor. Further, an observer is likely to make other evaluative judgments, such as allocating credit or blame for the consequences of the action taken. So whether or not—or to what degree—an observer perceives freedom in the actions of an actor has wide-ranging consequences for the attribution process.

## Some implications

At this point it should be made clear that the primary concern of the study of perceived freedom is precisely this—the effects of perceived freedom on the attribution process. The primary concern is not with an elucidation of human freedom, although there are many findings within studies of perceived freedom which are relevant to such an effort.

From the point of view of ethics and morality, we can examine the conditions under which observers attribute responsibility to others who act. These are the circumstances which are played out often in a courtroom—a jury being fed information which leads ultimately to a decision as to whether an accused was or is responsible for his or her action. The information provided, the way it is provided, as well as the inferential and attributional propensities of the jury have an impact on whether an accused is perceived to have acted freely or not. At the extreme, the attribution of freedom is the concern of an insanity defense (or the lack of it) and in such cases "expert" testimony is generally introduced. However, in cases where a defense based on "coercion" or "duress" is employed, such expert testimony may not be employed, and the more common everyday processes of attribution come into play. So the ways in which juries make attributions of freedom can be related to the conceptions of freedom which influence the practice of jurisprudence.

The conditions under which observers perceive freedom in the actions of others were summarized by Steiner in his 1970 chapter, and subsequently further findings and some data on the attribution of freedom to the self were summarized by Harvey (1976). For example, Steiner reported several studies (Steiner and Field, 1960; Jones and Harris, 1967; Jones, Davis, and Gergen, 1961) which showed that observers tend to believe that an individual is acting freely and revealing true personal dispositions when exhibiting behaviour which is at variance with a role which is explicitly expected (Steiner, 1970, p. 211). When an individual exhibits behaviour which is in conformity with role expectations, such behaviour is uninformative with respect to "true" dispositions. In the latter case, the role expectations are seen to be the principal determinant of the behaviour, whereas in the violation of role expectations, the individual is seen to be principal determinant. Therefore, it is reasonable to conclude that behaviour which violates known role expectations tends to be seen as more free than behaviour which is in conformity with such expectations.

When an individual behaves in such a way as to incur costs which do not appear to be necessary, such behaviour is seen to be freely chosen; an individual who is believed to be skilled and competent, but who is obstructionistic in a group enterprise is seen to be acting freely in this negative behaviour, and is blamed more than an individual who is merely thought to be an incompetent blunderer who accidentally obstructs (Steiner, 1970, p. 213). The other side of the coin is also represented—that helpful behaviours are appreciated more when they are seen to be freely given. However, we are more concerned here with the conditions under which they are perceived to be freely given than we are with how much they are appreciated.

Favours are seen to be freely given when they incur a cost, or are given in spite of evident restraints against giving them. An interesting dilemma arises at this point, for it is also reported that individuals receiving the benefits of a freely given and costly favour feel more indebted to the donor than do individuals who receive a favour which is demanded by the situation. Steiner cites a contention by Gouldner (1960), and evidence from Tesser, Gatewood, and Driver (1968) to this effect. The dilemma is that feeling appreciation and indebtedness for the bestowal of a favour is a serious erosion of behavioural freedom as described in the reactance literature. In effect, perceiving another to have acted freely toward one in a favourable way erodes one's own freedom. We should hardly expect this state of affairs to be appreciated. In fact, we can go to Nietzsche who said "Gratitude is hatred in a mask" (Gardner 1982, p. 32).

Steiner is quite explicit that much of the data cited in his review concerning the attribution of freedom is inferential. Little attention is paid, in most of the studies, to the actual cognitions and beliefs held by the subjects in the studies: "Many of the studies mentioned...provide only inferential evidence concerning the attribution process. They indicate that the affective reactions evoked by an actor's harmful or helpful behaviours depend on the amount of freedom the actor is *presumed* to have" (1970, p. 214) (Emphasis added).


### Attribution of freedom to the self


When we turn to the attribution of freedom to the self, Steiner (1970) asserted that there were far fewer data available than for the study of attribution to others. Bem (1965) had contended that the processes of reaching conclusions about the self were essentially the same as those used for reaching conclusions about others—e.g., observing oneself and deducing that one's consistent behaviours reveal dispositions. We would then expect that one would attribute freedom to oneself when acting contrary to role expectations, when violating norms, when doing things that are unnecessary and costly, when making choices between nearly equal alternatives and when having the skills and resources to maximize outcome freedom.

It is important here to make some conceptual distinctions, because we are again beginning to talk about the behaving human being as if he or she were a somewhat reflective automaton. We need to distinguish between attributing freedom to oneself *after the fact* as a result of observing what one did in a situation and attributing freedom to oneself *before the fact* by virtue of assessing the state of one's resources, the constraints of the situation, the equivalence of alternatives, one's intentions, and so on.

We usually think we know more about ourselves than we know about others, and than others know about us. This is particularly true with respect to what we (or others) *intend*. We are most likely to explain our own behaviour in terms of determining antecedent *causes* when we are not prepared to take responsibility for it and when we do not consider it free: "...the devil made me do it...". We are likely to explain our own behaviour in terms of *intentions* when we believe we are acting freely, whether or not we are willing to assume responsibility (either praise or blame) for the consequences: "I was trying to...", or if some negative consequence ensues, "I was *only* trying to...".

There are surely situations in which I may say that I must have done something freely and voluntarily because I can't think of any compelling circumstances: "It seemed like a good idea at the time...". There are just as surely circumstances under which I can identify appropriately compelling conditions which determined my behaviour, quite separate from anything I wanted to do: "How the hell could I get out of going to the boss's party...?" To assume that there is only one set of variables controlling whether one sees oneself or others as behaving freely or that "behaving freely" always has the same features is sheer nonsense.

Shotter (1981) has taken attribution theory to task for a narrow view: a view of attribution as having to do with identifying the *causes* of behaviour of oneself or of another person. Within attribution theory *causes* are generally seen in the positivistic, antecedent/consequent, material or efficient cause format. Shotter argues that while observers sometimes seek or generate explanations of this kind, they are more likely to seek explanations in terms of meanings, intentions, or reasons: causes which are more nearly in the format of formal causes and final causes. Rychlak (1975, 1977, 1980) has consistently argued that teleological explanation in the form of final causation is the appropriate model within which to talk about human behaviour.

## A second review

Only a few years later, Harvey (1976) provided another integrative review, this one titled "Attribution of freedom," in contrast to Steiner's "Perceived Freedom". Steiner had begun his review with a brief discussion of the status of the notion of freedom in psychology and had pointed out that whatever the

81

arguments for the reality or unreality of freedom, people often believe that they enjoy freedom — which he defined from Webster as "exemption from necessity in choice and action" (Steiner, 1970, p. 188). Harvey began his review with a quotation from Tolstoy, and referred to the "... unwavering consciousness of freedom ..." as a real phenomenon in human experience (1976, p. 73).

These two references represent quite different approaches: One is concerned with a belief that people can be exempt from necessity in choice and action — in effect, a belief in ontological freedom, or optative freedom — a belief in a real state of affairs. The second is concerned with a phenomenal experience of freedom. Steiner did not belabour his point and went directly to his description of the theoretical conditions under which people may be given to this general belief in freedom, and to the empirical evidence supporting such beliefs. In contrast, Harvey launches into a farrago of conceptual blurring and confusion. He leaps from Tolstoy's description of humans' experience of themselves to the notion of attribution of freedom to the perception of freedom, and treats the reader (in a footnote p. 74) to an explicit refusal to deal with any distinctions among the concepts of perceived freedom, perceived choice, volition, free will, etc. While he says it seems possible (and perhaps useful) to make such distinctions, no such distinctions will be made in his paper, and that all the terms will be considered as referring in a rather general fashion to the same phenomenological state. He cites Harvey, Harris and Barnes (1975) as indicating that subjects in psychological experiments do not appear to distinguish between at least the first two (perceived freedom and perceived choice) but there is no evidence in that 1975 paper to lead to any such conclusion. It is true that the data presented in that study show essentially the same values in response to a question about "how free an individual was to refuse..." and "how much choice an individual had in doing the job...", but it is a very tenuous leap to say that the *subjects* themselves do not distinguish between them — especially when the data are gathered on a single 11-point scale of "how much". This is an example of very limited data being used to characterize an entire conceptual structure, and a confusion between statistical differences and conceptual differences.

In addition, while these various terms are said to refer to a "phenomenological state" there is almost no investigation of any phenomenological states. Here, as we noted in reactance theory research, phenomenological or experiential states are said to be crucially important, but they almost never come under any direct and sustained inquiry. Typically, they are assumed to be perfectly correlated with experimental manipulations, which, of course, is a very shaky assumption.

Harvey provides a list of the conditions which should, theoretically, give rise to high subjective freedom. These are based primarily on Kelley's work (1967). It must be kept in mind that there may be several kinds of phenomena embedded in this one notion of "high subjective freedom", and they are worth exploring before looking to the conditions which are said to give rise to them.

Subjective freedom may be "self-attributed" freedom—a situation in which one assesses the circumstances of one's action and determines that one "is free" to one extent or another. This, too, may have many varieties: one may perceive an absence of restraints, a plethora of resources, a great variety of alternatives, or one may have a clear image of what is right and what one ought to do. Each of these (and other states of affairs) have been described in Chapter 1 and Chapter 2 as conditions contributing to an ontological state of freedom. One may appraise the world about one and come to the conclusion that one is free through a variety of different conditions.

On the other hand, subjective freedom may refer to experience rather than to attribution—one can *feel* free without necessarily meeting any or all criterial conditions which contribute to ontological freedom. Harvey has not distinguished between self-attribution of ontological freedom and reports of experienced freedom. We will attempt to do that in a later chapter, and will also present data showing that people do distinguish between them.

Harvey's list of conditions which are thought to contribute to high subjective freedom follows, obscure though the referent may be:

"1. When the constraints against a person's leaving a situation (of neutral or negative attractiveness) are low, and the person stays;

2. When the legitimate forces producing compliance are low and the person complies;

3. When alternatives are equal in attractiveness, and the person chooses one;

4. When the amount of pressure to make a choice between equally attractive alternatives is low, and the person makes a choice;

5. When the strength of illegitimate forces (to comply) is high, and the person complies;

6. When much conscious consideration is given to the choice;

7. When much uncertainty, conflict, and the potentiality of alternative responses exist in making the choice" (Harvey, 1976, p. 77).

There is clearly some redundancy in the list, and there are few data which respond directly to these as hypotheses. Some of the above conditions are thought to contribute to self-attribution of freedom, and possibly to the attribution of freedom to others, as well, and some are thought to influence feeling free. The distinction between self-attribution and experiential reports is made in only a very casual fashion.

Only a few of the hypotheses had been investigated at the time of Harvey's writing, and the evidence on these seems rather tangential to the notion of self-attributed freedom. For example, Harvey and Johnston (1973) and Jellison and Harvey (1973) presented subjects with descriptions of football teams and had the subjects choose between them.[2] One pair of teams was quite evenly matched with respect to their different strengths and weaknesses, while the other pair of teams was seriously mismatched. After choosing, subjects were asked to rate the extent to which they felt they had a choice between the two teams. Results showed that a greater sense of choice was reported when the teams were more nearly matched and some greater con-

---

[2] It is not clear in the report, but presumably the choice was as to which team would win a game; subjects were not given to believe that they could walk home with the franchise.

sideration had to be given to selecting a winner. This seems reasonable enough — that one should feel one has made a choice when there is some deliberation and some choosing to be done. However, to represent a sense of choice as a "feeling of control", "a self-attribution of freedom", or "a feeling of freedom" is to engage in conceptual mayhem. No questions about freedom were even asked of the subjects.

The present author investigated a similar problem in a more detailed fashion (Westcott, 1977). In an investigation of the conditions which lead to the experience of will, choices were posed, employing equivalences and differences, and several different varieties of choice were revealed by detailed interviewing. Informants reported "rational decision" and the experience of free will after examining all sides of a question, including one's own preferences, weighing the evidence in detail, reaching tentative conclusions, re-evaluating and ultimately reaching a final conclusion. Alternatively, free will was experienced in a "snap decision" when one feature of a choice situation stood out and none of the laborious consideration took place. In the face of a choice between two identical items the result was a "random choice" with no relevance to will, and when alternatives were grossly different in value, it was called "...no contest...no choice at all...", and experienced will had nothing to do with it. This last was called "coerced choice" (p. 256).

Steiner (1979) also reported a variety of forms of choice. Choices are not all alike, and a feeling of choice is not necessarily to be understood as a self-attribution of freedom, or perceived freedom, or as an example of the definition which Kelley adopted from Brehm and Cohen — "perceived freedom as the feeling of control over one's own behaviour" (Harvey, 1976, p. 76). It seems inappropriate to ask subjects questions about their feelings of choice, and to immediately translate the answers into a different set of terms. Why not ask them about feelings of control over their own behaviour if that is the format in which the answers are to be interpreted? Why not ask them about the extent of the freedom or volition felt under different conditions, rather than inferring these from responses to different questions?

The criticism leveled at reactance theory for never directly attempting to investigate the fundamental mediating experience of reactance itself, and to rely on dependent measures as the basis for inferring its existence applies here to attribution theory. The principal dependent variable is said to be self-attribution of freedom, experienced volition, free will, feeling of choice, or of control — often blurred one into the other — and it is a very rare event when these experiential conditions are examined in any detail, or even assessed superficially. We will return to studies of choice later in this chapter.


### Other selected studies


Several studies can be described which did make direct inquiry into subjects' individual sense of freedom. (I use the general term "sense" because the specific questions asked sometimes included the phrase "feel free" sometimes "was free", sometimes both.) One study used reinforcements in a "learning" task and one used punishments in a similar design. Harvey, Harris and Barnes (1975) employed a situation in which Ss were randomly assigned to be either *teacher* or *observer of the teacher* in a task where the teacher was to influence a (confederate) "pupil" in the learning of word pairs by the administration of mild electric shocks. The effect of these shocks on the pupil was reported to the teacher and to the observer on a "distress meter", ostensibly connected to GSR electrodes attached to the pupil. Actually, the pupil manipulated the meter directly by means of a rheostat, and two conditions were run: one where the distress reported was moderate, and the other where the distress reported was severe. The confederate "learned" on a regular, predetermined schedule.

The dependent variables were how free the teacher felt he was himself to refuse to continue the experiment, and how free the observer felt the teacher was to refuse. Questions were also asked concerning how much responsibility for the distress of the pupil the teacher attributed to himself and how much the observer attributed to the teacher. In the moderate distress condition there was no difference between the teacher and the observer in terms of the responsibility attributed, but from this baseline, the high distress condition increased the attribution of responsibility by the observer to the teacher and decreased the attribution of responsibility by the teacher to himself.

With respect to the attribution of freedom to discontinue the experiment, similar results were obtained, except that the observer always attributed more freedom to discontinue to the teacher than the teacher attributed to himself. As the distress condition changed from moderate to severe the observer attributed even more freedom to the teacher, while the teacher attributed even less to himself.

In their discussion, Harvey, Harris and Barnes state: "The results of this study provide generally strong support for the hypothesis that an observer would attribute more responsibility and freedom to an actor the more severe the consequences of his behaviour, but that an actor would attribute less responsibility and freedom to himself the more severe the consequences of his behaviour" (1975, p. 26). In this study "responsibility" was meant as "accountability" and the authors discuss their results within the framework of self-justification following an action. While their findings are fully in line with much of our traditional legal practice of prosecution and defence, they are contrary to our notions of the inverse relationship between responsibility and freedom when the former is taken as "obligation" and the latter as "lack of obligation" (cf. Benn and Weinstein, 1974). It is also evident that self-attributed freedom in the context of self-justification and accountability is quite different from experienced freedom in, for example, choice among attractive alternatives.

Gurwitz and Panciera (1975) have reported a similar study in which Ss were randomly assigned to genuine roles of teacher or pupil in an anagram-solving task, and rewards in the form of small amounts of money were given or taken away by the teacher for success or failure on the part of the pupil. The problem was to investigate the extent to which pupils and teachers made different attributions of freedom to themselves and to their partners under the same experimental conditions. In each case, participants attributed more freedom to the other than to the self. Gurwitz and Panciera note, in their introduction, "...we became aware of an interesting methodological issue relevant to any study measuring estimates of a concept such as freedom. Freedom is an abstract term that can be inferred from a variety of circumstances. A person can be perceived as having a great deal of freedom in one dimension but very little on another. This suggests that a subject's response to a question about perceived freedom is likely to depend on the precise nature of the question he is asked" (p. 532).

It is interesting to note that while Harvey, Harris, and Barnes (1975, p. 24) report only the general intent of their questions, Gurwitz and Panciera (1975, p. 534) list the precise questions asked. Their results essentially support their hypotheses, but Gurwitz and Panciera point out that "The data from the present experiment suggest that when measuring an abstract and complex concept such as perceived freedom one should carefully design multiple dependent measures that refer to different aspects of the term's meaning" (p. 539). In this comment they are responding to their belief that $E$'s "...choice of measure would...determine the conclusions he would draw from his research as well as his desire and ability to publish the results of the experiment. Interestingly, those measures which are most specific to the manipulations are most likely to find an experimental base from which to draw generalizations" (p. 539). They go on to point out that such generalizations which can be drawn confidently are likely to be of a more limited rather than of a broader nature.

This somewhat oblique observation is central to the evolution of psychological studies of human freedom. After a hundred years of avoidance, the study of freedom in an experimental context has leap-frogged over the diverse literature of freedom arising in the more extended traditions of philosophical, social, political and legal research and analysis, and has relied almost entirely on the positivist methodologies of attribution and reactance studies. The experimental studies have generally ignored the fact that human freedom is an extremely complex concept, and that there are differences between freedom as attributed (to others or to the self) and freedom as experienced. Consequently, systematic data have never been gathered on this diversity. As Gurwitz and Panciera (1975) point out, any generalizations to be drawn about human freedom from the experimental literature may be very narrow and have little consequence for human freedom anywhere except in the specific laboratory context.

Even with the focus which Gurwitz and Panciera place on the specificity of questions asked, and the importance of knowing *exactly* what $E$ is asking $S$, (and what $S$ understands $E$ to be asking) they provide a double-barreled question: "How free do you feel you were to refuse...?" Surely, the term "feel"

86

here means "believe", or does it? At any rate both "feel" and "were" arise in the same sentence, and cleaning this up would have been worthwhile.


## Choice, decision, and freedom


Harvey (1976) also summarized research on several other variables which affect the extent to which subjects report perception of choice. Choice is more likely to be reported when the options presented are positive than when they have negative valences. That is, the tendency for more choice to be reported between nearly equivalent alternatives appears only when the alternatives have positive valences. Between negative-valence alternatives relatively little choice is reported, and the extent to which the alternatives differ has little effect on this. To choose the lesser (or greater) of two evils seems hardly a choice at all (Harvey, 1976, p. 82).

Perceived choice is also related to the number of options made available, in a curvilinear fashion. More choice is reported with six alternatives than with 3 or 12, and this effect is moderated by the extent to which subjects are led to believe (actually do believe?) that they have evaluated the alternatives thoroughly and carefully. It should be noted that the choices employed in this research (Harvey and Jellison, 1974) were not choices in the usual sense of the alternatives offered in reactance studies. They were choices of what football teams should be selected for bowl games. The nature of the activity involved here is certainly decision making, but it seems a bit of a stretch to call these *choices* in the sense of something that an individual can actually do, have, or influence. However, the findings are directly generalized to the kind of situation in which an individual can have or do the thing decided upon. This seems an unwarranted generalization to me.

It must be pointed out again that Harvey's position is that perceived freedom is directly related to a sense of control over one's behaviour, (not necessarily the outcome of one's behaviour). Regardless of whether one can have or do or influence the thing decided upon (such as which teams go to the bowl) the action of deciding, and the feeling that one has done the deciding would contribute to perceived freedom whether or not one has any actual control of the outcome. This places the onus for the development of perceived freedom totally within the purview of decision freedom, and leaves outcome freedom—the probability that one can actually obtain or accomplish one's chosen goal—out in the cold altogether. Further, if one feels control of one's behaviour but no control of the consequences of one's behaviour one cannot even assess the valence of outcomes.

Harvey (1976) has more to say about the two studies described earlier (Harvey and Johnston, 1973, and Jellison and Harvey, 1973). He says they "...have examined the derivation from Mills' analysis that people will perceive a greater sense of freedom in their decisions if choice options are close together than if far apart in attractiveness" (p. 79).[3] However, in neither of the two studies cited do the derivations from Mills or the hypotheses tested make any mention of a sense of freedom, or perceived freedom. Both studies are studies of choice and perceived choice under conditions of greater or lesser similarity between options, and certainty or uncertainty of outcomes.

Jellison and Harvey (1973) do cite the notion of freedom in their abstract, and in the last paragraph of their discussion, where they simply imply that high perceived choice and high perceived freedom are intimately related (p. 382). No empirical demonstration of this relationship is provided, nor any compelling reasoning. They say "...in part, organisms may seek situations in which they feel free because it is in those situations that their competence motivation can be best satisfied" (p. 382). This is not a pure *non sequitur*, since perceived competence in decision making was reported to a higher degree when the alternatives to be decided between were nearly equal than when they were greatly different, and perceived competence was correlated + .40 with perceived choice. However, the transition from these data to the above quotation, seems more a preemptive strike than an inferential leap.

As described briefly earlier, the specific task employed by Jellison and Harvey (1973) involved the provision of elaborate "scouting" information about two football teams, assessing their relative strengths in various aspects of the game, and asking Ss to decide (choose) which one had won the game actually played between them. The teams were either closely matched or seriously mismatched. The hypothesis was that choices between closely matched teams would yield greater perceived choice than choices between teams that were very unequal. In fact, this turned out to be true — again, choice is perceived when there is a choice to be made.

But there is a curious note, as well. The Mills analysis focusses on differential attractiveness of outcomes; but the manipulation of the scouting reports so as to make the strengths of the two teams nearly equal or very unequal is surely more accurately a manipulation of probability of outcome than of attractiveness of outcome. Ss were told the game had already been played and one team had won. Neither team was named, so that personal preferences or loyalty could not play a part with respect to the favourite or the underdog; all that could be responded to by the decision maker was the assessment of the strengths and weaknesses, and a judgment of the probability of winning. In fact, one team (designated W) was slightly stronger in the nearly-equal condition, and was consistently chosen by subjects. How does the notion of "attractiveness" enter here? It appears to be completely confounded with probability of outcome. There was no pay-off of any kind for a correct judgment.

In these studies, "certainty" was manipulated by providing additional information in the form of a short or long list of players injured on each team. The long list decreased certainty more than the short list because the scouting reports had been made when the teams were at full strength. It is true that

---

[3]The Mills analysis referred to is cited as a personal communication in both studies, and as of 1979 had not yet been published (Harvey, Harris and Lightner, 1979).

this injury list would serve as a damper on the probability of outcomes, but the initial "attractiveness" can hardly be seen as anything but another estimate of probability of outcome. Thus, while the findings are in line with the hypotheses derived from Mills, it is doubtful that *attractiveness*, in any meaningful sense, was manipulated at all, and there is no evidence in the study relating to perceived freedom or a sense of freedom.

The Harvey and Johnston (1973) paper, also noted above, refers to freedom only in a passing comment concerning the similarity between Steiner's (1970) notion of decision freedom—maximized when alternatives are believed to offer approximately equal gains—and the Mills analysis which hypothesized perceived choice to be greater when alternatives are similarly attractive than when they are greatly different. This is certainly a paper on perceived choice, and comprises two different studies. In the first, $S$s were presented with the records of decisions made by a series of earlier $S$s in which both the magnitude of potential payoffs and the probability of these payoffs were manipulated. The $S$s in the present study were to judge how much choice the earlier $S$s had felt they had in the choices they made. Here is a repetition of an earlier convolution: $S$s are being asked to make an attribution to another, but the attribution is not of choice, but of perceived or felt choice; that is, the $S$ is not judging an ontological state but an experiential state in another. This distinction seems to escape the authors, for in their subsequent discussion they do nothing to disentangle the knot. We shall have data to present in a later chapter on precisely this point.

At any rate, the $S$s did indicate that the earlier $S$s had, or felt, or felt they had (it is not clear which) more choice in situations where the alternatives were nearly equal in attractiveness (payoff), and when the outcomes were relatively uncertain, as compared to situations in which the alternatives were greatly different or highly certain. There were also interactions among these variables.

The second study reported by Harvey and Johnston (1973) paralleled the football team study of Jellison and Harvey (1973), as noted earlier, but included some different manipulations. Again, the focus was on perceived choice under conditions of relative attractiveness (read: probability of winning) and certainty of outcome. There is no mention of perceived or felt freedom in the context of the experiments reported, nor any mention of freedom in the derivation of hypotheses from Mills. So data said to be concerned with freedom tend to be concerned with choice. Not necessarily the same thing, regardless of preemptive strikes.


### A further review


But all that was many years ago, and we can look to a more recent integration of the work on perceived freedom (Harvey, Harris, and Lightner, 1979) in which the concept is seen as central to psychological theory and research. These authors see the idea of perceived freedom as very important in a great many different areas of contemporary psychology, but the concept is defined in very different ways in different contexts, and definitions even shift and change within a single paragraph. They propose to distinguish clearly between perceived *freedom* and perceived *control*, and go on to say,

> "Although this distinction between perceived freedom and perceived control seems necessary to clarify their theoretical independence, research shows that these experiences often are positively related and occur in almost a simultaneous manner. For example, Harvey and Harris (1975) found a positive relationship (r = .38) between perceived choice in making a selection about which task to perform and expectancy about control over behaviour on the subsequent task. Also, these investigators found evidence that in conditions producing high perceived choice ... expectancy about feelings of internal control was higher than in conditions producing low perceived choice..." (pp. 276-277).

Without so much as a fare-thee-well or a thank-you-ma'am, perceived freedom has become perceived choice. And a correlation of .38 is usually called "moderate" in text books.

But the authors do go on to say that "As a dependent variable, freedom is often operationalized as perceived freedom of choice in selecting alternate behaviours, rewards, etc." (p. 279). No examples are cited, but we have noted several examples where "freedom of choice" is rendered as "how much choice". Again, not the same thing. Indeed, this semantic slippage is surely present, not only at the operational level but at the conceptual level as well. Most of the work cited by Harvey, Harris and Lightner in all areas of psychology is oriented around choices, the sources of choices, the possibility of choices, the consequences of choices — whether in environmental psychology, reactance theory, attribution theory, learning processes, decision theory, clinical diagnosis or psychopathological labelling. In effect, the concept of perceived freedom has become the concept of perceived choice. But Harvey, Harris and Lightner point out, for all its apparent promise, almost no research effort has been invested in the relationships between perceived or attributed choice — whether of the self or of others — and decision theory.

By 1979 this seemed to be the major development: that notions of perceived freedom had been subsumed under notions of perceived choice without any of the sophistication which decision theory might bring to them. But there is another direction, as well: a light at the end of a tunnel?

### Some brushes with experience: the subject as person

Steiner (1979), in the same volume as the Harvey, Harris and Lightner chapter, suggests that experimental social psychologists have been excessively reliant upon their own projections with respect to whether they actually create the desired or presumed psychological conditions by their manipulations. He refers to the fairly common "manipulation checks" in which subjects are interrogated after an experiment to determine if they understood the experiment the same way the experimenter did. He also describes "throwaway subjects" who are interrogated immediately after, or even during the manipulation, and then not included in the data. But he says,

"...I would go further and propose that we ought somehow to legitimize and dignify research in which all dependent variables are abstracted from subjects' responses to inquiries concerning their feelings of control and choice. Perhaps that seems outrageously phenomenological, but subjects' experiences are what determine whether our manipulations are doing what we want them to do" (pp. 20-21).

He also says,

"If we were as clever at eliciting subjects' appraisals of our manipulations as we usually are in staging them, we would gain useful information about whether we are really stimulating control and choice. And until we are pretty certain what our manipulations are doing to subjects, we can't be sure our experiments are identifying consequences of control and choice" (p. 20).

He goes on to point out that even when the crucial psychological variables — cognitive states, beliefs, perceptions — are central to the mediation of effects, psychologists have been more interested in the relationships between antecedent variables and consequent variables than in the psychological states that are supposed to mediate the relationships between them.

Here is a breath of fresh air in the experimental social psychological cellar: While Steiner is wary about what subjects can tell us about themselves, he does suggest that an inquiry into what they think about our laboratory manipulations might reveal information that could be taken seriously, and might even be data. It is remarkable the extent to which experimental social psychologists take seriously their own speculations about what might be going on in the heads of their subjects and refuse to take any account of their subjects' own reports of such goings on. But here is a break, and Steiner reports on three kinds of choice as described both by the individual choosing and from the perspective of the characteristics of the alternatives.

A "good" choice is one where the best alternative is really attractive to the chooser, and the quality of the other alternatives is not very important.[4] A "discriminative" choice is more directly related to the magnitude of the difference between alternatives, and not to the quality of the best alternative.[5] An "autonomous" choice is one where a great array of qualitative differences distinguish the alternatives, and the final choice is idiosyncratic, that is, related to the individual rather than to clear and unambiguous superiority of one alternative over the other[6] (Steiner, 1979).[7]

In a subsequent and much more extensive paper, Steiner (1980) reiterates this theme in a somewhat more subdued form, but does go on to describe

---

[4]This sounds like a low decision freedom condition.
[5]This is closely related to varying degrees of decision freedom.
[6]This clearly seems a high decision freedom condition.
[7]In these contrasting types of choice, the variable of availability is not entertained.

possible phenomenologies of decision making, and reports much more diversified ways of manipulating events to generate these diverse phenomenologies. However, the data reported remain entirely of the "dependent variable" sort: "How much choice did you have to refuse..." "How free did you feel to select the alternative...?". While the phenomenological state of $S$ is of interest, it is tapped in an extremely narrow way, and discursive explorations of the full-blooded phenomenology of choice remains beyond the scope of this form of research. While greater attention to the mental state of the experimental participant is paid in the theorizing and in the design of the manipulations, the data of importance can only be said to be "...consonant with..." the theorizing, and a direct inquiry which might actually show that the theorizing is *correct or incorrect* remains an unfulfilled hope. Perhaps it is, as Steiner suggested in the earlier (1979) paper — "...outrageously phenomenological...", but the mental states which are theorized to intervene between the manipulations and the stated "feeling of choice" are not merely abstractions or mathematical relations: They are real events, and while they cannot be observed publicly, they certainly can be reported upon. Indeed it is precisely such reports by the theorist which lead to the development of the theory. Is the theorist's phenomenology to be taken seriously, but not the subject's? Surely we can do better than that!

Indeed, we *have* done better than that, for Martin (1922), in a detailed study of types of voluntary choice, devotes fully half of his 115-page monograph to direct phenomenological reports of the experience of choice. Ultimately, he too, reports several kinds of choices, but focusses on the experience of choice rather than on the characteristics of the alternatives. There is "preferential" choice, where the individual is deeply and personally involved, really actively chooses, is confident of the choice, even enthusiastic, and may act later to justify the choice (p. 39). There is "conflict" choice which is quite different: the individual vacillates repeatedly in making it, and after a choice is made, the chooser may remain uncertain and the alternative not chosen remains in consciousness (p. 46). There is "indifferent" choice, in which the chooser is quite uninvolved, there is a lack of feeling, and it simply must be done for external reasons (p. 50). Finally, there is "judgmental" choice, which is cool and dispassionate, having little to do with preferences or commitments, and also lacking in feeling. It would seem that any set of alternatives might give rise to any of the varieties of choice which Martin describes, depending on the peculiarities of the individual doing the choosing. Steiner does not attend to the peculiarities of the person; only to the peculiarities of the alternatives.


## Summary: reactance and attribution


These two approaches to human freedom through experimental social psychology have both failed to deliver on their promises. Reactance theory,

from the outset, is conceived as being based on internal and subjective evaluations of behavioural freedoms and threats to behavioural freedoms, but the
research never provides any systematic direct account of these. Reactance as
an experience is central to the theory but never investigated, because it is likely to be either unconscious or denied. Direct efforts to reinstate one's behavioural freedoms are the most important consequence of reactance, but are
almost totally absent from the research literature because such efforts may be
"uncivilized". Over a period of more than two decades of research this
avoidance of the central issues of the theory has not changed.

Over a shorter period of time, studies of perceived or attributed freedom
have given birth to the study of perceived or attributed choice. Recently,
Steiner, one of the central researchers in this tradition, has called for fundamental attention to the study of the experiential state of the $Ss$ (1979). But
even he fails to take any direct account of these crucial processes (1980) when
he elaborates on various *possible* phenomenologies of choice. The point is, of
course, that experimental social psychology is not interested in, and cannot
come to terms with the experiential events on which their theorizing rests.
Experimental social psychology tends to be hamstrung by the aspiration to be
a non-human science, in the mold of a rather outdated physics.

### Overview

At the beginning of this chapter I suggested that we would deal with many
different issues, and indeed we have. We began with perceived and attributed
freedom and studies of the conditions under which individuals perceive
freedom in their own and others' actions or attribute freedom to these actions. We were concerned with the interchangeability of these terms, "attribution" and "perception", and noted several serious objections to the "perceptual model". We also noted the extent to which various terms were telescoped
into each other, with important conceptual distinctions being washed out in
the process: distinctions among whether $Ss$ *are free, feel free, feel that they are
free, feel that they have choice, believe that they have choice*, are simply not
made.

When the study of perceived freedom evolved into the study of perceived
choice, distinctions were blurred between conditions under which people
make choices which have consequences for them ("I'll take the one on the
left"), as compared to choices in which they are merely right or wrong about
something that already happened ("I think team W won"). In this evolution,
the concept of perceived, felt, or attributed freedom became the concept of
perceived, felt, or attributed choice, and then became perceived control over
one's behaviour, which is not the same as control over the outcomes of one's
behaviour. In effect, we have moved from the philosophical conceptual
labyrinth to the psychological conceptual morass.

Throughout, I have been critical of the extent to which the central explanatory processes — experiences, perceptions, cognitions — were only inferred from behaviour, and the extent to which the experimenter's phenomenology was taken seriously but the subject's phenomenology was not even sought. We did note one researcher's call from the mainstream to take $S$'s experience as primary data, but even he (Steiner) suspected that it was outrageous to do so and we found no following for that call.

## Prospect

In the next section, which is but one chapter, I will try to step back from the immediate subject — the study of human freedom — and place in a more general context the concerns I have already voiced. I will present a set of general criticisms of the kinds of constraints which have left barren not only the study of human freedom but the study of a wide range of other human processes as well. I will contrast the natural science approach to the study of complex human behaviour, which has dominated the last two chapters, with a human science approach, which will inform the subsequent chapters.

# PART III: METACONSIDERATIONS

*Chapter Five: Criticisms and Transitions*

# 5 Criticisms and Transitions

## The plan

In this chapter it is my intention to sketch out some of the more general criticisms which have been levelled at contemporary mainstream positivist psychology, and some of the inadequacies to which this point of view has led. I will then describe some of the alternative approaches which promise to lead to a more full and human understanding of human behaviour, and I will deal with the issue of volition. This latter concept, long suppressed and avoided in psychology, is fundamental to a humanly meaningful understanding of human behaviour.

## Crisis and alternatives

It is certainly no secret that psychology is in a crisis. Nor is it any secret that psychology has been in one crisis after another for most of its history. The crises have been over its identity, its unity, its relationship to other members of the scientific community, its proper subject matter, its methodology, its social responsibility. Recently added are crises of its licensure, its eligibility for third-party payments, its political stance with respect to everything from fluoridation to nuclear war, and in the A.P.A., the advertising carried in *Psychology Today*.

The principal focus of this chapter will be to explore the contention which currently exists concerning the *point of view* which mainstream psychology takes toward its subject matter, especially human behaviour, and most particularly human social behaviour. The points of view which we will explore are the contrasting perspectives of a *natural science view* and a *human science view*. We will take a brief look at the current dissatisfactions, some alternative solutions, and then a more historical view of the notion of volition — central to concerns about human freedom.

## Unhappiness

The literature of dissatisfaction with psychology as a positivist natural science has grown rapidly (e.g., Brandt, 1982; Braginski and Braginski, 1974; Johnson, 1975; Gergen, 1978, 1982; Giorgi, 1970; Harré and Secord, 1972; Koch, 1981; Miller, 1972; Reason and Rowan, 1981; Rychlak, 1975; Sampson, 1978; Sarason, 1981; Secord, 1982; Silverman, 1977; Smith, 1972; Westland, 1978), and alternative visions of a more sensible and sensitive approach to psychology have been offered. Both the critical literature and the proposed alternatives are too extensive to be dealt with in detail here, but certain points must be made.

Perhaps one of the most compact indictments of contemporary psychology has been made by Koch (1981). Koch can afford to be compact at this time because he has contributed consistently and extensively to the critical literature for nearly forty years. He accuses psychology of "ameaningful thinking" — thinking based on the rigid application of limited rules, and the torturing of phenomena into a format whereby rule-following can yield research results, however senseless or trivial the results may be. One of the principal features of ameaningful thinking is the "Tendency to accept any 'finding' conformable to some treasured methodology in preference to 'traditional' wisdom or *individual experience*, no matter how pellucidly and frequently confirmed the non-scientistic knowledge may be" (p. 258). Koch goes on to argue that the knowledge-generating and certainty - generating methodologies have deleted from psychology any means of capturing the antinomies, the ambiguities of human behaviour or experience. They have proceeded with preemptive finalism and, as such, have generated models of human behaviour which he considers morally bankrupt.

Others have taken on social psychology specifically (Gergen, 1973, 1978, 1982; Harré, 1981, 1984; Harré and Secord, 1972; Miller, 1972; Silverman,

1977; Smith, 1972), and have argued that the laboratory experiment, and the spirit of positivism which informs it, represent systematic distortions of any meaningful conceptions of human behaviour. Reason and Rowan (1981) in introducing their edited volume of sources for what they call "new paradigm" research say, "Through our balanced cool appraisal there comes an undercurrent of hatred and horror about what traditional research does to those it studies, those who do the research, and about the dreadful rubbish that is sometimes put forward as scientific knowledge" (p. xii). And further, "It is obscene to take a young researcher who actually wants to know more about people and divert them into manipulating 'variables', counting 'behaviours', observing 'responses' and all the rest of the ways in which people are falsified and fragmented" (p. xxiii). And to this end, they and their contributors provide a compendium of philosophical bases, methodological approaches, research results, and future directions which represent serious alternatives to the positivist natural science model of psychology.

The production of research results or "knowledge" under the mainstream conditions is not simply misleading. The problem goes further than this, for the knowledge produced in the laboratory is taken to be the "best scientific knowledge" concerning the phenomena in question. In fact the phenomena in question are systematically distorted and trivialized by the very laboratory experiments which are supposed to illuminate them.

Responses to criticisms of this kind have been provided by Berkowitz and Donnerstein (1982) and Mook (1983). The principal reply is that the critics simply do not understand the enterprise of experimental social psychology. Experimental social psychology is in the business of generating theories and testing hypotheses, and whether the findings of rigorous research map on the categories of ordinary common-sense psychology is entirely secondary. The enterprise is directed to establishing scientifically sound knowledge about human behaviour, which may have obvious relevance to real world events, but does not require this. Whether the events of the laboratory look like events in the real world or not is quite irrelevant: What does matter is whether honestly derived hypotheses can be honestly tested and confirmed or rejected. This kind of reply does not respond very tellingly to Koch's specific argument that the kind of knowledge generated is ameaningful: Ameaningful knowledge may be knowledge about what people can do under entirely artificial circumstances, and even to entertain ultimate relevance to the real world is to write a blank cheque on a bankrupt institution.

In contrast, understanding of human behaviour which is based on the human meanings of situations and the social meanings of actions is precisely the concern of ethogeny (Harré and Secord, 1972). Concern with human experience and how human experience directs and modifies human behaviour is the focus of phenomenological psychology (Giorgi, 1970; Keen, 1975; Kruger, 1981; Thines, 1977; Valle and King, 1978). A telic approach (Rychlak, 1975, 1977, 1980) is directed at the power of personal plans and intentions to govern actions toward the future. A respect for the context in which human social behaviour occurs (Gergen, 1982) presses us to understand this behaviour as a part of history and culture, which are human products, and contrasts with an understanding which emphasizes the inevitabilities of biology and physics. We will address each of these proposed alternatives in turn, and then explore the role which the concept of volition has had in psychology.


## Ethogeny


Harré and Secord (1972, chapter 3) detail their view of the shortcomings of laboratory studies of social psychological phenomena. They point out that there is loss of verisimilitude in that the experimental set-up destroys the possibility of the study of the very features which are essential to social behaviour in its natural setting. For example, stimuli are presented in relatively pure form — otherwise they cannot be controlled by the experimenter — and they rarely appear in pure form in the natural world. The *presentation of stimuli* (again, necessary if the experimenter is to control the experiment) renders the subject merely an information processing system rather than an information-seeking and information-generating agent. The immense complexity of many social psychological concepts is ignored, and simple operational definitions which can be plugged into experiments are substituted for the rich and often enigmatic phenomena they are supposed to represent.

They go on to point out that the psychological laboratory is a special kind of society and it is critical to include an understanding of the participants and the experimenters and their views of what is going on as "integral and idiosyncratic elements in each 'experiment'" (p. 46). The psychological experiment is seen as a peculiar kind of interaction between strangers during which it is unclear whether there is a high degree of protection of selves, or alternatively, excessive disclosure. In any case, they argue that it requires a suspension of disbelief to assume that social psychological experiments, as generally conducted, are representative of the processes in real life which they purport to study.

Harré and Secord (1972, chapter 5) go on to detail an anthropomorphic model of man, drawing on what they consider the best of contemporary philosophical thinking on the nature of persons from the work of Strawson (1959) and Hampshire (1965). They conclude that some of the most critical defining characteristics of human beings are that they have the power to initiate action and changes in action; they have the power to monitor their performances; they have the power to monitor their monitorings, to be aware that they are aware; they have the power of language and speech, and through this they have the power to provide meaningful commentary on their intentions, their actions, and their monitorings. Further, Harré and Secord reject the notion of a one-to-one correspondence between biological individuals and social individuals; instead, they argue that any single biological person can have many different social personae, each logically coherent, but possibly contradictory with each other.

"In the anthropomorphic model of man we not only have the person as agent but the person as watcher, commentator and critic as well. It follows from this that the most characteristic form of *human* behaviour is the conscious following of rules and the intentional carrying out of plans" (1972, p. 91). Unless social psychology takes account of these most fundamental and distinguishing characteristics of the human being as social actor, the pursuit of the scientific study of human social behaviour can be nothing but a charade.

So they go on to describe the open souls doctrine which advocates "...that all or very nearly all the kinds of things we ordinarily say about ourselves and about other people should be taken seriously as reports of data relevant in a science of psychology. This is not to imply that such statements are to be accepted uncritically, but rather to say that the phenomena which they purport to report both *really exist* and are *relevant*" (1972, p. 105).

Ultimately, the method for arriving at the understanding and explanation of social behaviour is through the negotiation of authentic accounts of social episodes. Negotiated accounts can contain both causes and reasons as explanatory, the accounts are negotiated among participants and observers, and such accounts always remain open to revision. While accounts may remain somewhat problematic, the unthinking assumption that they have *no* authenticity and can form *no* part of science is simply a mistake. The mistake is "...*exactly* parallel to the problem of induction in the natural sciences, which is created by supposing that if general laws cannot be proved to be true from the restricted kind of evidence which *can* be collected, then they have *no* title to belief, a supposition which, if accepted, would make natural science impossible" (p. 163).

Accounts typically are oriented around roles, rules, and plans, and as the different commentaries by actors and observers become more and more concordant, the authenticity increases. "Perfect authenticity will be said to have been achieved when there is full concordance between *all* accounts, both between anticipatory, monitoring, and retrospective commentaries, and between the accounts of all the people involved in the episode. Concordance does not of course imply identity. We should expect in many cases that some people's accounts will contain items not in those of another, but authenticity is preserved when the idiosyncratic items are concordant with the items in the accounts of others" (p. 163).

The negotiating of accounts of meaningful social episodes is an elaborate and time-consuming activity, but the aim is to develop the most accurate and meaningful explanation of human social behaviour in its richness, its ambiguity, its subtlety, and to attend to the human powers which make social psychology worth studying at all.

### Phenomenology

In the same vein, proponents of phenomenological psychology take a dim view of the restrictions which a natural science approach to the behaving human being imposes, and of the resulting narrowness of its findings.

"If anything, a phenomenological approach is even more rigorous than a traditional approach because it tries to account for more of the phenomenon. It does not deny the aims and ambitions of traditional psychology as such, but rather criticizes the way that traditional psychology tries to accomplish the very aims of science. It believes not that psychology should be less scientific, but that it should be scientific in a different way. It does not demand less; it demands more. Traditional psychology has avoided the major psychological issues by either ignoring the peculiarly human phenomena or by reducing them to such an extent to fit the strict scientific method that they were no longer recognizable. A phenomenological approach to human phenomena insists that the phenomena cannot be essentially distorted, which implies devising a method to fit the phenomenon" (Giorgi, 1971, p. 14).

The phenomenological approach attempts to study human experience as it is directly revealed to the experiencer, with preconceptions cleared or suspended, insofar as possible. It is more concerned with meaning than with measurement, and is perfectly prepared to come to grips with the complexity of human experience as lived. The effort is often descriptive (cf. Colaizzi, 1978), eliciting and analyzing detailed features of experience, from initial protocols, through significant statements, to recurrent themes. Much of the interest of phenomenological psychology is clinical, but a phenomenological approach to standard experimental laboratory situations is also possible.

For example, Colaizzi (1971) presented a standard nonsense-syllable learning task to 22 Ss. The list was made of 10 syllables and the task was divided into three phases for each S. The purpose was not simply to plot average learning curves for the Ss, but rather to make probe inquiries about the appearance of the learning materials and the experience of S at each phase of the study. The first probe was after the first complete presentation of the ten nonsense syllables; the second probe was after the first trial on which five or more syllables had been correctly anticipated; the third probe was after the trial on which all ten syllables were correctly anticipated for the second time. At each of these points, S was asked to write down how the material appeared to him, what his experience of the situation was. S was not to describe either the list or the individual syllables. Analysis of the descriptions was carried out contrasting the different experiences of the material at the different points in the learning process.

Typically, at phase one, after the first revolution of the memory drum, the list appeared to be an amorphous mass, confusing, very long, beyond description, tension-inducing, and so on. At phase two, when half the list had been learned, there was an incipient development of order in the list, the list appeared to be an incomplete whole, with blocks and gaps, the list appeared to shorten, the presentation seemed slower, some enthusiasm for the task appeared.  In the third phase, the material was described as "friendly", the list shortened again, the list flowed from item to item, tension was reduced.

These findings are of an utterly different order from the findings of an average learning curve, and some would argue that they tell us a great deal more about nonsense-syllable learning than do the aggregate data of learning curves.  They certainly tell us things about the human experience of learning nonsense-syllables that standard curves of acquisition never can.

We could go further, and inquire into the phenomenology of serial position effects, list length effects, and the experience of changing list lengths.  Colaizzi points out in his discussion that the problem explored here was described more than 30 years previously by Adams (1931) when he contended that "...not only the insight learning studied by Gestalt psychologists but all instances of learning consist of a re-organization of a field of perception and that it should be the task of experimentation to demonstrate this — a task which unfortunately has not been undertaken until presently because of the traditional bias of psychology to avoid experiential data" (Colaizzi, 1971, p. 106).

Here it is important to note that generalizations about experience may be appropriate but are not required.  Each respondent's phenomenological report can be taken as a datum in itself, a finding.  That different persons might well experience the materials differently from each other at any phase of the study is to be expected.  We know from day to day experience that different people do experience the world differently, and the kind of general laws sought in natural sciences as appropriate to their more-or-less interchangeable molecules or cells are just not appropriate when dealing with the experience and behaviour of complex human beings, even in the simplified and highly controlled world of the psychological laboratory.  To find that a group of $S$s requires a mean of x trials (S.D. = y) to learn a set of 10 nonsense syllables with z% association value under conditions A, B, ...n is simply not enough to find out, if we are studying human behaviour and experience.  It has been argued that psychologists of learning have almost never studied learning.  They have studied the *conditions* of learning, but not the *learning* itself.  Learning does not occur in the stimulus or in the response, but in the learner.

It should be clear that these alternative approaches to the study of humans acting as real human beings — even if in unnatural situations — tell us something different about human experience, human construction of the world, human rule following, than do the direct recording of narrow response categories, defined by $E$ rather than defined by $S$.  The people who come into the laboratory are no less human for the fact that psychologists reduce them from people into $S$s, or believe they do so, and the laboratory remains a human social situation, despite the intervention of tape recorded instructions and on-line computer recording of responses.

It certainly is true that the analysis of "what is going on psychologically" can be just as rigorous from an ethogenic point of view or from a phenomenological point of view as it can be from a natural science independent variable-dependent variable point of view.  And it would appear that the findings concerning "what is going on psychologically" are more humanly coherent and intelligible from the former points of view than from the latter. The functioning human being is simply not emitting an R to an S. He or she anticipates, monitors, changes behaviour on the basis of such monitorings, and perhaps above all else, is aware that he or she is *doing* these things. No mechanistic model can account for these processes. An alternative model is demanded by the evidence, if we take our evidence seriously.

Both the ethogenic and the phenomenological approaches employ a model of man which accepts and incorporates those features of human psychological functioning which are centrally human, "...pellucidly and frequently confirmed..." as Koch said. They also include the notion of meaning and ambiguity of meaning as central, with consciousness and experience at the core of the problems of psychology. This is no mere return to introspectionism, as some ill-informed critics have argued (Greeno, 1982; see also Giorgi, 1982), but the development of rigorous systematic approaches to human behaviour based on experience and attempting to capture not only its regularities but its rich variations as well.


## Teleology


Rychlak (1975, 1977, 1980) represents another force for more appropriate approaches to human psychology. As telic theorist he has argued for a more diversified conception of causality in human behaviour than the usual material/efficient causality which informs the positivist approach and which excludes a great deal that is peculiarly human in human behaviour. Rychlak argues that teleological causation is entirely appropriate. Individuals behave "for the sake of" something (final causation) as much as they behave "because of" something (efficient causation). He uses the term "telosponsivity" as a contrast to responsivity. While it remains true that many varieties of human behaviour can be considered in the realm of biology, and models from biological science are appropriate, there are many features of human behaviour – some would argue the most important features – which do not lend themselves to this natural science efficient cause model at all. When one looks to what is special about human functioning it is precisely this: that people do plan, that people do change their minds, that people have the very compelling experience of initiating their own behaviour, often in spite of external circumstances. They behave for the sake of ideas, principles, plans, which are not encompassed by the most stretched notion of "stimuli". Rychlak argues that humans can change "...that, for the sake of which..." they act; they can and do behave volitionally, and the explanation of the behaviour is a teleological one. This teleological approach has recently been brought to bear on cognitive psychology (Lamiell and Durbeck, 1987; Rychlak, 1987; Slife, 1987; Williams, 1987).

One other point of importance is that these contemporary approaches are not daunted by the early behaviouristic view that verbalizations about oneself are irrelevant, nor by the more recent behaviouristic notion that verbal behaviour is to be understood only as behaviour in its own right and not as reports about some other events, nor by the pervasive Freudian skepticism concerning what people say about themselves. Nor do the recent assertions by Nisbett and Wilson (1977) that people typically misreport their own mental processes trouble them. Morris (1981) points out, in contrast, that most of the processes and phenomena that Nisbett and Wilson are concerned with are behaviours which are not typically monitored at all and that it is not surprising that respondents might well have to fabricate bases for their behaviour and that their fabrications might be at odds with the evidence of manipulated variables. Morris argues that when the behaviour in question is closely monitored by the actor, the basis of behaviour — whether conceived of as causes or as purposes — can be described with reasonable accuracy by the actor. Others (Adair and Spinner, 1981; Cotton, 1980; Ericsson and Simon, 1980; Rich, 1979; Smith and Miller, 1978; White, 1980) have contested the Nisbett and Wilson findings from the point of view of cognitive processes and methodology. It remains true that there are aspects of human behaviour of which the actors cannot be aware (cf. Shevrin and Dickman, 1980), and many aspects which are simply not monitored. When called to account for these actions the actors are stumped. But in most human behaviour, the purposes, meanings, and intentions are available and serve as valuable components of intelligible explanation.

## Contextualism

Gergen (1982) develops further arguments for why the study of human social behaviour simply cannot yield to a positivist approach. His line of reasoning is that the phenomena in question are historically and culturally embedded at a particular place and time, and transhistorical "laws" are simply not possible. In contrast, the phenomena which have yielded to one or another form of positivist approach, as in physics or chemistry, while corrigible, are not inevitably transient, because the phenomena in question are not. No amount of physicalist, mechanist causal explanation of human social behaviour, however detailed and accurate, can render such behaviour intelligible. Intelligibility arrives — and very promptly — when even modest attention is given to the reasons, purposes, or functions of a social act.

Gergen details the dissatisfactions with current theory and method in psychology, and cites more than 70 references in two paragraphs, and more than 25 additional ones in a footnote (1982, pp. 190-191). He goes further, outlining several of the existing alternatives to a positivist approach — the hermeneutic-interpretive movement, the dialectical approach, the perspective of critical theory, and the ethogenic approach. From these alternatives to positivism, he derives a series of compatibilities which these perspectives all appear to share at the level of pivotal assumptions, very different from the traditional perspective.

From these compatibilities, Gergen takes heart that there are genuinely viable alternatives which arise from the dying ashes of positivism. There is even the possibility of unification at the metatheoretical level, and a new dream for a sophisticated science of human behaviour is at hand, a science which treats the subject matter at a level appropriate to its complexity, its transience, its historical embedding, its fundamental dependence upon language, and its all-important meaningfulness. These are crucial features of human social behaviour which the traditional approach can never capture (p. 200-209).

## The matter of volition in psychology

Most North American psychologists understand, at least roughly, that Wundt established an independent experimental science of psychology in 1879 and this discipline was principally concerned with matters such as psychophysics and the strict introspective study of the structure of consciousness. This is what writings on the origins of experimental psychology traditionally have told us. But much recent historical work has shown the origin myth to be just that: a myth (e.g. Danziger, 1979a; Blumenthal, 1980). Wundt opposed the separation of psychology from philosophy, "...holding that the most important problems in psychology were so closely connected with philosophical problems that a separation of the two would reduce the psychologist to the level of an artisan imprisoned by a covert and naive metaphysics" (Danziger, 1979b, p. 31). When a professional society of German psychologists was founded in 1904, Wundt would have nothing to do with it. In addition, experimental psychology was a mere fragment of psychology for Wundt, and he wrote at elaborate length on much broader issues of social psychology.

Quite in contrast to the hard-eyed experimentalist we have been led to see as our founding father, Wundt had broad human concerns beyond psychology, and quite in contrast to the relatively sterile mechanistic biological science point of view we attribute to him, he called his psychology "voluntarism" and took volition to be one of the fundamental human functions which are the core problems of psychology (Danziger, 1980). We are much more likely to attribute a concern with volition and will to William James, and properly so, but these concerns were central for Wundt as well.

But almost as soon as Wundt had developed his voluntaristic psychology, a wave of positivism swept over Europe and engulfed even its first generation of students. Volition was seen to be "metaphysical" and outside the realm of psychological study cast in a "scientific" mould. Positivism also captured the practical-minded North Americans, so that they were never even exposed to the full flesh and blood of Wundt's psychology. Interpreted to North Americans primarily by Titchener, Wundt's psychology was a mere fragment of its true self, and was tailored for a culture quite different from that in which it arose. So Wundt's fundamental concerns in psychology were repudiated or ignored (Danziger, 1979a), while a generation or so later, homage was paid to the founder as scientist. Notions such as volition were to be reduced to the status of secondary or derivative phenomena, explicable in terms dictated by the emerging positivist scientific psychology.

But of course, this move away from Wundt's original intentions was not universal, and protests were heard. As early as 1900, Buchner (1900) expressed great concern about the tyranny involved in the emerging trend that "The elements of conscious experience are to be reduced to those of one kind or quality only" (p. 495). Specifically, with respect to volition, Buchner went on to say "However many might be the detailed propositions that set forth the problem of volition, it must be put upon a par with the specific problems of sensation or of movement, and must be solved... with the aid of conceptions appropriate to itself rather than to other forms of consciousness... through this sweeping negation of certain data, psychology is cast into a form different from that which has prevailed hitherto" (p. 496). And indeed it was so. The voluntarism of Wundt was cast aside as just not acceptable. And while James's notions of will were better known in North America, they, too, were simply not acceptable. The positivist person became a purely reactive one, quite incapable of initiating action.

While strict positivistic behaviourism did effectively preclude a concern with volition with a conscious content worthy of investigation, motivation, as a reducible concept did persist, and indeed flourished. But the conscious component — volition — disappeared, and the scientific effort was to relate experimental manipulations to behavioural outcomes without the intervention of conscious contents, volitional or otherwise. What was left out was the notion of volition as a *source* of the initiation of behaviour — that conscious experience which gives rise to the notion in the first place. "Motivation", then, concerned itself with the effect of antecedents of a particular class on consequents of a particular class. Reports of conscious experience of choice were eliminated, and even when allowed in, as in psychoanalytic theory, they were suspect.

So the subject of volition or will was typically avoided by psychologists for most of the first half of this century. In 1942, Irwin (1942) said "For the general inadequacy of the experimental study of volition a number of reasons are assignable. Chief of these is the frequently described flight of experimental psychology from 'philosophical' or 'metaphysical' concepts ... The experimentalist, in his attempt to avoid those aspects of the concept which would hinder him or even be opposed to his program, has gone to such lengths as either to use terms with inadequate analysis of their meaning, or to avoid the problem altogether ... problems have been determined by methods rather than methods by problems" (p. 115).

107

Irwin argued that attempts to study volition in reaction time experiments and in attempts to distinguish voluntary movements from reflex movements in terms of latencies and response curves was not very satisfactory, although he was impressed by Bair's (1901) study of learning to wiggle one's ears. He was concerned about the great investment in simply trying to distinguish between volition and reflex in small muscle groups, and the triviality of the information gained: "... and we begin to wonder how we can have departed so far from the spirit of what once was regarded as willed or voluntary that it is now difficult or crucial to distinguish voluntary behaviour from the simplest and most mechanical of behaviours" (Irwin, 1942, p. 126). Supported by Woodworth's (1906) arguments, Irwin argued that the essence of voluntary behaviour is not in the movement itself but in the purpose or intention of the movement. He quoted Woodworth: "It would be much truer to speak of our voluntary move-ment of physical objects than to speak of voluntary bodily movements. If I wish to cut a stick, my intention is not that of making certain back and forth movements of my arm, while simultaneously holding fingers pressed tightly towards each other; my intention is to cut that stick" (Woodworth, 1906, p. 374-375). While noting that teleological concepts were not popular in con-temporary psychology at that time, Irwin went on to argue that voluntary be-haviour is controlled by purpose, and it is in this direction that one should look for its understanding.

Subsequently, Murphy (1947, p. 291) said, concerning self-initiated be-haviours, "The capacity of inner symbols to arouse muscular contractions...is perhaps not the full flesh and blood of the volition process." And indeed a greater understatement can hardly be imagined. But the unpopularity of teleological notions remained, and little experimental work in this direction was conducted, other than the Miller, Galanter and Pribram (1960) work on plans, and little of that was considered the study of will or volition. I submit that the reason little of this last work was considered to be related to volition or will was that such concepts simply were not respectable. Rather, the psychological community took eagerly to the cybernetic information process-ing view of human behaviour presented and to the possibility of rendering human intelligence and action in sophisticated machine-like terms, through the notion of plans and programs. But Miller, Galanter and Pribram also spoke to the issues of hierarchical organization, of control processes, of con-sciousness and will, of the formation and execution of plans. They included a chapter on suspension of will, using hypnosis as their model. Most people don't seem to remember that, and Hebb's review of the book in *Contemporary Psychology* (Hebb, 1960) didn't take these matters very seriously. But Miller, Galanter, and Pribram appear to have taken them very seriously. They said: "...what we call an 'effort of will' seems to be in large measure a kind of em-phatic inner speech... When we make a special effort the inner speech gets louder, more dominating. This inner shouting is not some irrelevant epiphenomenon; in a very real sense it *is* the Plan that is running our informa-tion processing equipment" (p. 71). An effort of will can be greater or lesser, can set one plan in a dominant position over a competing or conflicting plan, and in effect, "will" is the final arbiter of what planned action is carried out.

Finally, Miller, Galanter, and Pribram presented consciousness as the capacity to make one's own plans, and volition as the capacity to execute them. In saying this, they have explained neither capacity, but most assuredly, they have allowed these capacities to the human being.

However, the late 1960's and the early 1970's turned out to be bumper years. In 1968, at the American Psychological Association meetings in San Francisco, a symposium was held under the title "What ever happened to the will in American psychology?," and in 1970 several papers from that symposium were published (Gilbert, 1970; Royce, 1970; Strunk, 1970). The papers were primarily historical, and focussed on some of the points I have already made, but there was also focus on the contemporary influences of existentialism and notions of free choice which were nudging some sectors of psychology in new directions. And almost as if in answer to the question raised by the symposium, Kimble and Perlmuter published "The problem of volition" in 1970, and Kahneman published "Attention and effort" in 1973. We will return to the former shortly, but the latter is especially significant because attention and effort were precisely the achievements of will, according to William James: "The essential achievement of will is to attend to a difficult object and hold it fast before the mind" (James, 1890, Vol. II, p. 561). However, Kahneman did not index "will", "volition", or any related terms, and said that the term "attention" merely serves "...to provide a label for some of the internal mechanisms that determine the significance of stimuli and thereby make it impossible to predict behaviour by stimulus conditions alone" (1973, p. 2). However, he did distinguish between voluntary and involuntary attention. The former is effortful and determined by selection based on current plans and intentions; the latter is determined by stimulus properties such as intensity, and more enduring propensities of the individual.

At about the same time, in the context of studies of decision making, Broadbent (1973, pp. 26, 30) referred unashamedly, if metaphorically, to the "...fiat of the will..." in describing the shift from deliberation to action in reaction time studies. He did not index the term, but the fact that he needed to use it indicated a sensitivity to human functions which we need to refer to, however obscure they may be.

Both Kahneman (1973) and Broadbent (1973) did deal with notions that are historically issues of will and volition, and it seems that these functions of the human being are of abiding interest, even if we are deeply troubled about using them. They do have value, it seems, even if we are hard pressed to place them in a fully deterministic universe in a legitimate positivistic format.

But to backtrack a bit: Kimble and Perlmuter (1970) described the ways in which the cards had been stacked against the reintroduction of volition to psychology because theories had, for over a 150 years, focussed on volition as a special faculty of mind, doomed to ostracism as other faculties of mind were doomed to ostracism. They traced the history of conceptions of volition, and while they give Wundt rather short shrift, and Miller, Galanter and Pribram

(1960) are mentioned only in passing, Kimble and Perlmuter consider James's view, that images of the consequences of acts can serve as stimuli for those acts, and give rise to "volitional" behaviour. While there is evidence that when both kinesthetic and more remote kinds of feedback from behaviour are lacking, individuals can still perform the acts, albeit less well, there is also evidence that feedback plays a very large role in the control of voluntary behaviour under normal circumstances.

In every theoretical case that Kimble and Perlmuter describe, the effort was to eliminate something like will or volition: "The obvious goal of what we have called the classical theory of volition, as it has developed over the years, has been to replace the concept of will with a mechanism that could be subjected to experimental tests and conceivably reduced to neurophysiological status" (p. 368). James finally acknowledged that for the purposes of science, free will had to be abandoned in the study of human behaviour. But James, as everyone else, was a child of his times, and the conception of science he held was of the fully deterministic, positivistic stance of the turn of the century. It required him to be willing to adopt a model of the human being which gave lie to his own experience, and to the experience of others, if he was to be scientific. However James thought the science of psychology would provide a very limited view of human conduct (cf. Viney, 1986). While our present model is still dominated by this kind of notion, the possibilities for a science which can do justice to the basic phenomena of being human is much more tolerable now than it was then. But James also recognized that science was situated in a much larger context over which it had no dominion (cf. Fancher, 1979). He remained concerned with the experience of will, and argued in favour of a notion of free will if human life was to make any sense at all. James aspired to reconcile his psychology with his ethics and his experience, something that many psychologists of today can attempt only at their peril.

Kimble and Perlmuter were primarily concerned with the concept of volition in behaviour which goes from an initial reflex occurrence to a studiously monitored voluntary state, often guided by considerable attention, effort, and verbal monitoring, to an automatized condition, rolling off quickly, competently, and without attention or obvious direct motivation. They were subsequently concerned with what happens to automatized behaviour when it is interrupted or when attention is focused on it.

But automatized behaviour is only a limited kind of behaviour: behaviour which at one time required monitoring and subsequently does not normally require such attention. Other behaviours which involve the operation of voluntary activities or volition or will are legion. There are the very difficult decisions requiring great deliberation, there are the rather quicker and trivial choices of a necktie or how much mustard to put on your hot dog. Each of these is usually intentional, and one knows whether a proper choice has been made or not. There are the occasions on which one makes a great effort to persist in that which is unpleasant but necessary, or to forbear from doing that which is attractive but destructive or forbidden. These are very human and very important human actions.

Certainly it has been the committment to a particular format of scientific respectability that has hampered the direct investigation of volition and will as elaborate human psychological functions (cf. Irwin, 1942). Kimble and Perlmuter were quite explicit about this: In referring to the classical theories they say that "...most classical statements referred voluntary behaviour to a faculty of 'willing' or to 'consciousness' or 'intention'. Each of these interpretations suffers from an intransigence towards operational reduction to observables" (p. 381). In effect, they are all seen to be deficient because they do not conform to the notion that if one cannot reduce human psychology to natural science concepts, one cannot explain human behaviour. But more of this later.

Let me add one more windfall from these early years of the last decade. In 1971, a symposium was held at the University of Kent in England, on the philosophy of psychology. This was published in 1974 (Brown, 1974). One of the sub-sections of the symposium was on determinism, and included a paper by Mandler and Kessen (1974) on the appearance of will. The title was a *double entendre* since they treated the notion of will as a common experience or appearance arising from some identifiable sources, and they also treated this experience from a developmental perspective, discussing the kinds of events which progressively give rise to the appearance of such a belief system and to its maintenance. They argued that there is simply no place in an orderly universe for a concept such as will which renders events random with respect to evident determining variables. They argued that a great deal of the confusion and concern in this area is due to the intrusion of common language mentalism passing as psychology—which it is not. They argued that physics is not likely to advance very much through attempts to predict the exact course of falling leaves in a wind storm; and "Psychologists do not and should not claim explanatory powers for specific human actions *in vivo...*" (p. 311). They were clear that the determinist position is not one which is open to logical or empirical test or support: it "...is a metatheoretical convention—an axiom for theory and research—pragmatic in intent and often moral in its force" (p. 309).

Although Mandler and Kessen explicitly denied any "truth" for free will assertions they argued that such a belief has some probable positive outcomes—principally that individuals believing in free will are likely to delay decisions with the consequence that decisions based on maximum information are likely to show an increment in quality over those made more quickly. They were taken to task by several commentators at this symposium for the awkward assertion that belief in a false doctrine should be seen as a virtue. They also may be taken to task for the assertion that the adoption of a free will position is false, when its purported alternative, determinism, is explicitly presented as an unproved and unprovable metatheoretical axiom. However, their paper serves as a transition—from the study of volitional behaviour in the laboratory, focussing on reaction times and small muscle groups and reflexes, to something much more focussed on the totality of behaviour, influenced by beliefs, social situations, and so on.

111

Of all human concerns, human freedom cries out more loudly than any other for a serious voluntarist theory, in the context of which the subject can be taken seriously. Skinner (1971, p. 11) has said that talkings about human freedom are mischievous; Mandler and Kessen, (1974) have argued that there is simply no place in an orderly universe for a concept such as human will, and Lefcourt (1973) explicitly considered control and freedom as illusions. Recall that Mandler and Kessen speculate that belief that one is free and/or has control of situations may have positive consequences in the sense that greater deliberation and maximum use of information may lead to more suitable decisions, and Lefcourt cites data from Glass, *et al.* (1969) showing that such a belief has stress-reducing consequences. But voluntarism is simply not a serious matter for these writers.

However, in a human science approach, such as in systematic phenomenology, ethogeny, or telic theory, volition and freedom can be taken seriously and are considered to be central functions of human life. As we progressively come to believe that ordinary human behaviour in the typically complex context of ordinary human interaction is influenced not by events so much as by people's understanding of events, we come to the necessity of understanding the ordinary language mentalisms which are the framework in which these understandings are couched (Antaki, 1981). Whether or not we, as psychologists, credit people's assertions about themselves, the individuals making the assertions do credit them, and they go on to act in accord with them. To consider the notion of volition or will as a concept to be analyzed away is to deny a great deal of human understanding. To argue, as Skinner (1971) does, that talk about freedom and dignity is mischievous and counterproductive is to commit what Koch calls "...ludicrous prescriptionism..." (1981, p. 269).

Howard and Conway (1986) confronted the issue of volition directly, and treated volition as a process in its own right and as a significant contributor to human action. They treated their experimental *S*s as agents who could initiate and guide their own actions. The studies produced results which, on the one hand are quite remarkable, and on the other hand, not remarkable at all.

They engaged and manipulated volition by instructing *S* to "eat" or "not eat" peanuts. As a second independent variable, the peanuts were either in sight or out of sight. The quantity of peanuts eaten under each of these conditions was the dependent variable. In their first study *S*s were 22 volunteer university students studied over a period of 24 consecutive school days, weekends excluded. *S*s were given a 16-ounce jar of peanuts which was weighed and refilled each day. Each day they were given one of four instructions: "Keep the jar in sight in your dormitory room and eat as many peanuts as you wish," "Keep the jar in sight and try not to eat any peanuts," "Put the jar out of sight and eat as many peanuts as you wish," or "Put the jar out of sight and try not to eat any peanuts" (pp. 1243-1244). There was a very great difference in the quantity of peanuts eaten under the conditions of "Don't eat" and "Eat all you like". An analysis of variance showed a large and highly significant effect for volition, a marginally significant effect for sight, and a significant interaction effect for sight and volition. The effect size for volition exceeded the effect size for sight for all 22 Ss (p. 1244).

Since an "instructional variable" interpretation can be pitted against a "volitional" interpretation, a second study was conducted in order to establish one of these two interpretations as more plausible. This additional study had two conditions: one in which the "eat" and "not eat" days were determined by the toss of a coin, but only the Ss knew which condition was represented by heads and which by tails. In the second condition Ss alone decided which days were to be "eat" and which were to be "not eat". The only constraint on Ss in this second condition was that the two kinds of days were to be essentially equal over the 24-day period of the study. Further, on half of the days of the study a written reminder was sent to Ss about following the coin-toss results or their own decision concerning "eat" or "not eat". The results of this further study strengthened the findings of the first: The volitional component showed a large main effect, and there was no effect for the coin-toss vs. choice condition or for the reminder-no reminder variable, nor any significant interactions.

What is remarkable about these findings is that a variable characteristically ignored or avoided in psychological research, even said to be imaginary, can account for so much of the effect in an experiment. What is not remarkable at all about the findings is that in everyday life, we manipulate volitional variables with greater or lesser success all the time and produce large effects when successful, disappointing results when not successful. Why shouldn't this work in the laboratory?

Howard and Conway continued this line of studies by attempting to modify, volitionally, an increase in social skills among a group of thirty-five undergraduates who wanted to increase the frequency of their heterosexual social interactions. Each day the Ss received a set of instructions to "try to" or "try not to" a) initiate conversations with the opposite sex, b) spend time in social places, and c) make positive self-statements. As hypothesized, the behaviour tracked the volitional variable and yielded large and significant effects (p. 1247).

The authors interpreted their results with caution, primarily, I think, because the treacherous notion of volition is the central issue of their work. In more usual experiments we typically take volitional variables for granted, as when we ask a subject to "fixate a stimulus", or to "pay close attention to these instructions", or to "try to keep the pointer on the target..." How much different would be our experimental results if we didn't invoke these quiet volitional components? Indeed, many of our experiments could never even be carried out, and if carried out, would make no sense at all. It is preposterous to think that the simple presence of instructions (on a tape, on a piece of paper, in the experimenter's mind) is enough to influence psychological events on the part of a subject. The instructions must be conveyed to the subject, understood (or misunderstood), and acted upon through compliance or non-compliance.

113

Howard and Conway's caution was well placed, since just a year later, four commentaries on their paper were published (Ford, 1987; Hayes, 1987; Hershberger, 1987; Staats, 1987) together with a reply (Howard and Conway, 1987). All four commentaries found fault with the original article: either it went too far or it didn't go far enough; it missed the deterministic interpretation; it contributed to the disunity in psychology; it was not a unified theory; it missed the point by using a mainstream methodology. But there still is an undeniable optimism in the comments that there are highly desirable prospects for the development of theory and metatheory which will take account of contributors to human behaviour which have been ignored because of their awkward status within traditional views.

So the notions of volition, of will, of freedom, haunt us because they are so persistent and functional in human life while methodological commitments oblige many to deny their very existence (Cf. Westcott, 1985). As Gergen and Gergen (1982) point out, "...it may be ventured that the most significant theoretical undertaking at the present juncture should be... voluntarist theories of human action" (p. 149). With this, we come full circle because voluntarism was at the core of Wundt's psychology, and voluntarism has had a rocky road ever since.

Although the criticism and the line of reasoning developed in this chapter (and the resistance to it) has flourished during the past two decades, it is certainly not new. It is rarely noted explicitly, but a steady stream of objection to and criticism of the mechanistic interpretation of human behaviour flows in the work of Stern, Spranger, Munsterberg and the Gelstaltists, with its most recent and clearest exponent in North America in the person of Gordon Allport. This line of precursors to the present wave of passion for a human science approach seems to be ignored currently, very much as it was ignored during the dominance of behaviourism (Cooper, 1986).

So now we turn to some human science approaches to human freedom, to see what they can tell us beyond what the natural science approaches have told us.

# PART IV: PSYCHOLOGICAL STUDIES: The Hum Sci Variations

# 6 Systematic Personal Reports of Freedom

## The plan

In this chapter, some additional concerns and assumptions of a human science approach to psychological research will be dealt with briefly. The general issues were rather fully explored in the preceding chapter. Two programmes of research concerning human freedom will be presented. The first is a direct experiential report, the product of several years of self-study focussing on experienced freedom (Parmenter, 1980). The second is a presentation of open-ended reports from a wide variety of respondents (Zavalloni, 1962). A third and fourth line of research will be reserved for the following two chapters. It will become evident that direct, first-person reports are not only useful, but crucial, in moving toward a full explication of the psychological features of human freedom.

## The concerns of human science

Much as the phenomena of human freedom cry out for study from the human science viewpoint, there has not been much response. By a human science study, I mean systematic empirical study of the ways in which human freedom is experienced and the way human freedom affects and is affected by human life.

We have already reviewed a variety of studies of human freedom which meet some of these specifications, but none which meets them all. The philosophical studies are certainly systematic, and extensive, but they tend to be prescriptive, that is, identify what *true freedom is*, and they focus on analysis of the wide variety of abstract concepts of freedom. When human experience of freedom is brought in, it tends to be downgraded – for example, in talk about people wanting to *feel* free rather than to *be* free. The historical studies are also systematic, and are non-prescriptive. They focus on the forms of interpersonal and political behaviour which have been representative of the concept of freedom at different times and places. But here, too, there is no noticeable attention paid to how the common individual experiences freedom in these different contexts, and in these different times.

The experimental psychological work has also been systematic: the reactance literature and the attribution literature have pursued the careful manipulation of variables and have explored varying values of their parameters. But they, especially, have been criticized for the limited and often confused conceptualizations of what they are studying, and the extent to which their operationalizations distort or trivialize the phenomena in question.

In this chapter, we will focus on studies which attempt to take human freedom as an experience-in-context – that is, an approach which attends to both the nature of the experience of the individual and the circumstances under which it occurs. The approach is not prescriptive, nor does it attempt to define what freedom *is*. It does not make the reductive assumption that freedom is any one thing, or any one experience. The approach allows persons to speak for themselves, and allows for diversity.

Generalization is not required: any report of experienced freedom can be taken as a datum in its own right, and however idiosyncratic or even bizarre, such a report can be employed to illuminate the question of human freedom, in all its complexity. But at the same time, generalization is not to be ignored when it is possible. The human science approach does not fall into the quagmire of seeing every person as so different from all others that a totally idiosyncratic solipsism results.

Though generalization is not required, and at the extreme, each person's total experience may be unique, we are not so blind as to deny that humans do share in their experiences. Linguistic labels concerning those experiences are sufficiently social that communication is possible, empathy is possible, understanding is possible. It requires wit, wisdom, and care to extract essential truths from individualistic reports of experience, but no researcher in the arena of human behaviour would deny that it requires the same qualities to design good empirical research in the positivist natural science tradition. As Koch has pointed out, we seem to have lost sight of the necessary human qualities in psychological research, and have succumbed to the "ameaningful thinking" which results from the blind application of rules.

In the human science approaches there are rules, of course, one cannot go off doing anything one likes. But one is pressed to use the rules imaginatively, to use one's own human powers of observation and interpretation imaginatively, to incorporate the subject or respondent in the process of making intelligible the experience or behaviour in question. Far from ignoring what the participant thinks about what is going on, the participant's views are crucial in the human science understanding of what he or she experiences or does.

And it may be possible to generalize. With respect to the experience of human freedom there may be great variety, but the variety is not likely to be infinite. It may be possible to identify a half dozen or a dozen varieties of experienced human freedom just as it was possible for Adler to identify a limited number of conceptions under which the great array of philosophical conceptions of human freedom could be subsumed.

In each act of generalization, some of the richness of detail is lost, some of the concrete unique features of the various exemplars is sacrificed in favour of a focus on the commonalities. But in human science research, the categories for generalization are driven by the data or evidence gathered, not by a preconception of theory or a formal hypothesis which seriously limits the kinds of observations which are made and which can be made.

But, one can argue, the concept of human freedom, either as an abstraction or as an experience, is so diffuse and so variously defined that one can never be certain that two persons talking about freedom are talking about the same thing. The possibility of systematic data can be linked only to linguistic habits. And indeed it is so. The study of human experience, as communicated from one person to another is certainly an exercise in sociolinguistics, but so is the provision of instructions to an experimental subject — either in writing, by tape, or direct speech. There is no way that investigators of human behaviour can elude the fact that a study of human behaviour which directly involves investigators, *E*s, informants, participants or *S*s is a social linguistic interaction. Experiments can be rendered very non-human both in format and in intent, but there is no way that a participant is going to shed his or her entire history of human interaction to become a naive pure *S*. And of course, it is not the *intent* of *E*'s instructions which govern *S*'s behaviour. It is *S*'s understanding of *E*'s instructions — which may or may not be at variance with what *E* thinks is going on. Hence, the belated introduction of the "manipulation check" or the "throwaway subject" in the more contemporary of the traditional studies.

In the human science approaches, we require serious commitment on the part of both the investigator and the informant, serious commitment to trying to find out about something which may be enigmatic in nature. Reports and accounts are corrigible and always open to revision, but the attempt is made to render them as accurate as possible. Much of the history of psychology has been dedicated to the pursuit of the incorrigible (Gergen, 1982, with reference to Austin, 1962) – the uncovering of absolute knowledge – final and genuine psychological *laws*. This pursuit, it has been argued in the previous chapter, is a chimera, a charade, an engagement in rigid rule-following behaviour which produces ameaningful knowledge.

As Giorgi pointed out (1971), the human science approach requires much more than the natural science approach requires. Rigour must be maintained, and rigour in the human science approach cannot be guaranteed by the simple following of limited sets of rules, somehow guaranteed to produce knowledge. In the human science approach, the rich variety of human experience is respected, as is the rich variety of human thought processes involved in rendering human behaviour intelligible.

There are four different kinds of direct human investigations of human freedom to be reported in this tradition - two in this chapter and one in each of the next two chapters. They are all systematic and rigorous, but in different ways.

## Systematic autobiographical phenomenology

In what Ross Parmenter calls an autobiographical essay, with the somewhat unlikely title "School of the Soldier", he makes a systematic inquiry into the various ways in which he has experienced freedom, the various conditions under which he has experienced freedom, and into some of the various meanings freedom in the abstract and freedom in the concrete have for him.

For our purposes here, this essay has several special merits. First, it is systematic: It is a sustained inquiry by a reflective and literate man over a period of years. Second, it is humanly meaningful: It does not arise in a short term exposure to laboratory conditions or in circumstances which are highly specialized. Rather, it traces his essentially mundane life during the years he was a member of the U.S. Army as a wartime draftee. The essay is devoid of battles, devoid of heroics. Third, the writer was open to discovery. He held only the most commonplace preconceptions about freedom, and in examining his experience, he was able – or obliged – to suspend these preconceptions, and his openness to discovery allowed the full flowering of awareness of the antinomies, the paradoxes, the uncertainties which are the stuff of human freedom. Fourth, the essay is a personal report, and while it might just as well be autobiographical fiction, it is not. I'm not certain what difference this makes, but we do somehow think that a true story has more illuminating merit than fiction. That point of view is an open question to me, but the fact is, Parmenter has told a true story.[1]

In the following section, I will necessarily quote liberally from Parmenter's work, for the texture of it cannot be paraphrased. Parmenter says:

"It will be remembered that freedom was what we soldiers were told so repeatedly that World War II was being fought to achieve, and it was freedom we were assured that we were drafted to protect. More important, though, was the unexpected way the army made me look at freedom. In civilian life it had always seemed so obviously desirable that, when I encountered the word in rhetoric, I responded with the proper pleasurable feelings, and, like many of my generation, thought little more about it. As far as I was concerned, freedom was largely an abstraction" (p. 20).

Parmenter reports that prior to induction at age 30 his life was remarkable for its freedom. He was well-off, well-educated, well-employed in a career of his choice, a member of no disadvantaged minority group, had access to the resources of a large city, and as quoted above, typically he gave freedom barely a thought, as the fish gives no thought to the water. "I entered the army with practically no experience of what it was like not being free" (p. 20).

"My reception center was Fort Dix, N.J., and I am sure I shall always remember my days there as among the happiest of my life. They bordered almost on exaltation. It was because I felt so free" (p. 25).

While this quotation might be rather a surprise, he goes on to elaborate:

"After ten years of concentrated and incessant thought, the menial tasks and the manual labor freed me from the burdens of 'mental strife'... The good humored gregariousness freed me from much of the loneliness that is the inevitable price a man must pay for solitude. I was freed from even the most elementary decisions as to what to wear or to eat" (p. 25).

An especially important observation:

"More importantly, I was freed from the war because I was no longer concerned with what, unresolved, is the most disturbing of its claims — the problem of what to do about it personally. The responsibility for my activity was no longer in my own hands. I was also freed from two of man's greatest millstones — the past and the future: from the past because the break was so complete, and the future because it was so entirely unknown" (pp. 25-26).

Here we find an individual entering a condition of life which many, in their most sober hours, resented from end to end, yet he focusses on the features of it which provide him with a feeling of freedom bordering on exaltation. He is no longer enslaved by the complexities of his career as a journalist—

---

[1]It is interesting that convincing fiction (some of which I have quoted elsewhere in this book) tells us something that COULD happen in human behaviour, under certain circumstances. This is precisely how we have described a large body of psychological laboratory research: as showing what human behaviour CAN BE, given special conditions. Much fiction is more convincing than many laboratory reports.

telephones, deadlines, constant mental effort, decisions, review of one's past, planning of one's future, attempting to decide about his loyalties with respect to the war (Parmenter was born and raised and educated in Canada but as a U.S. resident, he was drafted there) and all this is replaced by menial physical tasks, easy comraderie, the sharing of a common fate which is out of one's hands. Clearly this illustrates one stark paradox of human freedom: Freedom is not one thing, it is an interpretation of one's relationship to events, the interpretation set in a context, and the context being personal and historical.

But Parmenter goes on in much greater detail to find other paradoxes. He describes one evening in his second week in camp. His tent mates were going to a movie, and he looked forward to an evening reading. It was winter.

"But I found when I started to read that I was cold. I poked at the fire in the antique stove in the centre of the tent and put on some more coal. I returned to my book, but I was still cold. I poked at the fire again, only to discover that the orange core of glowing coals had shrunk still further" (p. 26).

Events went from bad to worse, and he says, "...the experience taught me my first important lesson in freedom. Without heat, a man is a slave to the necessity of keeping warm" (p. 27). He reports a similar experience having to do with dirt and latrine orderly duties. After hosing and scrubbing to perfection, the place was as dirty as before shortly after the exercise. Similar experiences at KP duty showed him the amount of dirt even clean people cause in the course of living. He also observed the amount of wood, even green limbs that were burned to heat water to wash out garbage cans. "In those days, then, I learned my first important truth—that freedom is largely material. I learned that a man was a slave to his need to keep alive" (p. 29).

Even while he was thinking about the material basis of freedom, he was comparing the spartan life of the inductee with the spartan life of the monk: early rising, frugal eating, cold bare institutions with little comfort, rigidly regulated, secluded from the world, celibate, under orders from a larger outside force. The comparison

"...showed me that the peace of the monastery was not...a figment of pious imagination, but a reality. For what I felt was so extraordinary that I recognized in my own person for the first time in my life what others have called spiritual freedom...I realized that monasticism had the same psychological effects when it was prescribed for the military victory of the United States as when it was prescribed for the worship of God.
"With this discovery, I had another important truth to lay alongside my first one—namely, that the greatest freedom is essentially spiritual. For I had seen that it could be gained at the expense of bodily comfort; indeed that it positively flourished with the removal of material things. And I had seen that it was not just a matter of the removal of comforts and possessions; in an even deeper sense it was a suspension of the whole personal will" (p. 29).[2]

---

[2]How remarkably at odds this is with the taking of personal initiative, decision making, choosing, going from "being able" to "doing". It is rather more like "being perfectly integrated with one's culture" (cf. Chapter 2).

He became aware that there were no automobiles, no telephones, no buying or selling, no possibility of sexual gratification, no chance for advancement, no conflict of duties or loyalties, no possibility of changing the conditions, and no possibility of planning one's own work.

"...never in my life had I been so closely confined or so physically uncomfortable. Yet the sense of serene elation continued...Never in my life had I been so physically restricted. Yet still the feeling of freedom persisted" (pp. 32-33).

But upon moving from the reception center to basic training, he encountered

"...a sort of ever-present pressure from which the soldier is never free. I can only call it the Will of the Army. We had not really felt it at the reception center—especially those of us who were there long enough to learn how to stay hidden when they were looking for men to work. But we became aware of it the moment training started. There was no escaping it, no hiding place. The Will was everywhere and it held us like a vice...I saw its influence extending all the way from a small thing, like standing still, to a large one, like facing death. I do not say such a Will is not necessary in an army. But I do say a man can't have any affection for it, and as long as he is under its domination, he cannot feel free...I realized I had come up against something relatively new to me—the tyranny of external events" (pp. 38-41).

In the context of the Will of the Army and the tyranny of external events, Parmenter turned to prayer and poetry to sustain himself during the inevitable hours of trial and boredom, and he began to read nearly anything he could put his hands on. He began to collect pamphlets distributed by religious sects and other inspirational groups, and finally realized that "An inner life as a means to freedom, then, was my next important lesson" (p. 44). His inner life was systematic thought, and he engaged in this activity through countless hours of dreary work. In the process of breaking 1800 eggs for breakfast, and wondering at the magnitude of the task, he became aware of the fact that all the people being fed by this great pot of eggs would have eaten breakfast somewhere if they weren't in the army. Similarly, the mobs appearing for sick call led him to think there was a great deal of sickness about, and then led him to realize that a great deal of sickness was not unusual, only that it was all gathered to one place at one time. Following this, he concluded that the eating, the sickness, the restrictions are simply more nakedly exposed in the army than they are in civilian life. "The new question was: Were we really essentially any freer in civilian life?" (p. 45).

Although the Articles of War stripped members of the Armed forces of many of their normal rights, it also protected some, and Parmenter, as a conscientious objector, experienced this. During basic training, no matter how he was badgered by sergeant or captain, he could not be compelled to perform on the firing range. The scope and limits of rights and freedoms were much more explicit in the Army than out of it, and in the relatively primitive conditions of the Army camp, the dependence upon food, fuel, and water for the merest rudiments of freedom were writ large. And what he could and could not be compelled to do were similarly clear.

As a conscientious objector, Parmenter had chosen training as a medical technician, and was ultimately to learn that "...you cannot begin to be free without health. Sickness is enslaving" (p. 64). His prior experience had never included severe illness in himself or in any close associate. "I had thought only superficially of the way illness made a mockery of every other type of freedom that might be within reach of an afflicted man" (p. 65).[3]

In his training as a medical technician, he came to appreciate the ways in which medical knowledge had mitigated the enslavement by illness: "Knowledge as a means to freedom, then, was the next basic lesson I learned" (p. 67).

So far, then, Parmenter's personal odyssey has led him to identify several fundamental bases for the experience of freedom: First, the material basis — the availability of the elemental requirements of the bodily life — warmth, cleanliness, food, water. These, so that the mind can be free of the constant search. Second, the spiritual basis, possible when material needs are met minimally, and individual will is suspended. Third, health, so that the human being can engage in fundamentally human activities. Fourth, some guarantees of rights, so that the individual conscience cannot be invaded or denied. Fifth, knowledge as a means to freedom, in that knowledge may serve as the basis for mitigation of the incursions of otherwise unmanageable forces.

It is important to note that Parmenter is not talking as prescriptive philosopher, but as a reporter of his own experience and understanding. He makes it perfectly clear that his own exaltation during his time in the reception center was not necessarily the rule: "Indeed, many soldiers claim that those days were their unhappiest in the army" (p. 83), and indeed, most of them never turned their attention to the examination of the personal nature and conditions of freedom as Parmenter did. We have, nonetheless, made a distinction between Parmenter's reports of his own experience, and his surmises about others, for example, on the matter of health.

One of his examinations showed that some of the conditions which contributed to his exaltation and enhanced feeling of freedom were two-edged swords which subsequently cut the other way. The living in austerity, only in the present, the simple drudgery of eating, sleeping, surviving, the seclusion from the world were no longer enough. As a music critic for the New York Times before his induction into the army, his hunger began to mount, "...and what had at first seemed like protective covering came to seem like the lid of a coffin. I longed to be moved again by beauty. The absence of music was something that was always with me, like a parent's later grief at a child's death" (p. 93).

---

[3]Parmenter's observation of affliction from the outside stands in stark contrast to one set of observations from the inside. Stephen W. Hawking, a theoretical physicist at Cambridge University is afflicted with motor neuron disease, cannot write, can barely speak. He has said that he believes his illness has advanced his career because it has given him the freedom to think (Harwood, 1983).

His recognition that the protective covering had become the lid of a coffin made him realize that "...I had not been free during that period to anything like the extent I thought. I had merely exchanged an old slavery for a new one, and, in the joy of escaping the old one, had not yet recognized the nature of the substitute" (p. 95).[4]

Parmenter's self-observations turned to the nature of his new bondage, and he began to recognize the kind of freedom which the slave has—a freedom from the feeling that there are always projects to finish, always planning to be done, always management functions to perform. Instead, the slave has his tasks to carry out, and when done, he merely awaits further instructions. The strenuousness of the work of the slave and the soldier are such that he is even freed from most of the body's desires. "Stretching out and rejoicing in work-lessness is all that his heart craves" (p. 96). So he had enjoyed the freedom of the slave, and the romance with that kind of experienced freedom came to an end.

But there were new developments, for as he came to the end of training, where he had, for most of the time, experienced the freedom of the slave, he began to take on involvement in administration and was saddled with the continuous feeling that the work was never done: In effect, he traded the freedom of the slave, which freedom had become suffocating, for the bondage of a position in which he had time off but no real leisure, no time to look after his personal affairs, to get a haircut, or have his shoes repaired.

But this state of affairs came to an abrupt, if brief, end with his first three-day pass in Los Angeles. Back to an entrancing city, no responsibilities or orders, some money to spend, all led Parmenter to see that he was, at least temporarily, free of both kinds of paradoxical bondage he had recognized. But it was not satisfactory, for his seven months in the army had cut him off from his former life sufficiently that he was simply unconnected with the rest of the world, with the rest of life. His separateness from old obligations and old attachments was precisely what had made him free.

Through a series of steps he came to the conclusion and recognition that one could be objectively free but have no sense of freedom, and that one can be too free, too infinitely free, so that one is disconnected, so that one loses a sense of affiliation, a sense of being anchored (pp. 105-106). A further conclusion he reached is that no one wants to be really free,[5] but most want a sense of freedom, and that such a sense of freedom can come from a dizzying array of conditions which vary dramatically from person to person. To consider freedom one thing is utterly foolish. There are many paradoxical and contradictory truths about freedom as it is lived and experienced by ordinary people.

Parmenter has described a variety of these contradictions and paradoxes in his own experience—circumstances under which he has little objective freedom, but feels free to the point of exaltation; circumstances under which he has relatively great objective freedom, but no sense of freedom. He

---

[4]And here is Von Mering's conception of freeing and bonding.
[5]And here is the terror of the existentialist position.

describes his own experience of being too free, and the associated feeling of being disconnected; he distinguishes sharply between the more or less objective condition of freedom and the sense of freedom. One may be considered the province of the objective world, and one the province of the spirit: "...I came to see my particular experience in considerably more general terms. It became clear to me that what I had found true for myself was true for all men — namely, that the struggle for freedom is two-fold. Each man has to win the sense of freedom in two spheres: in his environment and in himself" (p. 122).

When Parmenter moves on from personal experiential reporting to generalization to all men, he moves out of the realm of psychological phenomenology into the realm of philosophy, and his writing becomes less germane to this chapter. However, his awareness of the crucial difference between objective and subjective freedom, and his awareness of the great diversity of conditions for and experiences of freedom save him from narrow prescriptionism and simplistic proposals.

The complexity, the subtlety, the contradictory and paradoxical nature of human freedom is revealed in this personal document in ways which have eluded the philosophers, the anthropologists and the psychologists so far described. While the philosophers are more sophisticated in their conceptual and linguistic analyses, and while the anthropologists employ a somewhat more diverse, and certainly more exotic information base, Parmenter's searching personal odyssey provides a richness the others lack. It illuminates the personal dimensions of paradox which prevents the oversimplification which results from enthusiastic generalization and the aspiration to work with a single concept of freedom.

It hardly needs saying that a comparison between Parmenter's living documents and the data from the experimental psychology laboratory is very difficult to make. They are both psychological, but in very different traditions, asking different questions, soliciting different kinds of evidence, arriving at different kinds of answers. Possibly they may be compared with respect to rigour: the rigour of the operational definitions, the experimental manipulations, the statistical analyses compared with the rigor of the sustained analysis of personal experience. But such a comparison is really meaningless. Possibly they can be compared with respect to fidelity to the phenomenon under consideration. Taking into account the vastly divergent kinds of evidence utilized in the two traditions, one could hardly call them the same phenomenon: one is human freedom as operationalized and minimalized for the laboratory, the other is human freedom as lived in the world.

A comparison of intelligibility might be more possible: To what extent is our understanding of the psychology of human freedom illuminated by the findings of the laboratory compared with the findings of the analysis of personal experience? The answer, of course, is moot. But that it should be moot is a great advance over the position that only positivist laboratory findings can tell us anything important about important psychological events.

## Systematic solicited reports

While Parmenter's approach is systematic in the sense of sustained examination of his own experience over an extended period of time, Zavalloni's approach (1962) is systematic in a different way. He attempted to tap into the experience of freedom by asking a large number of individuals to provide written statements in which they were "...to describe by means of a concrete example an experience which entailed the use of their freedom or its restriction" (p. 162). He solicited these statements from students, both directly and through other educators, and ultimately he received 173 usable responses from persons of both sexes ranging from 11 to 20 years of age, from various educational situations, home backgrounds, and in three different languages. In the above quoted request, it does not appear that he differentiated between the experience of "being free" and "feeling free" which Parmenter (and I) feel is so important.

It is also possible that the instructions were interpreted in different ways by different respondents. As a matter of fact, it is frequently very difficult to elicit statements which are useful examples of *personal experience* in this realm of inquiry. In my own research efforts, attempting to get people to talk about their own experiences of freedom almost inevitably leads into abstract statements and broad generalizations about the nature of freedom. One must be continuously alert to keep a respondent on the track of *personal experience* rather than conceptual abstraction, since the abstractions tend to dominate the statements.

As in the previous section, it is imperative to quote extensively from the original reports Zavalloni collected. Abridgements and paraphrases are often necessary due to space restrictions, but there is no proper substitute for the direct reports. Even in Zavalloni's original volume, he quotes from only about half the statements he found usable – and I will quote from a sample of his sample of a sample. Contrary to my earlier statement about human science research being driven by the data, Zavalloni did have a quite explicit hypothesis. This hypothesis was that there is a developmental hierarchy of human freedom ranging from simple autonomy – the capacity to initiate action, often impulsively – to self-determination, in which this capacity is informed not only by intelligence, but by morality and ethics.[6] That is, self-determination, the ultimate expression of human freedom, is by no means value free. Zavalloni is a priest, his work was translated from the Italian by two other priests, and the work bears the imprimatur of the Vicar General of the Archdiocese of Chicago.

This is not to imply that this is a religious tract: The depth and breadth of the psychological scholarship is staggering, and includes extensive reference to works in English, French, Italian and German, encompassing vast litera-

---

[6]Recall Adler's three notions of a) natural freedom of self-determination, b) circumstantial freedom of non-interference and c) acquired freedom of self-perfection discussed in Chapter 1.

tures which are beyond the scope of any work derived from English language sources alone. The hypothesis was derived from his analysis of experimental, clinical and philosophical literature and leads him to seek out the above progression in the personal reports.

On the other hand, my own predilection is toward neutrality in the value of one kind of expression or experience of freedom over another. I believe that is beyond the scope of a psychological work unless evidence can be adduced that one or another kind of experience or expression of freedom is psychologically superior. I made the same point in discussing the anthropological works that carry an implicit moral judgment concerning the expression of freedom in various cultures or in various historic times. My purpose is the description of commonality and variety in the experience or expression of human freedom, and consequently my sampling from Zavalloni's sampling will emphasize diversity rather than progression. Later on we will have something to say about the relationships between experienced freedom and psychological well-being, but it will not bear on the value of one kind of experience or expression of freedom as superior to another. We will also have something to say about the experience of and expression of freedom in persons of different ages (Chapter 8), but it will show only very little of the kind of progression from lower to higher forms which is the substance of Zavalloni's hypothesis.

But Zavalloni does provide a wealth of first-person material, and it appears that providing these reports was taken seriously by the informants. Some respondents found it necessary to turn down the task altogether, and wrote their statements to that effect:

*"I confess that this assignment has given me the opportunity to do a little thinking about myself. However, no matter how hard I've tried, I've been unable to recall an incident or something like that in which I had the feeling of freedom or the restriction of it. Perhaps such a reaction will surprise you, for I know that it's hard to imagine that in all my past twenty years I never once found myself in a circumstance in which the operation or violation of my freedom was involved. But this can be easily explained in that I left my family at the age of eleven, to follow what I believed to be my vocation. As a result, the circumstances of my life changed completely... To tell the truth, I can't seem to concentrate on this topic. Something is bothering me. It's a problem that is growing more serious every day; I know I should get some advice, but I can't seem to talk about it to anyone. I am awfully sorry if I haven't been of much help to you" (p. 163).

Another:

*"From the little I've heard it seems that some importance has been attached to this task. And because I'm supposed to give the subject some serious consideration, I'd rather not answer. I feel that it's better to write nothing than to write something asinine. Therefore, since the problem seems so important, I'll refrain from answering. I can't see any reason for leading the experimenter into error" (p. 164).

---

*In this section, to distinguish clearly between quotes from Zavalloni and quotes from respondents, the latter will each be preceded by an asterisk.

But most of the statements were usable, and while they varied from the concrete to the abstract, they illuminate many features of freedom, as lived and experienced. Specific examples provide the flavour of the responses which were fairly loosely categorized by Zavalloni, for example, contact with nature:

> *"Once I had a feeling of complete freedom, when I was alone up in the mountains. I felt that I wanted to stay out there forever. I was experiencing a strong feeling of freedom within me. I felt freer than I had ever felt in my life in those small backyards around my home" (p. 164).

> *"The sun was shining high in the sky and it gave me a feeling of great joy and well-being. Everything invited me to run and to enjoy the happy freedom of that moment" (p. 166).

> *"Although presumptuous, I believe I can overcome the sea and test my feeling of complete freedom" (p. 166).

When at home alone or without parental supervision:

> *"Nobody else is at home: a drop of water breaks the silence. Father and Mother went to Milan. The housekeeper is sick. Finally, I am free" (p. 167).

> *"Only then, when we are not kept under control by the vigilant eyes of our mother, without worrying over her disappointment in seeing us return home late all covered with dust, we experience the feeling of freedom, which is so vivid in us boys... The joy which makes us happy is based mainly on the thought of not having anyone who can prevent us from doing what we like" (p. 167).

Interestingly, one report from a fifteen year old girl which recalls an experience at the age of six is essentially discounted by Zavalloni, who says "...There is not and cannot be — at the age to which the remembrance refers — a true experience of freedom" (p. 167). The report says:

> *"I was only six years old when my mother told me that from tomorrow on I would have to go to school by myself. This was a great event for me. My joy was unlimited. The maid who used to come every day to pick me up and was my guardian angel was not enjoying my sympathy any more in those days. She used to hold my hand too tightly, she dragged me now by the right, now by the left hand. She treated me as if I were a doll. I found this coercion exasperating. Certainly, for her it was a great responsibility, but I believed that I was big enough to take care of myself. Consider, therefore, with what pride I went to school alone for the first time. I believed I was somebody. This freedom which I desired was given me suddenly, without a thousand warnings even though the road was very dangerous. My whole being was filled with happiness. I felt like a bird that is freed from the cage where it was a prisoner" (p. 168).

Zavalloni discounts this report because from his perspective this is simply the desire for, and experience of, mere autonomy, as contrasted with self-determination which involves much more in the way of planning and decision making. In this chapter, we are not concerned with more or less abstract definitions as were dealt with in the section on philosophical considerations, but with the reports of actual human beings concerning their experience. From the perspective of this chapter, the above is a perfectly valid and useful report of experienced freedom, perhaps appropriate to a six year old, and perhaps not appropriate to a mature adult. We shall have more to say about the reports of younger persons in Chapter 8.

Zavalloni is concerned with reports which show a kind of social awareness, and the working out of compromises between one's own direct desires and the expression of responsibility. The examples range from the very simple to the very complex, elaborate, and in some cases, barely credible:

> *"Sometimes when I get up in the morning and I feel happy, I would like to sing. But I cannot do that, because I feel the duty of restricting my freedom for the freedom of others, and in this case for that of my little sister, who must be free to sleep as long as she wishes" (p. 168).

> *"There is nothing more beautiful than an act of charity which is performed with human understanding. Christmas was near, and I insisted on having an electric train as a present. My mother tried to convince me that the toy was too expensive, and that I was already too big for such toys. She told me there were many people who were suffering and who lacked everything. There was no reason therefore to waste money this way. But I did not let her convince me. I insisted so much that my father, who was tired of being annoyed, gave me the money to buy the train. Overjoyed, I left our apartment immediately to buy it. But on my way downstairs I met the poor widow who lived upstairs all sick and tired and bent under the weight of a sack of wood. I then remembered the words of my mother. At once I approached the poor woman, grabbed the sack of wood from her hands, and climbed the stairs without paying any attention to her weak protestations. I entered the attic and set down the bag of wood. On standing up, I noticed her children lying close together in bed, perhaps to keep warm. I did not hesitate for a moment—I handed all the money my father had given me to the poor woman, who in her complete confusion could find no words to thank me. With that money Christmas would be a day of joy for them also. At that moment I felt my heart become lighter and I was filled with a great happiness" (p. 170).

While Zavalloni notes that the episode is reported by an eleven year old boy and seems to be inspired by a short story by De Amicis, he credits it because it represents to him a high level of self-generated moral decision making, which, as noted above, is central to his notion of self-determination. The reader can take it or leave it.

A somewhat more prosaic example, again reflecting decision making of consequence is perhaps more representative:

> *"A few days ago I had a clear example of that freedom which makes us boys so proud. One evening at suppertime we were talking about the studies I would pursue after my secondary education, and about my future. My parents gave me permission to choose the path I would like to follow. My answer, which expressed my desire to begin studying at an institute of technology, was favorably received by them. With great satisfaction I became aware that what I said had been very well thought out. In this way I had an example of the freedom that each individual possesses. I must add, however, that I so presented my reasons only because I knew them well, and that I had made my decision after much meditation" (p. 171).

### An example which focusses on relief from boredom and sameness:

> *"This was not simply a trip to go a long distance and see new places, but to show ourselves what freedom meant, after having been in college for one year. We were annoyed at seeing the same places every day from one vacation to the next. How happy we were to get away from difficult studies, from the ordinary life of school! It was as if the nausea and pains of life did not exist for us. We felt as free as birds" (p. 174).

And one which reflect's Lee's notion of the movement from *being able to* to *doing*:

> *"I made an effort; I was happy. It is certain that we have freedom, but freedom is often opposed by our environment, by human respect, etc. What counts is the effort we make to show our freedom" (p. 175).

And finally, one which reflects the use of one's freedom to impose constraint based on a higher principle. It is interestingly reminiscent of the example we drew from G. B. Shaw in Chapter 2:

> *"A friend of mine came to my house to pick me up for a walk in the open fields. Both of us were very serious. After a long walk, we had a lot of fun in an innocent way. We came back home after three or four hours. There had been no flirting, but there was a tendency towards it. I could have gone further than that very quickly if I did not have a little bit of will power. And if the occasion would present itself once more, I would certainly involve myself more seriously and engage in petting, because there was a real sexual attraction and much sympathy between the two of us. Conclusion: I hope that I will never go again with him alone, because I am afraid of myself and fear that I might lose, little by little, my simplicity and innocence. I am glad that I was able to use my freedom, but the next time I will use my freedom by telling him two things: that I consider him a very good friend of mine, and that I do not want to be alone with him in the fields... In fact, freedom for me is obedience freely accepted — obedience to duties of one's state, to moral and religious laws in my entire conduct. This will still constitute the use of my freedom" (pp. 175-176).

Is Hypatia exchanged with Percival?

Finally, Zavalloni reports protocols on the experience of freedom in the activity of self-determination — planning and choosing (and ultimately, pursuing) one's future. We have protocols concerning the first two aspects, but since the respondents were all students, the possibilities for evidence on the third were relatively meager. But we should still recognize that the carrying out of an immediate future — as in the example of the 15-year old recalling her experience as a six-year-old — may very justly be called the active management of one's future. A relevant report:

> *"Freedom, in some cases, is something which demands much effort, and consequently much will power. The only time in which I can say that I experienced being really free is when I had to choose my future. After having finished my secondary education, I expressed the desire of entering a professional school in order to continue my education and obtain my degree. This is the only proof of freedom that I can quote at the present time, because I cannot say that I was really free in any other case. To say that I was free in other cases would constitute a lie" (pp. 176-177).

> *"I must choose my career. What shall I do? Since I am in my classical studies, the problem of choosing my career has to be faced with decision. I feel free, horribly free. I hesitate. I cannot make up my mind. I think of this, of that, but no decision. I think that I would really be happy if somebody else would choose for me. But it is I who must choose — and upon this choice my entire life will depend" (p. 177).

A truly existential crisis.

> *"When I chose my vocation I felt completely and truly free. I chose the vocation to the priesthood. I could have refused or accepted this vocation without any actual sin. No force

of any kind was determining me to follow it, while, on the other hand, carnal links were keeping me tied up with the world. I assented to this vocation and accepted. In my acceptance I felt really free because I cut as with a sword every link that was yet tying me to the world" (p. 182).

Different degrees and kinds of conflict and stress are evident in these decision making events, and while the third example reiterates the freedom of being cut off from the rest of the world which Parmenter described, the anxiety and conflict associated with the freedom of decision making is a matter we will take up again later.

In accord with his original request, Zavalloni also received reports of examples of freedom being interfered with. He notes:

"...Limitations on freedom can be of an external or internal character, of a moral or social nature. They can proceed, in other words, from environment and society, and from circumstances within the individual himself and from his psychic functions. While in the subjects from eleven to fourteen years of age the external limitations prevail by far, in the subjects from fourteen to twenty, on the contrary, the references to internal limitations are seen to be more stressed in the protocols. This is an evident sign of that process of interiorization which begins during childhood but which develops during the late stages of adolescence" (p. 183).

This progression may be peculiar to the time of gathering these findings, or the place, or the fact that many of the protocols came from boarding and parochial schools, and some from Catholic seminaries. Data to be reported later do not show this trend in contemporary Canada. At any rate, contrasting examples include, first, some of the more elementary external impingements on freedom:

*"How furious I was because I could not go out. If I had been alone at home, I would have left my homework unfinished, and I would have followed my impulse to freedom; I would have gone out, but my mother repeatedly insisted that I study, and then I would feel the burden of the lack of freedom" (p. 183).

More impersonal conditions, e.g., economic ones, may also serve as external blocks to freedom:[7]

*"But how great was my disillusionment when my mother told me, with sadness, she could not afford it because we were too poor. ...I wished that I had the power to be free, to act freely, to satisfy my desire! The beautiful yellow soccer ball was there, behind the thin glass window, and seemed to invite me! But I could not do anything. I couldn't because I was poor, because I was not as rich as many other boys, and therefore I was not free to satisfy my desire" (p. 184).

But strong moral features also appear:

*"A violation of my freedom happened when I was still a boy and was unable to choose and to will. At that time I was taught to perform something bad, in other words I was taught to do

---

[7]Zavalloni does not distinguish between personal and impersonal threats or obstructions to freedom as is done in reactance theory.

an immoral act. This was for me a true coercion, a real limitation of my freedom. On the part of the individual who taught me that bad thing, it was an irrational act. This bad act which he had taught me proves that my freedom had been violated. Could he really do this at the expense of my freedom?" (p. 187).

In this context of infringement on freedoms, some reports are centrally relevant to the concept of reactance. Many of the reports speak principally of strong emotion, and a desire to rebel in the face of continuous restriction:

*"I do not know how mad I was when I was confronted with these continuous denials. I thought I also had the right to the freedom that so many other boys were enjoying" (p. 192).

*"I was exasperated, I almost wanted to rebel. Looking out the window, I thought, 'When I grow up, I will do everything in my own way and I will be free to go where I want to, as the others do.' Meanwhile I saw a swallow flying happily and the other boys playing... I envied them, as a hungry person envies one who is eating" (p. 192).

Zavalloni, however, goes on to say,

"Some subjects, after having described some concrete facts of limitation of their freedom, write reflections which are very interesting from the pedagogical viewpoint. An excessive control and coercion have the effect of exasperating them and inducing them to search illicitly for the freedom of which they believe they were unjustly deprived. But this is not the only damaging consequence. Deprived for too long of a moderate exercise of freedom, these youngsters will find themselves suddenly in an occasion where they will have to make full use of their freedom, and then they are unprepared" (p. 193).

However, his example is of a nineteen year old, reflecting on his experience as a fifteen year old. When the lad was fifteen, he had been a faithful Christian and was inclined to follow the vocation of a priest, but his parents opposed this and he began to lead a morally reprehensible life. After his parents opposed him, the respondent says,

*"From that time on, I began to grow cold toward my vocation. After that, I erred along the path of my life and fell from one precipice to another...in the mud. I was so bad that I became a scandal to my friends. I did not go to Mass on Sunday; my daily Communions became annual ones (and they were bad Communions!). My favorite pastime was card playing. I occupied myself in looking for English soldiers and taking them to the whores, in inciting my friends to do evil, and in spending at the movies the money my mother (sick in bed with shock) had given me to buy her prescriptions" (pp. 194-195).

This is somewhat problematic from the point of view of reactance theory, since his pursuit of the lower life could hardly be considered an increased desire for, or renewed efforts to pursue the priesthood. On the other hand, his reprehensible behaviour may be considered symbolic of pursuing a course which would be opposed by his parents at least as strongly as they opposed his vocation. Or, the pursuit of the lower life could be considered angry aggression toward the parents. However one cares to consider it, it does appear that the infringement of his freedom of choice had negative consequences.

Other negative consequences of consistent restriction of freedom and the development toward self-determination are less dramatic, but of great concern to Zavalloni from a pedagogical and general human development point of view. He argues that the capacity for freedom, in its elemental form of autonomy or the self-generation of action is inherent in the human being, but the development of self-determination — autonomy informed by intelligence and morality — must be acquired through practice. When this practice is denied, the capacity for self-determination is inhibited in its development, or never develops at all. Several examples are provided in which respondents bemoan the restriction and authoritarian structure of their schools and predict (or report) the excesses and abuse of freedom which they would indulge in or have indulged in when given the opportunity.

*"Some individuals are not very much preoccupied by the limitation of their freedom. They are very willing to let their parents, as their guardians, always keep them away from every danger in life. But what will happen when their mother no longer observes them, when they will be without guidance and must face the turbulent waters of an unscrupulous world? Are their characters strong enough to face the great temptations that they will certainly encounter? I say no! A man won't learn to swim, no matter how hard he studies from a book the required way of moving his body in the water. He must go into the water and undergo that experience" (pp. 193-194).

*Oh, certainly, I can think of an event of my life in which I experienced a limitation of my freedom: the fact that I am locked up in a boarding school, among religious persons, from whom we must hide what we think, because, naturally, what we think is not always too good and beautiful. If I could choose, certainly I would not go to Mass every day. Faced by this obligation, I went to Mass out of habit, which changed into indifference and perhaps even into disgust. Doubtless, this is not very Christian. I should profit by this opportunity and try to find a personal delight in attending Mass, but I am forced to think of the mechanical aspect of the duty: to get up in the morning, to be controlled by nuns, to be counted when we go to Mass and Communion, etc., etc. Actually, we are forced to go to Mass and Communion. I detest life in a boarding school. After having been treated in this way, when we enter into the world with all its attractions, only defeat awaits us. If freedom is offered to me all at one time, I will use and abuse it in every way. Here is what the limitation of freedom produces" (p. 196).

Zavalloni's purpose was to illuminate the proposition that true freedom lies in the use of the capacity for self-determination, informed by intelligence, morality and ethics. It is not at all clear that these self reports generally do this, although there are clear examples where these are precisely the circumstances under which freedom is experienced. The kinds of loose and perhaps overly-large categories which he employed can be usefully broken down by reference to their actual content rather than to the principles they illustrate: either simple impulsiveness or self-determination, properly informed.

Imposing a somewhat more strict ordering, I have attempted to derive a series of categories of circumstances under which Zavalloni's respondents report feeling free. Needless to say, my categorization is informed by the kinds of categories I developed before reading Zavalloni's work (Westcott, 1978, 1981, 1982a). From Zavalloni's work then, it appears that experiences which give rise to reports of freedom — either being free or feeling free — include the following:

(1) Situations in which the individual is in contact with nature—both placid, as on a mountain top, and vigorous, as in being buffeted by wind or wave;

(2) Absence of parental surveillance, as when parents are away or one goes out without a chaperone;

(3) Some reports include a growing awareness of social balance and responsibility, as freedom experienced precisely when one voluntarily restricts one's own freedom, in order that the freedom of others may be guaranteed;

(4) Doing gladly what one ought—freedom experienced through altruistic acts carried out gladly;

(5) When making a personal decision about one's future—many respondents spoke directly about decisions concerning a career or further education;

(6) Experiences of being independent and meeting a challenge successfully—this feature of independence and challenge can be in a decision situation, a moral dilemma, a physical challenge, an interpersonal one;

(7) The final achievement of a goal which involves specific self-expression, as in ultimately learning to fly an airplane;

(8) The more primitive freedom experienced when one can finally go outside after a long illness;

(9) The simple freedom of engaging in a novel experience, such as going to an unfamiliar city;

(10) The clear recognition that one is free when becoming aware of the opposite side of freedom—responsibility and conflict.

These ten categories capture at least some of the essence of the kinds of situations which give rise to reports of feeling free or recognition that one is free, at least for the respondents to Zavalloni's question. Some responses fall outside these categories, of course, and some experiences that have been included in each category differ very much from each other. Zavalloni does not provide much context for the responses—merely age and sex (sometimes) and the language in which the report was written. He states that the findings do not lend themselves to any statistical treatment, but one of his respondents submitted a survey rather than a personal report: A 19 year old girl surveyed a youth group of which she was a member, and reported that a feeling of complete freedom had been experienced by 20% of the girls while alone or in contact with nature, 20% during vacation or leisure time, 20% when not under any control or chaperonage, and 12% after they had overcome some obstacle or performed a good act (p. 174). We are not told the number surveyed, nor whether the above percentages are independent, but they certainly reflect some of the categories mentioned previously.

The point to be taken is that a systematic survey is possible, and that some statistical treatment is also possible, and that one can inquire directly into the conditions which give rise to one feeling free or to one recognizing that one is free. I continue to use these two phrases because they are not equivalent, although they are often used by Zavalloni as if they were (cf. Westcott, 1982b).

Caution in the interpretation of these findings is needed. In addition to the selective bias under which Zavalloni worked in illuminating his hypothesis through examples, we must also be aware of the demand characteristics of the method used for gathering the reports. Although we have little information on this, we do know that the reports were gathered through teachers' and administrators' requests to students, primarily in Roman Catholic boarding schools. To what extent this setting contributed to reports tainted with social desirability we cannot know, although we have examples which seem to reflect this aspiration. We also have examples which appear to avoid this. We also have direct, thoughtful rejections of the task, so this must have been an option. The fact is, of course, that informants took on the task with different orientations, and as we have pointed out, the instructions of the request are only a fragment of the determinants of how the task is construed. It is not clear how justifiable it is to generalize from these data in support of Zavalloni's developmental hypothesis, but it is evident that the personal reports illuminate many facets of the lived conditions and experiences of freedom.

### Summary

In summary of the empirical material presented in this chapter, we have the autobiographical phenomenology of Parmenter and the solicited personal reports provided by Zavalloni. Both are systematic, but both tend toward a blurring of both concepts and data. Specifically, there is no consistent distinction made between *being free*, as an ontological state, and *feeling free*, as an experiential condition. These, of course are not the same thing at all. The former requires some recourse to external criteria, usually philosophical or political in nature, while the latter requires recourse to one's own evaluation of one's experience. The distinction is made, at least at times, by Parmenter, who pointed out that he believed people didn't want to *be* free, they wanted to *feel* free. But the distinction disappears elsewhere. Zavalloni simply doesn't make the distinction.

Another way in which data are mixed has to do with reports of oneself either being free or feeling free, on the one hand, and on the other hand, commentary or abstractions about freedom. I noted earlier that it is difficult to get people to talk or write about their own experiences of freedom without eliciting broad generalizations about the nature of freedom. The research to be reported in the next chapter attempts to maintain the distinctions between being free and feeling free, between reports of experience and commentary on experience.

# 7 Systematic Surveys of Experienced Freedom

## The plan

In this chapter, the systematic investigation of human freedom, informed by a human science perspective, continues. However, the material to be presented in this chapter is systematic in a way quite different from that presented in Chapter 6. It begins with open-ended interviews, but moves rapidly to the development of a questionnaire which attempts to gather quantifiable data on human freedom from a conceptual base much wider than the bases employed by reactance theory and attribution theory. The questionnaire attempts to capture both quantitative information (how free people feel) and qualitative information (how "feeling free" is construed) in a variety of theoretically important kinds of situations. Relatively simple statistical analyses are used to provide descriptive summaries of the findings.

It may be argued that the use of questionnaires and statistical summaries violates the very spirit of human science research. In some respects this is true, but the questionnaire developed and used is informed by a sensitivity to the variety of situations in which persons experience themselves as free, the variety of ways in which freedom can be experienced, and also solicits open-ended qualitative responses. However, even the qualitative data gathered are treated statistically, through frequency counts, correlations and coefficients of concordance. But the question is not whether the incantations performed over the data are orthodox, but whether they produce informative and illuminating understandings. The pursuit of this latter goal is fully in keeping with the spirit of human science research — adapting the methods to the phenomena and the purpose rather than adapting the phenomena and the purpose to methodological orthodoxy. Here, the phenomenon is the human experience of freedom, and the purpose is to sketch some broad general outlines.

The chapter concludes with some data illuminating the distinction between being free and feeling free, and some cross-cultural reflections will be offered, bringing focus again to the historical and cultural setting of the experience of human freedom.

## Systematic survey research

This research programme began (Westcott, 1978) with a series of interviews which focussed on the conditions under which respondents feel free. These early studies yielded the following observations: First, many people interviewed were obviously troubled by the question, "Do you think your behaviour is genuinely free, in any significant respect?" Most of them were psychology faculty or students, or at least somewhat psychologically sophisticated, so the question was loaded, and they expressed a genuine conflict over it. However, when asked, "Do you ever feel free?" there seemed to be no problem at all about the forthcoming positive answers. That is, while they were very noncommittal about believing that they were actually free, they indicated without hesitation that they sometimes, at least, felt free.

When pursued to find out some of the conditions under which they did feel free, quite a variety was revealed. The following are some examples of the specific responses to the question, "Under what conditions do you feel free? Try to be as specific as possible and think of a concrete case."

"I feel free when I have three martinis in me and I don't know what is going to happen next..."

"I feel free when I tip onto an unfamiliar ski slope and start down..."

"I feel free when I do something I haven't done before, like taking off for a weekend in Montreal..."

"I feel free when I think of something I can really do myself..."

"I feel free when I decide something trivial, like taking a different route to work..."

"I felt free when I realized that the bind I was in was the result of a positive choice on my part in the past..."

"I feel free when I am doing something which contributes to the accomplishment of my long term plans..."

These statements represent only the first few moments of interviews which
typically lasted for well over an hour. It is interesting that the initial statements about freedom elicited from these informants do not appear to be explicit statements about the negative liberty of the philosophers. This could
well be because of informants' social and political status: None were under
any grinding heel of oppression, either external or internal. Indeed, findings
here may tap the experience of freedom well above the floor, that is, well
above the point where people are in some sort of clear bondage and negative
liberty is made crucial by its absence. We can, however, note that in several
of the examples given, the individuals could well be conceived of as feeling
free when they transcend the bondage of the ordinary, and one person
reports freedom experienced in terms of reconceptualizing the perceived
bondage of an earlier decision. So while there is only an occasional explicit
statement that release or negative liberty is a central part of the experience of
freedom for these people, it is implied in some cases where it is not explicit.

Next, positive freedom is more often either clear or implied. Informants
frequently feel free when doing something specific: skiing an unfamiliar
slope, finding "something which contributes to my long term plans," "doing
something I haven't done before." Each of these activities is an active use of
skills, an exploitation of resources which one can count on. A further implication is that doing the routine with one's resources does not give rise to
the experience of freedom to the same extent as doing something unfamiliar
or unusual with one's resources. Thus, it appears that the availability of opportunities and the use of resources is of central importance, as posed by
MacCallum (1967) and in spite of the criticism of Berlin (1969) and Parent
(1974b). Sometimes it seems important that the doing be coupled with at
least moderate risk. The informant who said he felt free when he didn't know
what was going to happen next indicated later that under these conditions he
had every confidence of coping with whatever it might be. Another common
feature is that resources referred to most were personal skills. William James
was especially impressed with novelty in the expression of free will (cf. Viney,
1986).

It is interesting that the norm-breaking found in studies of freedom attributed to the behaviour of others, (cf. Chapter 4) enters these self-reports
only in the mild form of doing something a little bit out of the ordinary, and
the feature of unpredictability of behaviour also receives an interesting twist.
The informants' reliance on personal resources or skills and their confidence
in outcomes indicate that the conditions which give rise to a sense of personal
freedom involve considerable predictability, from the point of view of the person carrying out the behaviour. So while unpredictability of behaviour is important when observers are asked to rate the freedom of the behaviour of
others, it appears that unpredictability of one's own behaviour may not be a
contributor to feeling free oneself. In fact, it might well detract from such a
feeling by implying an experienced loss of control.

In the examples above, there is only one which refers to specific choice behaviour as a central situation in which freedom is experienced. The informant stated it specifically as being a trivial choice — choosing a route to work — and in further discussion he pointed out that the alternatives among which he chose were typically almost identical in costs and benefits, and were high in availability. A choice of this kind would be perceived by others as free because of the high "decision freedom" component as well as the high "outcome freedom" component.

Looking at individual interviews in greater depth, it appears that each informant tended to focus on a theme of freedom which is an elaboration of a central point or central experience. This theme, for each individual, tended to become an abstraction which seemed to serve as a personal definition of freedom for that person. As each interview progressed, informants tended to move more and more closely toward such a personal abstract definition. The following can be deduced as some examples of the concept of freedom which appear to be meaningful and important to different persons:

Freedom is experienced in facing uncertainty with skill.
Freedom is experienced in self-discipline.
Freedom is experienced in the achievement of steps in a long-term program.
Freedom is experienced in the recognition of one's own realm of influence.
Freedom is experienced in getting the most out of existing limits.

While some of these examples overlap with each other, and while the quotations offered earlier show common threads, it would be preposterous to assert that experienced freedom, even in this relatively homogeneous sample of informants, is unitary, scalable on a single dimension, or can be conceptualized under a single definition. On the other hand, it is reasonable to suppose that there is some finite variety of personal definitions and conditions which are associated with experienced freedom.

At this point, it would be presumptuous to even guess what the most commonly held concepts of freedom or experiences of freedom are, or to guess whether they actually exist in a hierarchy of maturity or growth, or in any other systematic relationship to each other. However, it does appear that the findings reported here are useful starting points of meaningful and systematic investigation (Westcott, 1978, pp. 287-289).

## Development of a questionnaire

The more systematic study took the form of a questionnaire which went through many developmental stages before being used. From the philosophi-

140

cal and psychological literatures, as well as from the interviews, seven different types of situations, asserted to contribute to either prescribed, attributed, or experienced human freedom were derived. The seven types of situations were: (1) Self Direction; (2) Absence of Responsibility; (3) Release from Noxious Stimulation; (4) Recognition of Limits; (5) Active Decision Making; (6) Presence of Alternatives; (7) Exercise of Skilled Behaviour. Four specific examples of each kind of situation were progressively developed and refined by an iterative process of requesting university students to sort the specific situational descriptions into their presumed parent categories. Following each sorting, the situational descriptions were revised in the light of sorting "errors" and a new sample of sorters attempted the task again. Four cycles of this kind ultimately yielded 90% accuracy of sorting by a sample of 30 university undergraduates. Each group of four examples of the parent category was called a *cluster*. The specific situations described were tailored to the population of respondents — university students — and were situations in which they might commonly find themselves. The seven cluster names and an example of each appear below:[1]

1. *Self Direction* (S.D.): I am taking successful steps in working my way to a long-term goal.
2. *Absence of Responsibility* (A.R.): Sometimes I have no responsibilities.
3. *Release from Noxious Stimulation* (R.N.): All day long I have had a nagging headache, and I have just realized that it is gone.
4. *Recognition of Limits* (R.L.): Sometimes I restrict or reduce my desires to fit with what I believe a situation allows and to what I believe my abilities to be.
5. *Active Decision Making* (A.D.): I am faced with two important, valuable, and apparently equal choices. I am now deciding between them.
6. *Presence of Alternatives* (P.A.): Every year when I go through the university calendar and lecture schedule, I find a very large number of attractive courses which are open to me.
7. *Exercise of Skilled Behaviour* (S.B.): At times I engage in activities with skill and confidence in my ability to perform well.

Next, the 28 situational descriptions were cast into a questionnaire format as in the example shown in Figure 1. Respondents were instructed to consider carefully each of the 28 situations in turn, and decide whether it had anything to do with feeling free and/or feeling any opposite to free for them, individually. If so, they were to indicate the extent to which the situation contributed to either or both feelings by checking the appropriate point on the scale or scales chosen. In addition, if the OPPOSITE scale was used, each respondent was to supply the opposite for himself or herself for that specific

---

[1]A complete list of the situational descriptions can be found in the Appendix.

I am doing something at which I am skilled - something I do very well.  I feel:

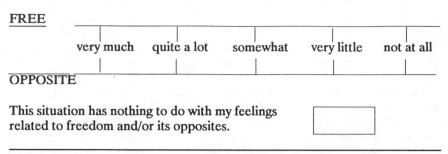

FREE

very much    quite a lot    somewhat    very little    not at all

OPPOSITE

This situation has nothing to do with my feelings
related to freedom and/or its opposites.

Figure 1.  An example of the questionnaire format.

situation by writing a word or phrase on the line marked OPPOSITE.  A final
alternative was to declare the entire situation not relevant personally to feeling free or any opposite to free.[2]

Because the questionnaire was administered in group settings, the investigator "walked through" an example of a situation and several possible options for responding to it, showing various ways in which respondents might
indicate their feelings.  In addition, while the questionnaire was being filled
out, the investigator and his assistants circulated throughout the group to
answer questions and to insure that respondents were following the format of
the response sheets accurately.  Maximum flexibility and thoughtfulness were
emphasized, so that the respondents could most accurately report their reactions to the situations, within the constraints of the questionnaire format.

Using this basic format, with several variations, a variety of studies have
been carried out and reported in detail (sometimes tedious detail) elsewhere
(Westcott, 1982a, 1982b, 1984).  They have been designed to answer a series
of questions concerning human freedom and the psychological investigation
of human freedom, so the questions are both conceptual and methodological.

### Utility of the questionnaire

The first few questions are methodological:  Can respondents actually use
the questionnaire format, and do the situational descriptions appear to have
anything to do with feeling free or any opposite?  Answers to these questions

---

[2]The inquiry into opposites to free was carried out in order to explore some qualitative
features of feeling free in the various situations.  The elicitation of opposites rather than
synonyms or elaborations was employed in order to focus on the bipolar dimensions
along which freedom was construed.  This inquiry is treated later in this chapter.

appear in the original data collected from two samples of respondents (n = 69, 139). Overall, the situations were rejected as *not applicable* to the question on 16% of the possible occasions; that is, 84% of the time, respondents were able to give what they considered meaningful answers to the questions posed within the questionnaire format. Different clusters of situations seemed more relevant than others, with Cluster 1 (Self Direction) being seen as relevant 92% of the time and Clusters 3 and 7 (Release from Noxious Stimulation and Exercise of Skilled Behaviour) being relevant only 79% of the time. On average, it can be said that respondents typically found approximately 24 of the 28 situational descriptions relevant to questions about experienced freedom. Of the total of 208 respondents cited here, the lowest frequency of relevance was 17 situations of the 28, and the highest, of course, was 28 of the 28. Occasionally an individual who had volunteered for the study would ultimately reject the task by failing to complete the form at all or by writing that he/she could not see how human freedom could be studied under these conditions. In addition to the great majority of respondents who (as usual) simply filled out the form and left the room, a surprising number approached the investigator to say that it was an unusually interesting, provocative, or difficult task. As I had found out in the earlier conduct of the interviews, almost no one had been asked about their feelings of freedom or the circumstances under which such feelings arise. Almost no one had ever thought about these matters before, either.

### Basic quantitative features: how free do you feel?

Respondents indicated on the five point scale how free they feel in each situation they thought relevant to the question. The mean score was calculated for each item and then means were calculated for each cluster, i.e., each group of four conceptually related items. Whenever an item was declared irrelevant it was simply excluded from the data. Table 1 shows the cluster means for two samples for how free respondents say they feel (Scale F) and for how strongly they feel an opposite to free (Scale 0). The same data are plotted as profiles in Figure 2.

First, it is evident that the two samples are essentially the same. They came from the same parent population, so we can consider this as replication. Of the fourteen comparisons between the two samples, only three show marginal statistically significant differences in cluster means. It can also be seen from Figure 1 that the profiles are almost identical for the two samples both on Scale F and Scale 0. It is also evident that Scale F profiles are almost perfect mirror images of Scale 0. For the aggregate data there is an almost perfect negative correlation between Scale F and Scale 0 — how free people feel in a given type of situation as compared with how strongly they feel opposite to

Table 1. Cluster means and S.D. s for Scale F and Scale O for two samples, t-values and significance of differences between the two samples.

| | SCALE F (FREE) | | | | |
|---|---|---|---|---|---|
| CLUSTER | Sample 1 | | Sample 2 | | |
| | $\overline{X}$ | S.D. | $\overline{X}$ | S.D. | t |
| 1. S.D. | 3.87 | .71 | 3.93 | .70 | .53 |
| 2. A.R. | 3.87 | .70 | 3.82 | .88 | .42 |
| 3. R.N. | 4.32 | .55 | 4.25 | .83 | .79 |
| 4. R.L. | 3.06 | .85 | 2.92 | .80 | 1.22 |
| 5. A.D. | 2.76 | 1.02 | 3.08 | .98 | 2.19* |
| 6. P.A. | 3.47 | .86 | 3.35 | .86 | .92 |
| 7. S.B. | 4.22 | .69 | 4.16 | .70 | .54 |

*$p < .05$

| | SCALE O (OPPOSITE) | | | | |
|---|---|---|---|---|---|
| CLUSTER | Sample 1 | | Sample 2 | | |
| | $\overline{X}$ | S.D. | $\overline{X}$ | S.D. | t |
| 1. S.D. | 2.10 | .97 | 2.11 | .84 | .12 |
| 2. A.R. | 1.88 | .78 | 1.96 | .82 | .73 |
| 3. R.N. | 1.27 | .46 | 1.44 | .73 | 2.04* |
| 4. R.L. | 2.64 | .90 | 2.92 | .90 | 2.14* |
| 5. A.D. | 2.89 | .88 | 2.81 | 1.26 | .51 |
| 6. P.A. | 2.30 | .87 | 2.55 | 1.02 | 1.69 |
| 7. S.B. | 1.42 | .54 | 1.60 | .65 | 1.90 |

*$p < .05$

free in the same situation. This should surprise nobody, but there are some interesting findings in a more microscopic analysis.

When a product moment correlation for each respondent is calculated, across the 28 items, between scores on the F Scale and on the 0 Scale, a distribution of correlations is obtained. This distribution ranges from a perfect −1.00, parallel to the findings on the aggregate data, through zero-order correlations, to +.69 in Sample 1, and from −1.00 to +.39 in Sample 2. These positive correlations for individuals are quite different from the findings on the aggregate data.

The medians of these distributions of correlations are −.37 and −.75 respectively, and they are skewed strongly toward the positive end. Thus, for the bulk of individuals, the relationship between experienced freedom and its

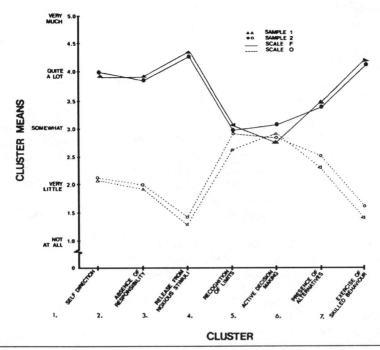

Figure 2. Profiles of cluster means for two samples of university students on Scale F and Scale 0. (Sample 1, n = 69; Sample 2, n = 139).

opposites is clearly inverse, but for some, the two are essentially unrelated, and for a few, the two covary positively in the situations explored.

From an Aristotelian point of view, the presence of experienced freedom should be negatively correlated with the experience of its opposites; however, from a decision making point of view, uncertainty and conflict should be associated with experienced freedom; from an existential point of view, freedom is not only inevitable, but also disturbing. It appears that some of our respondents experience freedom from an Aristotelian perspective, others from a decision theory perspective, and yet others from an existentialist perspective. This reflects the complexity of the problem, and the fact that the complexity can be described.

*Quantitative differences among clusters.* The statistical significance of differences in cluster means for the different clusters on both the F Scale and the 0 Scale are large, and are just about as they appear to be in Figure 2. For example, Clusters 1 and 2 on Scale F are not significantly different, but they are both significantly different from Cluster 3 (t-values range from 5.87 to 6.84). Cluster 4 is significantly different from Clusters 1, 2, and 3 (t-values

145

range from 4.16 to 15.35), and so on. Cluster 4 is not different from Cluster 5, but both are significantly different from Cluster 6 and Cluster 7, which are also different from each other. These details of Scale F, and similar comparisons concerning Scale 0 are presented in detail elsewhere (Westcott, 1982a). Essentially, those that *look* different in Figure 2 *are* different.

But the point to be kept in mind is that these different clusters of situations were designed to be conceptually, *qualitatively*, different—not simply different in a quantitative way along a single dimension. Even when significant differences are not shown in the quantitative data of Table 1 and Figure 2 (as between Clusters 1 and 2) there may be very important qualitative differences in the basis for these data. We will take this up later in more detail, but note for the moment that the conceptual characteristics of Cluster 1 (Self Direction) and Cluster 2 (Absence of Responsibility) are very different, and persons may report the same degree of feeling free for very different reasons, and feeling free in these kinds of situations may be very different, qualitatively.

The different clusters of items yield large and replicated differences in mean scores. According to our informants, they feel free to very different degrees in different types of "freedom inducing" situations.

*Intercorrelations of clusters.* The next question is to what extent the quantitative data for the different clusters intercorrelate. A matrix of all pair-wise intercorrelations shows that more than 75% of cluster means intercorrelate positively and significantly, indicating that the different clusters tend to tap the same domain without being redundant. Overall, the correlations range from $-.01$ to $+.60$. Some of the pairs of clusters which are conceptually quite different (e.g., Clusters 3 and 5—Release from Noxious Stimulation and Active Decision Making) correlate not at all (r = .02, $-.01$ for the two samples) while some that are conceptually quite similar show fairly high positive correlations: Clusters 5 and 6, Active Decision Making and Presence of Alternatives correlate to the extent of $+.60$ and $+.44$ for the two samples.

Keep in mind the difference between similarities in the levels of aggregate response for pairs of clusters and the correlations between them. For example, Clusters 1 and 2 are not significantly different in their mean scores, but they are correlated only r = .14 and .19 for the two samples. Similarly, Clusters 4 and 5 are also not significantly different in their scores, and show correlations of only r = .21 and .15 for the two samples. In contrast, Clusters 5 and 6 are significantly different from each other in their levels of feeling free, but they show correlations of r = .44 and .60 for the two samples. Thus, the aggregate data show relationships among cluster scores which can be viewed in a variety of ways and show important complexities.

The intercorrelations of cluster means for Scale 0 do not yield as stable a picture because Scale 0 is actually a collection of different scales, each uniquely defined by a respondent who provides a specific opposite. The intercorrelations range from $-.07$ to $+.54$, and nearly half the correlations in the matrix are significant beyond the .05 level. It can be concluded that the domain "opposite to free" is being tapped in more diverse ways than is the

146

domain "free". As noted earlier, the content of the opposites will be taken up later.

*Sex differences.* It might be expected that within the realm of human freedom there would be some differences in socialization for males and females, that the kinds of situations which produce the most — or least — degrees of feeling free might differ. The evidence from the present studies is that there are no such differences. In fact, no analysis of any kind yielded any sex differences in the quantitative data reported here, nor in the qualitative data to be reported later.

*Relationships to other findings.* With the above descriptive features of the data established, it is now possible to explore the relationships of the present findings to ideas found in other literatures. The results indicate that situations in which individuals are released from noxious stimulation or frustration (Cluster 3) and can engage in skilled behaviours (Cluster 7) generate the strongest experiences of feeling free. These two kinds of situations are parallels to the basic negative freedom ("freedom from") and positive freedom ("freedom to") discussed in the philosophical literature. MacCallum (1967) has argued that both components must be present in order to make a sensible statement about freedom. In contrast, Berlin (1969) and others, in developing a logical definition of freedom, have argued that if the negative component is socially guaranteed, the positive component can become socially prescriptive, and impose obligation rather than providing freedom. However, from the individual, experiential point of view tapped here, it appears that if the two components are combined, maximum freedom is likely to be experienced. These two clusters, Release from Noxious Stimulation and Exercise of Skilled Behaviour, so far, yield very similar data, (they are not different on Scale F or Scale O, and they are positively correlated) but they are conceptually very different.

The next most highly contributory pair of clusters, Self Direction (Cluster 1) and Absence of Responsibility (Cluster 2), are similar to the first pair in several respects. They are both relatively high on Scale F and low on Scale 0. They are not significantly different from each other on either scale for either sample, but they are conceptually quite different. Absence of Responsibility is a negative type of freedom, similar to Release from Noxious Stimulation, while Self Direction can be considered positive freedom as it entails action, similar to the Exercise of Skilled Behaviour. However, as presented in the descriptions in the questionnaire, the situations in Clusters 1 and 2 are neither as sudden in the implied affective changes, nor are the outcomes so rapid and certain as in Clusters 3 and 7. This may be the primary difference between these two pairs of clusters and it is possible that the statistically reliable differences between them could be explained by subtle but important shades of meaning and the time spans involved in the described situations. Further qualitative differences between these two clusters will be discussed later.

147

The two least powerful contributors to experienced freedom on Scale F are Active Decision Making (Cluster 5) and Recognition of Limits (Cluster 4). They are also the highest contributors on Scale 0. With respect to Active Decision Making, the attribution literature predicts theoretically (Steiner, 1970) and shows empirically (Harvey, 1976) that a high degree of freedom is attributed by observers to actors when the actors are making choices among alternatives which are almost equally attractive and available, that is, when there is both high decision freedom and high outcome freedom. The findings of the present study, while quite different, do not necessarily contradict those predictions or findings. Rather, the present data may point to a marked contrast between attributed and experienced freedom, at least with respect to decision making situations. In decision situations, where choice is not coerced by discrepancies in attractiveness or availability, actors may be seen to "be free" to a high degree by others, but they themselves do not "feel free" to a high degree, according to our data.

In 1973, Steiner asserted his belief "... that people feel they have decision freedom — a real choice — when the options between which they choose are about equally attractive, that is, when the options offer fairly equal net gains after calculating the costs and payoffs" (Steiner, 1973, p. 52). This quotation itself indicates the kind of potential for confusion which plagues the field, confusion between the feeling of having a real choice and feeling free. To say that an individual feels he or she has a real choice is not to say that an individual feels free. The present studies indicate that in choosing among reasonably balanced alternatives, respondents feel less free than in any of the other conditions described. If it were possible to render decision making a skilled behaviour, a considerable advance in experienced freedom might follow.

The data for Recognition of Limits (Cluster 4) fall into line with that body of philosophical thinking which asserts that maximum freedom resides in the maximum fulfillment of desires, and which argues that a reduction of desires cannot enhance freedom (cf., Berlin, 1969; Parent, 1974b, p. 151). This point of view is reflected in the reports of respondents in both samples. The recognition and acceptance of existing constraints on one's choice, while identifying the limits within which one can operate unencumbered, is a feeble contributor to feeling free, despite its importance in the formulations of anthropologists (cf. Chapter 2). This appears to be so in spite of the fact that such recognition can forewarn one about possible blunders, failures, and punishment. In this case, from the philosophical and experiential viewpoints respectively, knowing the "truth" does not make one "free," nor does it do much to make one "feel free".

The Presence of Alternatives (Cluster 6), with one marginal exception (see Table 1), is significantly different from all other clusters on both scales for both samples. It falls between the high and medium groups (Clusters, 1, 2, 3, and 7) and the low group (Clusters 4 and 5). Conceptually, it partakes of both.

While the situations described in Cluster 6 related purely to the presence of alternatives, with no choice or decision required (in contrast to Cluster 5, Active Decision Making), some respondents commented that they couldn't consider the Presence of Alternatives without considering making a choice between them. To these respondents, Cluster 6 is more or less a replication of Cluster 5, or at least confounded with it. With the implication of unpressured choice, Cluster 6 may also exhibit some of the features of Self Direction (Cluster 1). Thus, Cluster 6 is in a somewhat indeterminate position – differences between this cluster and both the high and low groups can be attributed to subtle differences among respondents in their interpretation or meaning, a point also made with respect to the differences between pairs of Clusters 1 and 2 versus 3 and 7.

The Presence of Alternatives (Cluster 6) is more conducive to reports of experienced freedom than is Active Decision Making (Cluster 5) or Recognition of Limits (Cluster 4). These are precisely the relationships which are implicitly predicted by reactance theory (Brehm, 1966; Brehm and Brehm, 1981; Wicklund, 1974). Reactance theory argues that when previously available alternatives are withdrawn, as in the recognition of limits on one's alternatives, or the elimination of alternatives by virtue of actually choosing among them, one's motivational state organizes behaviour toward the reestablishment of those alternatives. The present findings may be taken as a demonstration that the theoretical predictions of reactance theory are paralleled by the reports of experienced freedom. Research within the reactance paradigm has not shown this.

But the present data also support a more extended argument which relates to ordinary life: individuals move from situation to situation, and their actions or conceptualizations change with given situations from moment to moment in the ordinary flow of life. The present data indicate that an experiential process can be constructed for at least the short term maximization of experienced freedom: The mere presence of alternatives contributes to a modest degree of experienced freedom, but when limits are recognized and one is obliged to make a decision, the experienced freedom is diminished. However, if one is free of distracting responsibilities and can engage in skilled behaviour to gain relief from the frustration of the constraints and reestablish the alternatives, and then further engage in skilled decision making, one experiences self direction and experiences oneself as maximally free.

It is possible that the sequence described above can be truncated to include what may be the minimum conditions for a maximum experience of freedom: the presence of alternatives and the exercise of skilled behaviour in the decision making process. It seems that if (and only if) decision making is a skilled behaviour, can this shortened sequence be effective in generating a high degree of experienced freedom.

The data indicate that for the samples studied here, decision making does not seem to be a skilled behaviour and is not a striking contributor to experienced freedom. The age of the respondents may be a factor in this, although it is probable that most people find choices difficult among alternatives which are almost equally available and attractive. However, a paradox remains: The only way to exercise freedom in a choice situation is to give it up by selecting one alternative while abandoning the other alternatives. Thus, any kind of choice behaviour among attractive alternatives has both positive and negative features, and skilled decision making may be the action of defeating high decision freedom — the equality of the alternatives — so as to "coerce" a choice upon oneself one way or another (cf., Westcott, 1977, pp. 256-257).

A first priority for enhancing the experience of freedom for oneself or for others seems to be the development of skilled behaviours, and especially skilled decision making behaviours. The provision of alternatives, e.g., in educational settings or political or social settings, without the necessary training to make decision making a skilled behaviour, does not appear to be a suitable method of enhancing the experience of freedom. Difficult and unskilled decision making seems to do exactly the opposite. Our society has been preoccupied with providing alternatives without noticeable concern for the development of skills for choosing between alternatives in ways which enhance the experience of freedom (Platt, 1973). Enhancing the experience of human freedom is a central concern of humanistic psychotherapies (Enns, 1980), and one may find, paradoxically, that behaviouristic interventions which emphasize rapid symptom relief and the teaching of skills may be uniquely valuable in serving this end.

Finally, with respect to enhancing the experience of freedom, comes the ethical question as to whether this is simply the enhancement of an illusion. Lefcourt (1973) has explicitly called freedom an illusion, but has also pointed out the adaptive consequences of perceived freedom in human behaviour; Steiner (1970) has called freedom "at least an important illusion"; and Skinner (1971) has called the study of this illusion "mischievous." There is, however, a distinction to be drawn between he concept of social freedom and the concept of freedom of choice as a metaphysical truth.

The former ideally involves an enhancement of alternatives, the skill to choose among them, and the accompanying experience of oneself as free; the latter is a metaphysical contrast to determinism in human affairs (cf., Chapter 1). The two notions come from very different realms of discourse and should not be confused. Multiple realms of discourse represent another of the plagues of this area of inquiry. Making these points certainly does not resolve the ethical dilemma, but it may point to some complexities which are not immediately obvious.

## Qualitative features of experienced freedom

Throughout this chapter I have referred to features of experienced freedom which we would explore later. Now is the time. The philosophical literature tends to use the generic term "unfree" to refer to circumstances or conditions where freedom is abrogated or absent. But that term is not common in our ordinary language and seems to be particularly unsatisfactory when attempting to study the psychological construction of human experience. Therefore, the investigation to be reported here followed other leads, ranging from folk wisdom through epistemology, to psychological theory.

The folk wisdom is reflected in the classic two-liner:[3]

Morris: How's your wife?
Max: Compared to what?

The epistemological lead is represented in one of the primary meanings of the term "dialectic" (Rychlak, 1975). This classical meaning focusses on the elucidation of a concept by reference to its contrasts and opposites, and asserts that any concept may have a multitude of such contrasts and opposites.

The third lead, rooted in psychological theory, relies on the psychology of personal constructs (Kelly, 1955). Kelly argues that humans construe their experience along bipolar dimensions, and that every assertion about one's experience implies a continuum ranging from the stated qualitative feature of a situation, or person, or thing ("nice," "frightening") to some contrast. The former is the explicit pole of the bipolar dimension and the latter (contrast) is often, or even usually, implicit. The hierarchical network of these bipolar dimensions along which individuals construe their experience are their personal construct systems by which they anticipate events. For any explicit pole, there may be different implicit poles for different individuals under what appear to be the same conditions, or different implicit poles for the same individual under different conditions. Kelly's point of view is consonant with the broader notion that human consciousness is dialectical in nature (cf. Basseches, 1984; Lamiell and Durbeck, 1987).

Recall that in situations where respondents reported feelings opposite to free (Scale O), they supplied *their own specific descriptive adjectives or phrases*. These opposites are viewed as the implicit poles of various bipolar constructs of feeling free. The resultant dimensions along which respondents construe feeling free are taken to represent some of the qualitative features of experienced freedom.

Through repeated examination by two observers, the opposites supplied gave rise to seven content categories, plus an "uncodable". The raw frequency with which each code category was represented in each cluster of situations was determined, and the rank order of use of each code category was determined within each cluster for each sample. Comparisons among clusters in terms of the opposite code usage was carried out by means of coefficients of concordance and rank order correlations.

---

[3] de Charms (1968, footnote p. 343) attributed the response to a psychologist. I believe I heard it from the silver lips of Myron Cohen, which accounts for the change in characters.

*The variety of opposites to "free".* The first sample of 69 respondents provided opposites a total of 841 times. The second sample of 139 respondents did so 1740 times. For each sample, these figures represent about 45% of the possible opposite responses that could have been made. In total, the first sample provided 170 *different* words or phrases as opposites to "free" and the second sample added 45 *new* terms. Thus, we had a total of 224 variations on the generic term "unfree". No wonder the philosophers use the generic term.

Many of the terms supplied were very similar, such as "boxed in," "boxed up," "cornered," "trapped," or "anxious," "uneasy," "worried," "upset." These similarities, of course, are what made it possible to develop code categories at all. As noted, the codes were established by examination of a sample of the opposite responses, and then two independent coders attempted to code all the responses. For the first sample of 841 opposites, the two coders reached an initial agreement of 93% on specific codings. The differences were resolved by discussion and convention, and on the second sample of 1740 opposites, 98% agreement was reached initially, with the few remaining differences again resolved by discussion. The great variety of terms and phrases was reduced to the categories shown in Figure 3, which also includes a few examples of each.

1. *Diffuse unpleasant affect*
   (anxious, bored, overwhelmed)
2. *Diffuse pressure*
   (rushed, burdened, hassled)
3. *Prevention from without*
   (restricted, stifled, trapped)
4. *Prevention from within*
   (dormant, inhibited, incompetent)
5. *Coercion from without*
   (scheduled, controlled, dominated)
6. *Coercion from within*
   (obligated, responsible, committed)
7. *Conflict and indecision*
   (conflicted, undecided, uncertain)
8. *Other, uncodable, illegible*
   (dieting, changes, introspective)

Figure 3. Code categories for opposites to "free" and examples of each.

The frequency with which terms falling into each of the coding categories was calculated for each cluster; within each cluster, the rank order of the different kinds of opposites was determined. Such an ordering of the findings can show what are the most frequent kinds of opposites supplied for each kind of situation. This, in turn can lead us to an understanding of the ways in which "feeling free" is construed, that is, along what bi-polar dimensions the experience is comprehended in each kind of situation.

*The distribution of opposites.* Table 2 shows the complete distribution of opposites by clusters for the two samples separately, together with their rank orders within each cluster. These are the columns. The column totals are also ranked, reflecting the relative total use of all opposites within clusters. Finally, the row totals are ranked, reflecting the relative total use of the various opposites collapsed across clusters.

Before proceeding with a detailed description of the patterns of opposites, it should be noted that the rank-orders of the row totals (overall use of each opposite code) for the two samples are highly correlated (rho = .93; p < .05). In addition, the rank-orders of the column totals (combined use of all opposites within each cluster) for the two samples, are correlated almost perfectly (rho = .97, p < .01). Thus, Table 2 shows a very strong replication of the overall opposites data for the two samples.

The same can be said, generally, for the individual clusters. The rank-order correlations between opposite code use by the two samples in the different clusters range from .45 to .96, with only Clusters 3 and 7 being below .80. Thus, the cluster-by-cluster replication is also strong. Clusters 3 and 7, it should be noted, have the lowest raw frequencies of opposites which would lead to less stable patterns across samples. Thus it appears that the terms supplied as opposites to free can be coded reliably, and that the distribution of opposites found in the first sample is replicated strongly in the second.

Several different statistical analyses were performed to summarize the patterns of opposite use in the different clusters. First, an overall coefficient of concordance (Kendall's *w*, cf., Siegel, 1956, pp. 229*ff*), and subsequently, rank order correlations (rho) were employed to compare pairs or groups of clusters with each other in terms of the rank order of use of the various opposite code categories.[4]

*The clusters considered collectively.* The data in Table 2 yield highly significant coefficients of concordance among the rank orders of opposite code use across all seven clusters for both samples. For Sample 1, *w* = .564, (p < .001) and for Sample 2, *w* = .583 (p < .001). This means that there is significant general agreement on the nature of the opposites to feeling free, regardless of the kind of situation in which the opposite is expressed. *Prevention from Without* (code 3) is by far the most frequently used opposite, and always ranks first or second, while *Diffuse Unpleasant Affect* (code 1) never ranks lower than fourth. *Conflict and Indecision* (code 7), while somewhat more variable in its ranking from cluster to cluster, is third in overall use. These statements are true for both samples. Thus, it can be said that there is something like a "G" factor in feeling free—the contrast with feeling *Preven-*

---

[4]In the following discussion, for the sake of clarity, opposite code names will be presented in italics while cluster names will be standard face type.

Table 2. Distribution of opposite code use by cluster for two samples. The upper entry in each cell is Sample 1 and the lower is Sample 2. The entries are raw frequencies and rank *within clusters* in brackets. Cluster totals (column sums) are also ranked as are code totals (row sums).

| | 1 S.D. | 2 A.R. | 3 R.N. | 4 R.L. | 5 A.D. | 6 P.A. | 7 S.B. | Total |
|---|---|---|---|---|---|---|---|---|
| 1. Diffuse unpleasant affect | 25 (2) / 38 (3) | 62 (1) / 110 (1) | 10 (2) / 38 (1) | 23 (2) / 47 (2) | 15 (4) / 34 (3.5) | 21 (3) / 39 (3) | 11 (2) / 19 (3) | 167 (2) / 325 (2) |
| 2. Diffuse pressure | 10 (5) / 22 (6) | 0 (8) / 8 (7) | 2 (6) / 3 (6) | 1 (8) / 7 (8) | 27 (3) / 34 (3.5) | 14 (4) / 31 (4) | 2 (7) / 12 (5.5) | 56 (4) / 117 (5) |
| 3. Prevention from without | 38 (1) / 71 (1) | 24 (2) / 45 (2) | 18 (1) / 29 (2) | 121 (1) / 189 (1) | 79 (1) / 126 (1) | 58 (1) / 101 (1) | 19 (1) / 30 (2) | 357 (1) / 591 (1) |
| 4. Prevention from within | 1 (8) / 12 (8) | 14 (3) / 21 (4) | 3 (5) / 1 (8) | 8 (4) / 19 (5) | 0 (8) / 5 (8) | 8 (5) / 5 (8) | 5 (5) / 11 (7) | 39 (7) / 74 (8) |
| 5. Coercion from without | 9 (6) / 24 (5) | 2 (5.5) / 1 (8) | 5 (3.5) / 2 (7) | 11 (3) / 35 (3) | 7 (5) / 14 (6) | 4 (7) / 9 (7) | 3 (6) / 12 (5.5) | 41 (5.5) / 97 (7) |
| 6. Coercion from within | 20 (4) / 52 (2) | 5 (4) / 24 (3) | 0 (8) / 6 (5) | 2 (7) / 13 (6.5) | 1 (7) / 24 (5) | 5 (6) / 19 (5) | 8 (3) / 31 (1) | 41 (5.5) / 169 (4) |
| 7. Conflict and indecision | 22 (3) / 29 (4) | 1 (7) / 9 (6) | 1 (7) / 7 (4) | 7 (5) / 31 (4) | 50 (2) / 93 (2) | 33 (2) / 76 (2) | 6 (4) / 8 (8) | 120 (3) / 253 (3) |
| 8. Other, uncodable, illegible | 4 (7) / 14 (7) | 2 (5.5) / 18 (5) | 5 (3.5) / 28 (3) | 3 (6) / 13 (6.5) | 5 (6) / 9 (7) | 1 (8) / 14 (6) | 1 (8) / 18 (4) | 21 (8) / 114 (6) |
| Total | 129 (4) / 262 (4) | 110 (5) / 236 (5) | 44 (7) / 114 (7) | 176 (2) / 354 (1) | 184 (1) / 339 (2) | 144 (3) / 294 (3) | 55 (6) / 141 (6) | 841 / 1740 |

154

*tion from Without*, the contrast with feeling *Diffuse Unpleasant Affect*, and the contrast with feeling *Conflict and Indecision*. Both Berlin (1958, 1969) and Parent (1974) emphasize that from their philosophical viewpoints, external obstructions and/or interventions are the primary sources of the erosion of freedom. In a complementary fashion, Enns (1980) has argued that from the point of view of psychopathology and psychotherapy, fears and anxieties are fundamental blocks to effective behaviour and to the experience of oneself as free. The data show that *Prevention from Without* and *Diffuse Unpleasant Affect*, then, are conditions that one must be "free from" in order to experience oneself as free, attesting again to the primacy of negative liberty or non-interference.

*Conflict and Indecision*, which ranks third overall in use, suggests an inability to get on with action, a lack of "positive liberty" or "freedom to" as described by MacCallum (1967). Thus, we find basic negative liberty (the lack of interference) and positive liberty (the ability to act) as the primary components of experienced freedom. While this is in accord with much philosophical reasoning and clinical theorizing (cf. Enns, 1980; Westcott, 1978), it has not previously been demonstrated through systematic empirical study of reported human experience.

In spite of the highly significant overall concordance reported above, a matrix of pair-wise rank order correlations of opposite code use for all pairs of clusters for the two samples shows both significant and non-significant correlations ranging from rho $= -.13$ to $+ .97$. That is, there are both similarities and differences in the qualitative features of experienced freedom in the different clusters.

To summarize the preceding analyses, the opposites supplied can be coded reliably into meaningful categories, and are distributed across the clusters in patterns which are replicated in the two samples. There is general agreement concerning the nature of the opposites to feeling free, and the most frequently cited opposites are *Prevention from Without, Diffuse Unpleasant Affect*, and *Conflict and Indecision*. There are both similarities and differences among the clusters in the patterns of opposites use, and these are the focus of the next section.

*Clusters which are qualitatively similar and quantitatively different.* Most pairs of clusters show non-significant correlations in their patterns of opposites use. However, Self Direction, Active Decision Making, and Presence of Alternatives (Clusters 1, 5, and 6) show large and significant positive intercorrelations (rho ranges between $+ .74$ and $+ .97$), replicated in both samples. These three types of situations are highly interrelated qualitatively, while they are all significantly different from each other in the quantitative data, i.e., the cluster means, shown in Table 1. These three kinds of situations evoke reliably similar qualities of feeling free to reliably different degrees. The same can be said for Cluster pairs 7/1 and 7/2. The quality of the experience of feeling free in the Exercise of Skilled Behaviour overlaps with the feeling evoked under conditions of Self Direction and conditions of Absence

155

of Responsibility (rho ranges between $+.64$ and $+.81$). Yet, Cluster 7 is quantitatively different from both Cluster 1 and Cluster 2 (Table 1, Figure 2).

*Clusters which are quantitatively similar and qualitatively different.* In contrast to the preceding observations, Release from Noxious Stimulation and Exercise of Skilled Behaviour (Clusters 3 and 7) are not significantly different in the quantitative data of Table 1, yet are not significantly correlated in the rank order of use of opposites (rho $= +.27$ and $+.52$ for the two samples). That is, feeling free is reported to the same high degree in the two kinds of situations, but is construed differently. The same statement can be made about Self Direction and Absence of Responsibility (Clusters 1 and 2): Feeling free in these situations is quantitatively the same (Table 1) but qualitatively different in opposite code use for both samples. This is also the case for Recognition of Limits and Active Decision Making (Clusters 4 and 5). Thus, the qualitative similarities and differences shown in Table 2 are not systematically related to the quantitative similarities and differences shown in Table 1.

*Comparisons of attributed and experienced freedom: the difference between being free and feeling free.* Repeatedly, I have made heavy weather about the conceptual differences between *being* free and *feeling* free, and about the fact that most writers do not attend to this nicety. Now it is worthwhile to see if, and in what ways, ordinary respondents recognize the difference. In order to do this, the basic questionnaire described earlier was modified slightly in several ways. For the first modification, the situational descriptions remained the same but the stem of the response was changed from "I feel" free to "I am" free. The responses remained on the same five point scale ranging from "very much" to "not at all".

The second modification moved to a third-person format, with proper names inserted instead of the first person pronoun in the situational descriptions. Half the proper names were male and half were female, and two forms were developed: one in which the stem of the response was "He feels" free, or "She feels" free and the second form in which the stem was "He is" free or "She is" free. A final modification retained the same situational descriptions, and respondents scored on the five point scale in response to "I like this situation" — again, from "very much" to "not at all". One of the samples described earlier was used as the base line ("I feel") and four additional samples from the same parent population were employed for the modifications.[5]

Table 3 shows the mean scores for each of the seven clusters for each form of the questionnaire, and Table 4 shows the comparisons among forms, excluding Group E. Of the 14 direct comparisons between the "feel" and "be" forms (A/B, C/D) 7 are significant at or beyond the .05 level; of the fourteen direct comparisons between first- and third-person forms (A/C, B/D) only two are significant. The additional fourteen comparisons which vary both

---

[5]Different samples were employed with each form of the modified questionnaire to minimize contrast effects which would be likely if the same respondents were given all 5 modified forms. The replicability of the basic findings justified this decision.

156

person and format yield another seven significant differences. The indications are that these results are more dependent on format than on person.

Table 3. Cluster means and S.D.s for five formats of the questionnaire.

| Format | 1st Person | | | | 3rd Person | | | | 1st Person | |
|---|---|---|---|---|---|---|---|---|---|---|
| | Feel | | Be | | Feel | | Be | | Like | |
| | n = 135 | | n = 61 | | n = 52 | | n = 69 | | n = 25 | |
| CLUSTER | $\overline{X}$ | S.D. | $\overline{X}$ | S.D. | $\overline{X}$ | S.D. | $\overline{X}$ | S.D. | $\overline{X}$ | S.D. |
| 1. S.D. | 3.93 | .70 | 3.76 | .73 | 3.84 | .68 | 3.77 | .67 | 3.98 | .73 |
| 2. A.R. | 3.82 | .88 | 4.06 | .74 | 3.60 | .79 | 3.94 | .83 | 3.69 | .74 |
| 3. R.N. | 4.25 | .83 | 3.96 | .72 | 4.21 | .62 | 4.21 | .69 | 4.07 | .72 |
| 4. R.L. | 2.92 | .80 | 3.01 | .91 | 2.87 | .59 | 3.10 | .72 | 3.04 | .94 |
| 5. A.D. | 3.08 | .98 | 3.66 | .87 | 2.96 | .73 | 3.45 | .78 | 3.32 | .87 |
| 6. P.A. | 3.35 | .86 | 3.75 | .58 | 3.31 | .78 | 3.92 | .66 | 3.64 | .58 |
| 7. S.B. | 4.16 | .70 | 3.82 | .69 | 3.71 | .60 | 3.82 | .63 | 4.09 | .69 |
| Group | A | | B | | C | | D | | E | |

In the first person form respondents report that they "feel free" to a greater extent than they "are free" in Cluster 3 (Release from Noxious Stimulation), and Cluster 7 (Exercise of Skilled Behaviour). In contrast, they say they "are free" to a greater extent than they "feel free" in Cluster 2 (Absence of Responsibility) Cluster 5 (Active Decision Making) and Cluster 6 (Presence of Alternatives). In the third person format, where the respondent is attributing an ontological state on the one hand (He/She is free) or a probable feeling (He/She feels free) the same relationships hold for Clusters 2, 5, and 6. In Cluster 7, the direction is the same, but statistical significance is not reached. It is interesting that no differences were found by varying either person or format, or both, for Cluster 1 (Self-Direction) or Cluster 4 (Recognition of Limits) — the former quite high in contributing to all forms of the questionnaire, and the latter quite low in contributing to all forms.

Thus, respondents do make significant distinctions between being free and feeling free, and they make essentially the same distinctions in attributing these states to others as they make in reporting their own experience and self-attribution.

*Being free and liking it.* The differences between the self-attribution of being free and the self-report of feeling free may be mediated by the extent to which the different situations are liked. Table 3, Column E, shows the cluster means for "liking" the different situations. It is evident that the situations are

157

Table 4. t-values for differences between cluster means for all pairs of formats A-D shown in Table 3.

| Comparison | A/B | A/C | B/C | B/D | C/D | A/D |
|------------|-----|-----|-----|-----|-----|-----|
| CLUSTER | t | t | t | t | t | t |
| 1. S.D. | 1.32 | .79 | .60 | .08 | .51 | 1.57 |
| 2. A.R. | 1.77 | 1.57 | 2.60** | .87 | 2.26* | .94 |
| 3. R.N. | 2.37** | .32 | 1.96* | 2.02* | .02 | .35 |
| 4. R.L. | .70 | .34 | .95 | .63 | 1.79 | 1.58 |
| 5. A.D. | 3.98** | .19 | 4.59** | 1.45 | 3.49** | 2.73** |
| 6. P.A. | 3.31** | .29 | 3.43** | 1.55 | 4.59** | 4.84** |
| 7. S.B. | 3.18** | 4.09** | .90 | 0 | .90 | 3.41** |

\* $p < .05$
\*\* $p < .01$

differentially liked, and that there are strong rank order correlations among Columns A, B, and E. When we look at the 28 individual item scores rather than cluster means we find that *being free* is strongly correlated with *feeling free* ($r = .82$, $p < .001$); *liking a situation* is strongly correlated with *feeling free* ($r = .79$, $p < .001$); and *being free* is correlated with *liking a situation* more moderately ($r = .54$, $p < .01$). Together, the *being free* and *liking* scores account for 84% of the variance in the *feeling free* scores ($r = .92$, $p < .001$) with unique contributions of 58% and 52% respectively. It should be noted that the three clusters in which "feeling free" is higher than "being free" (Clusters 1, 3, and 7) are the three kinds of situations which are best liked (Table 3).

It appears that reports of feeling free in a situation derive from perceiving oneself as free in that situation and liking that situation. The two features make separate and approximately equal contributions to the result. Our popular literature and music tells us that "feeling free" is an unalloyed good and pleasure. "Being free" is not quite so delightful. Parmenter made this point through his observation of concrete lives; Fromm made the point historically; the existentialists made the point theoretically; the above data support it. There seems to be some substance to it, and it deserves further direct inquiry.

### A glance back at the bridge: some cross-cultural observations

In Chapter 2, I made much of the view that concepts of human freedom and experiences of human freedom are deeply embedded in historical, cultural, and linguistic webs. It would be compelling now if we could place the data presented in this chapter in a full anthropological context. But we cannot. The most that I can provide is a modicum of cross-cultural data, and even the crossing of cultures is modest.

While on sabbatical in India, a colleague, Richard Goranson, solicited responses to my questionnaire from students at the University of Banglore. The questionnaire was modified only to the extent of using less paper, and one question (the one about going to the cafeteria) was modified to make local sense. The respondents answered only the question concerning how free they feel in each situation.

The sample of respondents numbered 53, with 50 female, 2 male and one unidentified. They were students in an introductory psychology course, and all were fluent in English. The mean age was just over 21 years, not unlike the Canadian university students. Because religious affiliation may very well mean more in terms of world view in Asia than it does in Canada, their religion was identified. One failed to report, 6 were Christian, 42 Hindu, 3 Buddhist, and one was Moslem. I cannot pretend to know what these identifying characteristics may have to do with explaining the findings, reported below. Goranson reported that, in his opinion, the respondents were highly Anglicized (Goranson, 1981).

The cluster means for the Indian sample appear in Table 5, together with a statistical comparison with Canadian sample 2. The profile of the Indian cluster means is shown in Figure 4 together with the profile of the Canadian sample. It is evident that the responses of the Indian sample are different from the Canadian sample in five of the seven clusters. The statistical significance of the differences are sufficiently large that there may well be psychological significance entailed as well.

Table 5. Comparison of cluster means for a sample of Indian university students and a sample of Canadian university students.

| | Indian | | Canadian | | |
| | n = 53 | | n = 139 | | |
| CLUSTER | $\overline{X}$ | S.D. | $\overline{X}$ | S.D. | t |
|---|---|---|---|---|---|
| 1. S.D. | 3.70 | .74 | 3.93 | .70 | 1.95 |
| 2. A.R. | 3.10 | .83 | 3.82 | .88 | 5.37* |
| 3. R.N. | 3.67 | .95 | 4.25 | .83 | 3.92* |
| 4. R.L. | 3.44 | .57 | 2.92 | .80 | 5.04* |
| 5. A.D. | 3.28 | .76 | 3.08 | .98 | 1.50 |
| 6. P.A. | 2.94 | .71 | 3.35 | .86 | 3.36* |
| 7. S.B. | 3.77 | .74 | 4.16 | .70 | 3.30* |

* p < .01 (two-tailed)

159

With respect to the profiles, it remains true that the three highest cluster means for the Canadians are the same as for the Indian sample (Self Direction, Release from Noxious Stimulation, and Exercise of Skilled Behaviour), but all three of these are lower for the Indian sample than for the Canadian sample. The greatest differences between the Canadian and Indian samples are in Clusters 2 and 4 (Absence of Responsibility and Recognition of Limits). In the former, the Indian sample is almost a full standard deviation below the Canadian sample, and in the latter, the Indian sample is nearly a full standard deviation above the Canadian Sample.

In contrast to the generally depressed cluster means for the Indian sample, they are above the Canadian samples in the extent to which they report feeling free in Clusters 4 and 5 (Recognition of Limits and Active Decision Making). Overall, it can be said that the Indian sample shows a somewhat flatter profile than the Canadian sample shows.

On the surface, it might be possible to say that the flatter profile indicates that the dimension of feeling free is not as highly differentiated in the Indian

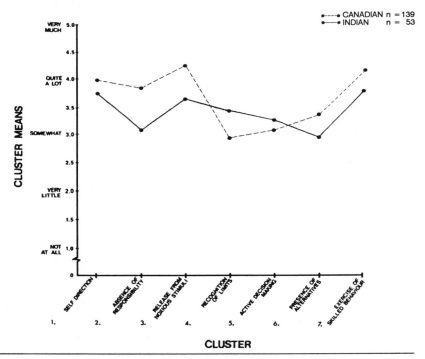

Figure 4: Profiles of the Indian sample in comparison with a Canadian sample.

sample as it is in the Canadian sample. That is, the former do not pay as much attention to it as the latter do. But this must be purely speculative, as must be the possibility that the Hindu orientation contributes to the differences. It is beyond my competence to illuminate the evident similarities and differences between the two samples from different cultures, but I can invoke the virtue of a research yield which provides both questions and answers.

The internal analyses of the Indian sample, i.e., intercorrelations among the cluster means are quite similar to the parallel analyses of the Canadian samples. Earlier in this chapter I reported the majority of cluster means intercorrelations for the Canadian samples were positive, modest, and significant. For Canadian sample 1, 15 of 21 correlations were significant, positive and moderate, and for sample 2, there were 19 of 21. The total for the two samples being 34 of 42. For the Indian sample, 9 of 21 such correlations meet the criteria of being positive, significant and modest. In no case was there a significant correlation in the Indian sample where there was not a similar significant correlation in the Canadian samples, and in both cases where neither Canadian sample showed a significant correlation (Clusters 4, 7 and Clusters 3, 5) the Indian sample showed correlations of .02 and –.03 respectively. The fact that the Indian sample shows fewer significant correlations than the other two samples may simply be a function of the smaller number of respondents. In general, the magnitudes of the correlations are similar for the three samples.

We can conclude tentatively that the structure of relationships among the extent to which the various situations contribute to feeling free is similar in both the Canadian and Indian samples. On the other hand, we have already pointed out that the absolute intensities of reported feeling free in each kind of situation differ considerably for the Canadian and Indian samples. In the next chapter we will have more to say about the nature of feeling free in different cultural contexts and at different ages.

## Retrospect and Prospect

In this chapter I have presented research findings based on a questionnaire derived from both theory and previous empirical research. The attempt was to explore the extent to which a variety of real life situations give rise to the experience of feeling free and/or feelings opposite to free. As a research instrument, the questionnaire showed considerable promise: Successive samples of respondents drawn from the same parent population showed very similar aggregate results; samples drawn from different populations showed very different aggregate results; both quantitative and qualitative data could be derived from the questionnaire, and small, but theoretically significant modifications of the wording of the questionnaire yielded coherently different results.

The relationships of these findings to earlier findings and earlier theoretical predictions are various. Some earlier findings are confirmed, some contested, some extended; but what is clearly shown is that a simple one-shot, one-situation approach to the study of human freedom will never capture it. The human experience of freedom is in the context of process, the moving from one state to another, and must be conceived as scenario or script. What is also evident is that different kinds of situations and scripts contribute differentially to the experience of freedom, and that very few of these analytically separable situations occur in isolation in real life.

It is also evident that the human experience of freedom is by no means a unitary affair, and is conceptualized and described quite differently in different situations. While this is true, it is also true that experiencing external prevention and unpleasant affect are dominant contrasts to feeling free, while other subtle contrasts are also present.

With all the variety—both quantitative and qualitative, and the demonstrated differences between different cultural groups and between being free and feeling free, it must be remembered that the situations to which the respondents reacted were provided for them. The situations in the questionnaire were derived rationally and were diverse, but they still did not give the respondents the opportunity to provide spontaneously their own unique experiences of feeling free or their own unique conditions under which the experience arises. The next chapter will be devoted to exploring and describing the conditions under which people report feeling free when the method of inquiry is open-ended interviews. Even greater variety will be evident, and some new dimensions will appear.

# 8   Further Direct Inquiry

## The plan

The plan of this chapter is quite straightforward. It is
to provide the rationale for a more direct and systematic
phenomenological inquiry into human freedom, to
describe such a study, and to compare the results with
findings from other research approaches.

## The rationale

It should be evident by now that human freedom is a
complex, subtle, and diversified notion. It is both an
abstract concept and a concrete lived human experience.
It should also be evident that to approach a conceptual
understanding of human freedom from a single perspective is an error, and that to seek a psychological understanding of human freedom without attention to the lived
experience is meaningless.

My aim in this work is primarily psychological, of course, and I see no way to explore the human experience except by direct inquiry of articulate and cooperative human beings. What are the conditions of freedom for living human beings in the ordinary, or even extraordinary, world? What does it feel like to feel free? What is the structure of the experience—the combination of conditions and experience? The pursuit of these questions by direct inquiry rests on a few common sense and useful assumptions, often simply ignored or elaborately refuted by psychologists: I assume that people ordinarily have some worthwhile awareness of their own experience, and when focussed, can have more than usual; with careful inquiry, human beings can tell each other meaningful things about this experience. These are assumptions that are entirely congenial to the newer psychological perspectives and methodologies described in Chapter 5, and they are assumptions on which our very lives as social beings are based.

Physicists cannot talk to their magnets, chemists cannot talk to their sulphur, biologists cannot talk to their cells; zoologists cannot talk to their animals (or can they?), and psychologists in the standard research tradition, imitating the "real" sciences, have too long pretended that they could not talk with their subjects. Personal reports of experience can surely be taken as data—not as uncritically accepted veridical meter readings—but as data to be interrogated. The use of meter readings as "hard" data rests on a dizzying set of assumptions about the nature of the meters and the nature of the relationships between the meter readings and the phenomena they are meant to represent. So too with verbal reports of experience. They are available for interrogation, and since they typically have meaning, they are open to negotiation. If we keep these principles in mind, and acknowledge that all knowledge is the result of negotiation, we can proceed with direct inquiry into those aspects of human freedom which have been systematically ignored by psychologists.

In many respects, that is what I thought I was doing in the questionnaire studies reported in Chapter 7. I began with interviews, moved to the philosophical and psychological literatures, and provided, I thought, a decent spectrum of kinds of conditions of human freedom. I asked people how free they feel in each situation, and I asked them about opposites to feeling free in the same situations, but I didn't ask them about their own unique conditions of freedom in an open ended inquiry. The kinds of situations I posed were ones they would be likely to find themselves in, and the data presented in Chapter 7 certainly indicate that the findings are reasonably robust. But an open ended inquiry provides an additional perspective on this many-faceted question.

Asking the respondents about their unique "opposites" to feeling free provided much more diversity—diversity limited only by linguistic imagination. Yet, through this diversity there was order, there was some sharing of the reported opposites to feeling free in the various situations. And when I asked the various samples of respondents to indicate the extent to which they felt free or were free, differences appeared—that is, some subtle distinctions could be made by asking people about their experiences on the one hand and their commentaries on their situations, on the other. In my view, this is sufficient rationale and justification for direct inquiry into human freedom, with the data sought from informants being personal reports of concrete experience rather than abstractions.

In the course of presenting and discussing the findings of this study, I will often have many speculations about the mental states of the respondents when gaps need to be filled or interpretations offered. This may seem strange, considering the extent to which I criticized the more traditional research for speculating in Chapters 3 and 4. The point is, however, that speculations about mental states in the present context represent genuine researchable hypotheses given the kind of assumptions made and the kind of methodology adopted, i.e., that personal reports of experience are data that can be interrogated. In the traditional approach, mental states are not researched directly, the methodology does not allow it, and hence speculation is indeed idle.

## Respondents

The primary findings to be reported in this chapter are based on interviews with 24 respondents. Nine were secondary school students 16 to 19 years of age; ten were in university, between 19 and 25 years old, and five respondents were retired. In the younger group, there were three males and six females; in the university group, there were six males and four females; in the retired group, two males and three females.

Some findings from additional interviews will be introduced for comparison purposes later, and the additional respondents will be identified and described at that time. The secondary school students and the retired respondents were interviewed by the present author, and the university students were interviewed by Greg Taylor as part of his Honours Thesis work (Taylor, 1986). All interviews were conducted in an open ended fashion, focussing on several questions: Do you ever feel free? Under what conditions do you feel free? What does it feel like to feel free? Occasionally respondents would introduce other material, such as descriptions of the conditions which militate against feeling free, and often these negative conditions were implied by their positive statements. The interviews typically took from a half hour to an hour and a half, they were taped and transcribed. From the transcripts, significant statements answering the relevant questions were extracted. Often these were perfectly clear, as in direct answers to direct questions, but often they had to be extracted from the context of longer discursive elements. This extracting process was carried out by two readers, checking each other and consulting, and negotiating, when the limits of a significant statements were not clear.

165

By this method, a total of 231 significant statements were derived. The number of statements given by each respondent varied, of course, and all were included in the data, even when a single individual gave several responses which were highly redundant.


## Coding


The crucial procedure for negotiating some order in these 231 different statements from the respondents was the development of a coding system. The coding system had to provide a level of generality and a level of individuality which made both the aggregate and the individual data intelligible and meaningful from a psychological perspective. There is no set of rules which one can observe which will provoke universal agreement. Through interacting with the data, one must determine rationally the level of generality or specificity which makes the data intelligible. The kinds of codes and the levels of codes which one uses are surely determined by prior conceptions and biases, whether one's own or those enshrined in the existing literature. But the dialogue is two-way. The researcher may impose some categories on the data, but the data, too, impose categories on the researcher.

In the present case, the researchers set out with some preconceptions from some of the existing literature: the broad categories which Adler (1973) found in the philosophical literature, the categories of situations which Westcott (1982a) employed previously, and the kinds of categories Westcott (1984) found in Zavalloni's work. Then, with these preselected categories in mind, they dialogued with the data. This dialogue involved seeing to what extent the predetermined code categories could encompass the statements of the respondents, and to what extent the statements of the respondents demanded modification of the coding categories, either by expansion or contraction.

The coding system derived by this procedure is shown in Figures 1, 2, and 3, and its evolution is described below. But before presenting or describing it, it must be pointed out that any ordering adopted remains open to further negotiation. There is no one final truth to be found in these data.

We began with the three broad abstract categories of theoretical conceptions of freedom provided by Adler's (1973) research. Throughout this work I have pointed out that the abstract notions do not, typically, represent clear realities of human experience, and so these three were taken merely as first organizing principles, and further specification was demanded. These three first principles appear as the major headings in Figures 1, 2, and 3 respectively: *Circumstantial Freedom, Acquired Freedom, and Natural Freedom.*

*Circumstantial Freedom.* The second level of specification under Circumstantial Freedom (Figure 1) took account of the frequent distinction

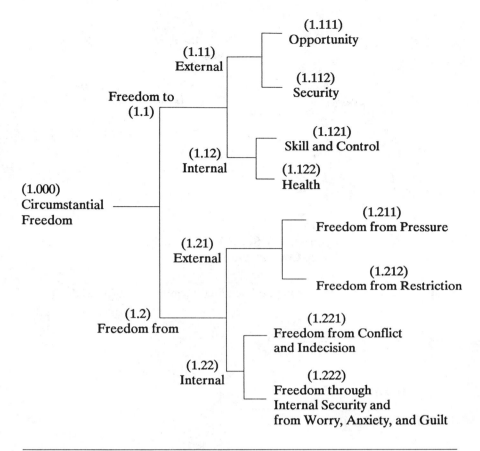

Figure 1. Codings under the general heading Circumstantial Freedom (1.000).

made between positive and negative freedom, i.e., *freedom from* and *freedom to* (cf. MacCallum, 1967). The third level of specification was derived from Westcott's (1981, 1982a) earlier work with opposites to free: the locus of facilitating or inhibiting events as being *internal* or *external*. The final levels of specification were derived from the statements of our informants as to exactly what kinds of circumstances, what kinds of positive and negative freedom were expressed, and what was seen as the locus of these contributors.

*Acquired Freedom.* With respect to Acquired Freedom (Figure 2) the theme of self-perfection was shown in previous data to appear in two quite distinguishable forms: the form of accomplishment or mastery of a task or a skill and the form of moral awareness or transcendence or commitment. Further specification of both of these varieties of acquired freedom were demanded by the statements from our informants.

167

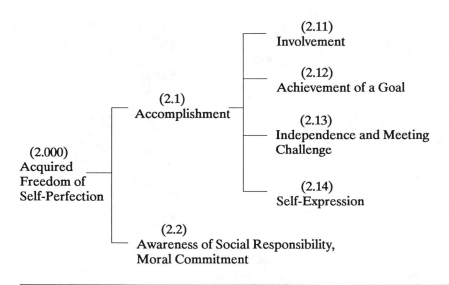

Figure 2. Codings under the general heading Acquired Freedom (2.000).

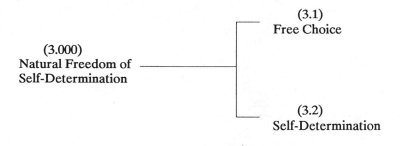

Figure 3. Codings under the general heading Natural Freedom (3.000).

*Natural Freedom.* For Adler, this general category referred to abstract notions of individuals having the capacity to initiate action and to direct that action. Most people, it seems, take this for granted, as a given in their own experience, and attend to it only under conditions of special restraint. It is important in the conceptual analysis of human freedom, and was hence included. However, among the respondents studied here, it was not very important as a specific category of experience. There were some examples provided, however, and the category was further divisible into two subcategories (Figure 3).

Ultimately, fifteen concrete categories were identified ranging under three main headings and the second-level headings. Each category is represented in Figures 1, 2, and 3, and a prototypical example of each is given in Tables 1, 2, and 3. Each statement is identified as to its source, as follows: high school student is identified as HS; university student is identified as U, retired person is identified as R; male is m, female is f; for the two younger groups, ages are included, and each individual is given an identifying number within the subsample. Recall that the quotations are taken from interview transcripts, and because the interviews were open ended and flexible, the syntax differs from statement to statement. Each statement refers to conditions under which the informant feels free.

As the reader can readily note, many of the coding categories blend into one another, multiple coding was sometimes necessary, and human experience does not come very neatly packaged.

### Results

Two kinds of tabulations were carried out: First, tabulations were made of the number of different individuals who offered one or more statements which fell into each category; second, tabulations were made of the total frequency of statements which fell into each code category, regardless of who offered them or how many were from a single respondent. The results of these two kinds of tabulations appear in Tables 4 and 5. The code categories are presented in the same order in which they are presented in tables 1, 2, and 3, and the entries are broken down by sample or origin and sex. Subsequently, in Table 6, the code categories are re-ordered in terms of decreasing frequency of respondents or statements.

In Table 6 it is evident that the two orderings are highly correlated and tend to confirm each other. For those who don't believe their eyes, the calculated correlation is rho = .88 between the frequency of respondents and the frequency of responses. There is an important dimension not assessed here, however: the intensity or importance of a particular set of conditions for the experienced freedom of different individuals. We will have more to say about that later, and will refer to the evidence on intensity which was a focus of the previous chapter.

The combined lists from Table 6 can be divided rather naturally into three groups in terms of the frequency with which the various code categories are employed. Codes 1.211, 1.111, and 3.2 are reflected in the experience of between 75% and 92% of the respondents, and comprise a total of 64% of all of the statements provided. These are obviously important conditions of experienced freedom for the samples studied, and are called *major categories*.

A second natural grouping according to frequency of use includes the next five categories, reflected in the experience of between 29% and 37% of the respondents, and together containing about 20% of the total responses.

169

Table 1. 1.000 Circumstantial Freedom.

1.1. Freedom to
  1.11  External
    1.111 Opportunity
    "...being allowed to be what you want to be" (U1, f, 19).
    1.112 Security
    "...house is paid for. We seem to be living within our income, the bank account seems to increase, which is nice" (R3, m).
  1.12  Internal
    1.121 Skill and Control
    "...you know, doing things that you're good at..." (HS2, m, 19).
    1.122 Health
    "...when my health is good and I have energy..." (R5, m).
1.2 Freedom from
  1.21  External
    1.211 Pressure
    "...free from school, work, the pressures of something..." (HS1, m, 17).
    1.212 Restriction
    "...I don't feel held down in any way..." (R4, f).
  1.22  Internal
    1.221 Conflict and indecision
    "...go to a wine and cheese party and there is no decision to make..." (R1, f).
    1.222 Worry and Anxiety
    "...when school is over, you've written your last exam, and there is stability to look forward to in the summer meaning you have a job lined up and you have a girlfriend or something and everything is going right..." (HS3, m, 19).

These categories are less general, but are certainly of some interest to the description of the conditions of experienced freedom. They are called *subsidiary categories*.

The third group comprises the remaining seven code categories reflecting the experience of from one to five of the 24 respondents, and together contributing the remaining 15% of responses. These are obviously less important, in the aggregate, but any of them may be extremely important to the individual for whom they are present. For the aggregate they are called *minor categories*.

Table 2. 2.000 Acquired Freedom of Self-Perfection.

2.1 Accomplishment, Mastery
    2.11    Involvement
        "...listening to music. I get absorbed by the music. I tend to forget a lot of things..." (U10, f, 19).
    2.12    Achievement of a goal
        "...just finished doing a project. Did a half decent job on it. Made me feel good..." (HS4, f, 17).
    2.13    Independence and meeting challenge
        "...It's when you've discovered yourself and in trying and dealing with people in growing and maturing and having all these different challenges..." (HS2, M, 19).
    2.14    Self-expression
        "...express yourself as freely as you can..." (U1, f, 19).
2.2. Social responsibility, moral commitment
    "...when my relationship with God is right..." (HS7, f, 18).

Table 3. 3.000 Natural Freedom of Self-Determination.

3.1 Free choice, decision making
    "...feel free that I can pick the classes and not go to ones if I feel tired. I was free to choose them..." (U4, m, 21).
3.2 Self-determination, self-direction
    "...it's just when you have nothing to do except whatever you want to do, like you can really let yourself go and do whatever you want to do..." (HS2, m, 19).

## The major categories

*Freedom from Pressure (1.211).* Twenty-two of the twenty-four respondents mentioned some conditions which could be coded into this category. It is very general, and pressure can imply such things as school work, responsibility, routine, supervision, and so on. Eight of the nine secondary school respondents referred to pressure and frequently to school as the principal source of pressure.

Table 4. Number of respondents providing one or more statements for each code category.

| | Sample | | | | | | | | |
|---|---|---|---|---|---|---|---|---|---|
| | HS n=9 | | U n=10 | | R n=5 | | Total n=24 | | Total % |
| % Code Category | M | F | M | F | M | F | M | F | |
| 1.111 Opportunity | 3 | 4 | 5 | 3 | 1 | 2 | 9 | 9 | 75 |
| 1.112 External Security | 1 | 0 | 1 | 1 | 2 | 0 | 4 | 1 | 20 |
| 1.121 Skill/Control | 1 | 3 | 0 | 0 | 0 | 1 | 1 | 4 | 20 |
| 1.122 Health | 0 | 0 | 0 | 0 | 1 | 0 | 1 | 0 | 04 |
| 1.211 From Pressure | 3 | 5 | 6 | 4 | 2 | 2 | 11 | 11 | 92 |
| 1.212 From Restrictions | 0 | 1 | 2 | 1 | 0 | 3 | 2 | 5 | 29 |
| 1.221 From Conflict/ Indecision | 0 | 1 | 1 | 1 | 0 | 1 | 3 | 1 | 16 |
| 1.222 Internal Security | 1 | 1 | 2 | 2 | 2 | 0 | 5 | 3 | 33 |
| 2.11 Involvement | 1 | 2 | 1 | 3 | 0 | 0 | 2 | 5 | 29 |
| 2.12 Achievement | 0 | 1 | 1 | 0 | 1 | 0 | 2 | 1 | 12 |
| 2.13 Independence/ Challenge | 2 | 1 | 1 | 1 | 1 | 1 | 4 | 3 | 29 |
| 2.14 Self-Expression | 2 | 0 | 4 | 3 | 0 | 0 | 6 | 3 | 37 |
| 2.2 Social responsibility/Commitment | 1 | 1 | 0 | 0 | 0 | 1 | 1 | 2 | 12 |
| 3.1 Free choice | 1 | 1 | 2 | 0 | 0 | 1 | 3 | 2 | 20 |
| 3.2 Self-Determination | 2 | 5 | 4 | 3 | 1 | 3 | 7 | 11 | 75 |

For example:

HS2, m, 19: "...Okay, well with me being in school...freedom is when there are no assignments, no pressures from home, to do things..."

At the university level, all ten respondents referred to freedom from pressure, again frequently in the educational context:

U21, f, 25: "...I can feel free from the pressures of responsibility at home, free from school..."

Four of the five retired respondents also identified freedom from pressure as important, but of course the sources of pressure were not school:

Table 5. Number of statements codable into each code category.

| | | HS | | U | | R | | Total | | |
|---|---|---|---|---|---|---|---|---|---|---|
| | | n = 9 | | n = 10 | | n = 5 | | n = 24 | | Total % |
| % | Code Category | M | F | M | F | M | F | M | F | |
| 1.111 | Opportunity | 7 | 8 | 13 | 4 | 3 | 4 | 23 | 16 | 17 |
| 1.112 | External Security | 1 | 0 | 1 | 1 | 2 | 0 | 4 | 1 | 02 |
| 1.121 | Skill/Control | 1 | 3 | 0 | 0 | 0 | 1 | 1 | 4 | 01 |
| 1.122 | Health | 0 | 0 | 0 | 0 | 1 | 0 | 1 | 0 | 01 |
| 1.211 | From Pressure | 12 | 10 | 23 | 17 | 4 | 5 | 39 | 32 | 31 |
| 1.212 | From Restrictions | 0 | 1 | 2 | 1 | 0 | 3 | 2 | 5 | 03 |
| 1.221 | From Conflict/ Indecision | 0 | 1 | 1 | 2 | 0 | 1 | 1 | 4 | 02 |
| 1.222 | Internal Security | 1 | 1 | 5 | 3 | 6 | 0 | 12 | 4 | 06 |
| 2.11 | Involvement | 1 | 2 | 1 | 4 | 0 | 0 | 2 | 6 | 03 |
| 2.12 | Achievement | 0 | 1 | 1 | 0 | 2 | 0 | 3 | 1 | 02 |
| 2.13 | Independence/ Challenge | 2 | 1 | 1 | 1 | 1 | 1 | 4 | 3 | 03 |
| 2.14 | Self-Expression | 2 | 0 | 5 | 4 | 0 | 0 | 7 | 4 | 04 |
| 2.2 | Social respon- sibility/Commit- ment | 1 | 4 | 0 | 0 | 0 | 2 | 1 | 6 | 03 |
| 3.1 | Free choice | 1 | 2 | 2 | 0 | 0 | 2 | 3 | 4 | 03 |
| 3.2 | Self-Determination | 6 | 10 | 11 | 6 | 1 | 4 | 18 | 20 | 16 |

R4, f: "...I guess when you get off and you're driving out and you're going on a holiday and you have no responsibilities around the house..."

Although a very large proportion of each group is represented in this category, it should be noted that the university respondents gave a much larger overall frequency of responses codable as freedom from pressure. The eight secondary school respondents provided 22 such responses; the ten university respondents provided 40 such statements; the five retired persons gave 9 such responses. In effect, it may be that the university students are more preoccupied with this kind of freedom than the others.

**Table 6.** Code categories ordered by frequency of informants and statements.

| % Code Category | | % and rank of number of informants | | % and rank of number of statements | |
|---|---|---|---|---|---|
| 1.211 | From Pressure | 92% | 1 | 31% | 1 |
| 1.111 | Opportunity | 75% | 2.5 | 17% | 2 |
| 3.2 | Self-Determination | 75% | 2.5 | 16% | 3 |
| 2.14 | Self-Expression | 37% | 4 | 04% | 5 |
| 1.222 | Internal Security | 33% | 5 | 06% | 4 |
| 1.212 | From Restrictions | 29% | 7 | 03% | 8 |
| 2.11 | Involvement | 29% | 7 | 03% | 8 |
| 2.13 | Independence/ Challenge | 29% | 7 | 03% | 8 |
| 1.112 | External Security | 20% | 10 | 02% | 12 |
| 1.121 | Skill/Control | 20% | 10 | 01% | 14.5 |
| 3.1 | Free choice | 20% | 10 | 03% | 8 |
| 1.221 | From Conflict/ Indecision | 16% | 12 | 02% | 12 |
| 2.12 | Achievement | 12% | 13.5 | 03% | 8 |
| 2.2 | Social responsibility/ Commitment | 12% | 13.5 | 03% | 8 |
| 1.122 | Health | 04% | 15 | 01% | 14.5 |

*Freedom in Opportunity (1.111).* The kinds of opportunities mentioned by the different informants are quite various, and when opportunity resides in having the time to do something, this category becomes a mirror-image of the previous category, freedom from pressure:

HS1, m, 17: "...there's not really all that much around you, so you can go off by yourself..."

But there are more specific kinds of opportunities cited by other respondents:

U1, f, 19: "...being allowed to be what you want to be..."

U4, m, 21: "I have the opportunity to do something I want to do. Get aggression out in any manner I want..."

R2, f: "...when I'm out in nature..."

Altogether, the kinds of opportunities which contributed to the experience of freedom ranged through educational opportunities, recreational opportunities, having a car, time, or the unspecified opportunities which came with retirement. Seven of the high school students appear in this category and give a total of 15 responses; eight of the ten university students are present, and give a total of 17 responses; three of the five retired persons give a total of 7 responses. So opportunity as a vehicle for experienced freedom appears to be of about the same importance for each group, based on the frequency counts. Again, we have not assessed possible differentials in intensity. It might well be that younger individuals find the availability of opportunities more contributory to experienced freedom than do older persons who have had previous experience of this kind. Alternatively it may be that for individual persons, retiring from a highly demanding and restricting job may make alternative opportunities more compelling as a source of freedom. The range of kinds of possible opportunities is wide, the range of possible importance is also wide.

*Freedom in Self-Determination (3.2).* One of the examples given in the preceding section had to do with the opportunity to be what one wanted to be. Clearly there is an overlap with the present category. As noted earlier, human experience does not come neatly packaged. But this category is most clearly differentiated from the previous one by virtue of the emphasis on the active doing, rather than on the opportunity or permission to do, keeping in mind that a lack of other pressures and the opportunity must normally be available in order for the doing to take place. But even that is not always true. For example, an individual can experience freedom through self-determination, even when doing what he must do, if:

HS7, m, 17: "...and I sort of do it my way..."

But the examples did usually state or imply the necessary lack of pressure and the presence of opportunity.

HS9, f, 17: "...you can come in when you want, go when you want..."

U5, m, 21: "...just go about doing the stuff I enjoy doing ..."

R3, m: "...do what you want when you want. Do things which were impossible when you were working. Like make a trip for two days or two weeks..."

As noted, the emphasis here is on the doing, regardless of what gets done. There is a great variety of doings reported by the seven secondary school respondents who gave 16 codable responses, by the seven university students who gave 17 codable responses, and by the four retired respondents who gave 5 codable statements. From the frequency counts it appears that the retired group are less preoccupied with self-determination as a route to experienced freedom than are the other two groups. It may well be that this just doesn't occur to them very much – they have little in the way of restrictions or prior commitments, and they may be rather continually involved in doing what they want when they want, without noticing it very much.

The above three categories are what we have called *Major*, and they represent the lion's share both of the respondents and the responses. It would be possible to make a relatively low order generalization that freedom is experienced by more than 75% of all of our respondents when pressure is off them, when they have opportunities, and when they do the things they want to do. The matter of pressure seems most frequent for the university sample, but for the other conditions, there is nothing to differentiate the three age groups.

### The subsidiary categories

The next group of five categories (see Table 6) reflects the experience of a much smaller proportion of our respondents than did the first three *Major* categories. We find between approximately 30 and 40 percent of the respondents from each sample represented in this group of categories and the frequency of responses comprising about 20% of all responses given.

*Self-Expression (2.14)*. This code category may be seen as a subset of self-determination, but involves more than the doing. It tends to involve some kind of uniquely personal doing, putting one's stamp on an activity, being creative. It is interesting that some of the younger respondents spoke particularly of team sports as a place for self-expression and experienced freedom. When questioned about the constraints involved in team sports, one replied:

HS8, m, 18: "...yeah, but in a lot of sports you can be creative. There are so many creative moves you can do on your own..."

A university student describes this in more intellectual terms:

U2, f, 25: "...so you start spilling out ideas and just anything that you want to think and say. That's something I get excited about. I like doing that and it's a release and a sort of a feeling of freedom..."

It is interesting that no statements from the retired group could be coded in this category, while two high school students provided two statements, and seven university students provided nine statements which could be so coded. It appears that this is clearly a concern of the university students particularly, in their experiences of freedom.

176

*Internal Security (1.222).* This category involves an absence of uncertainty, guilt, and worry, a contentment with oneself, and 33% of the respondents provided statements about this state of affairs as a contribution to experienced freedom. The kinds of internal security were various:

HS3, m, 19: "...when school is over, you've written your last exam, and there is stability to look forward to in the summer, meaning you have a job lined up and you have a girlfriend or something, and everything is going right..."

U3, m, 24: "...I feel that before I go to sleep that's going to be relaxing and there won't be anxieties..."

R5, m: "...I'm free of the 'old hellfire and damnation' which people become afraid of..."

Here, In these examples, the individuals refer to external events, but more particularly to their reactions to them — the security they feel under the conditions described. The security and peace of mind giving rise to feeling free.

*Freedom from Restrictions (1.212).* Statements codable were given by a total of seven respondents, some from each sample. It is interesting that this is only a subsidiary category inasmuch as restrictions (Prevention from Without) appeared to be the main source of erosion of freedom suffered by respondents in the research reported in Chapter 7 (Westcott, 1982a). In both the previous research and in the present study, the statements offered were spontaneous: each respondent supplied his or her own statements. However, in the present study, a more fine grained analysis is possible because we are working with phrases and statements in context, while the previous research asked respondents to supply only a word or phrase without much personal context. Here the respondents said:

HS4, f, 17: "...no restrictions from the job..."

U9, f, 22: "...It's nice to be at university where there's lots of space and you can walk freely. It's not confined physically like a high school..."

R1, f: "...no family restrictions, responsibilities..."

Once again, it may be that the general tenor of life for most of the respondents is sufficiently free of restrictions that they barely notice it, and the absence of restrictions does not become a major contributor to experienced freedom. It is essentially a background condition. Later, in a re-analysis of the Zavalloni (1962) data, we shall see that the issue is not so simple for some other respondents.

*Freedom through Involvement (2.11).* This category of responses entails getting so immersed or involved in an activity that all else disappears, and one is freed from other thoughts, other troubles, other pressures. The activity it-

177

self may involve its own restrictions, demands or pressures, but the involvement releases the participant from the routine:

HS1, m, 17: "...like I forgot about school, forgot about everything, what's important is just what you're doing right now..."

U10, f, 19: "...playing the piano, I get like that. Your mind is only on one particular thing, the music in front of you..."

None of the retired respondents provide statements which could be coded in this way. This category falls under the general heading of Acquired Freedom through Self-Perfection, and it may well be that they have perfected themselves as much as they are going to. On the other hand, these retired respondents were all members of a seniors educational group, all were healthy and very much involved in activities, and the difference between them and the younger samples might well be a cohort effect: The older people grew up in a time when the kind of single-minded involvement to which current younger people refer may have been seen as self-indulgence.

*Freedom through Independence/Challenge (2.13).* This category overlaps with the categories of freedom in achievement of a goal and freedom through skill and control, but has the particular emphasis on individual activity and on meeting challenge. The emphasis is on the *individual* doing rather than on the achievement. For example:

HS2, m, 19: "...It's when you've discovered yourself and in trying and dealing with people in growing and maturing and having all those different challenges..."

U7, m, 21, "...something I can do on my own..."

R2, f: "...control the mountain, learn to work with nature..."

A small number of respondents in each age group provide examples of this kind. The examples seem to involve some uncertainty about outcomes and the marshalling of one's resources to bring about favourable consequences on an individual basis.

### The minor categories

As the name implies, these categories represent relatively small numbers of respondents, ranging from a single person to about 20% of respondents. Relatively few statements are involved, ranging from a single example to a total of five within an individual code category. Altogether, these categories represent 14% of all responses given. Again note that while the frequency is low, the importance in any single case may be high.

178

*Freedom through External Security (1.112).* Obviously, the presence of external security may give rise to a report of internal security, and indeed some respondents make this connection in their statements. The specific categorization we assigned depended on the apparent emphasis (cf. Freedom through Internal Security). The single example we have for this category from a high school student is already coded in the former category, but is also reported here because of the double focus.

HS2, m, 19: "...when school is over, you've written your last exam and there is stability to look forward to in the summer, meaning you have a job lined up and you have a girlfriend or something, and everything is going right..."

The university sample and the retired sample give examples which are more explicitly external:

U2, f, 25: "...money makes me feel free..."

R3, m: "...house is paid for, we seem to be living within our income, the bank account seems to increase which is nice..."

It is evident that the kinds of security mentioned here are not typically ends in themselves, but make possible relief from many kinds of pressure and make available opportunities which might not otherwise be available.

*Freedom through Skill and Control (1.121).* This category has only four responses in it, and one of them has already been coded under Independence and Challenge. As noted earlier, there is this overlap, as well as overlap with Achievement of a Goal, to be discussed later. This specific category was initially included because the importance of such a category (Exercise of Skilled Behaviour) was shown in the earlier research (Westcott 1982a) reported in Chapter 7. It appears much less important in the present study. Nonetheless, the statements presented are central to the category, although it should be noted that of the four codable statements, three came from high school respondents, none appeared in the university sample, and the one from the retired sample has already been coded elsewhere:

HS2, m, 19: "...you know, doing things that you're good at..."

HS4, f, 17: "...when I did this well, I felt free in doing it..."

R2, f: "...control the mountain, learn to work with nature..."

The contrast between the importance of this kind of contributor to feeling free in the earlier research and in the present study will be discussed later.

*Freedom through Free Choice (3.1).* Statements coded into this category naturally assumed the availability of options or opportunities and the capacities to exploit them, and raised the problem of finding the emphasis of a statement. Staying close to the explicit content and wording of the statement led to coding a total of seven statements from five respondents, some from each sample:

HS3, f, 18: "...I was free to make a decision there. As it turned out, now I'm going to grade 13 but because of my own choice, there again, not just because of what other people tell me..."

U4, m, 21: "...feel free that I can pick the classes and not go to ones if I feel tired. I was free to choose them..."

R1, f: "...to make my own choices..."

In our society, making choices may have essentially the status of "background noise" and not be noticed unless the choice is threatened either implicitly or explicitly. This is certainly what reactance theory would suggest. It is certainly implied here that for the secondary school student and the university student, choices of the kind reported were not generally open to them, and conceivably could be threatened or taken away again.

*Freedom from Conflict and Indecision (1.221).* This category was initially suggested by earlier research (Westcott, 1982a) reported in Chapter 7. Conflict and Indecision was one of the major opposites to feeling free reported there, and was the principal incursion on experienced freedom in decision making situations. In the present study, five persons gave a total of 16 statements which can be so categorized.

HS9, f, 17: "...and you know your limitations..."

U9, f, 22: "...I think I feel more confident and that could be a source of freedom..."

R1, f: "...go to a wine and cheese party and there is no decision to make..."

Here lack of conflict comes from various sources, such as recognition of limitations, feelings of confidence, and prior decisions, but the common theme is that the respondent is not in conflict.

*Freedom in the Achievement of a Goal (2.12).* In this category we have examples in which the achievement of a goal is important, and others in which the progressively successful pursuit of a goal is important.

HS4, f, 17: "...just finished doing a project. Did a half decent job on it. Made me feel good..."

U6, m, 22: "...I imagine if it's something I'm in pursuit of and I reach that goal..."

R5, m: "...when I'm doing something I consider worthwhile..."

In total there were only three respondents providing statements of this kind, and a total of four statements which could be coded here.

*Freedom through Social Responsibility and Moral Commitment (2.2).* Here we have freedom experienced through an individual doing something good for someone or by making a moral commitment. We had only three respondents and seven statements in this category. None of them came from university students. The responses range from the relatively mundane to the relatively cosmic:

HS7, f, 18: "...when my relationship with God is right..."

HS6, m, 17: "...that is something that I feel in my house that I should do, to help out around the house and cutting the lawn is part of that..."

R1, f: "...you are free to accept and do the things that you feel are going to make all the better world than what we are supposed to be living in, there's a freedom..."

In each of these examples there is a kind of action which makes one part of a larger whole—the family, the Godly, the world, and the purpose is to a higher perfection, meeting worthy obligations, participating in a valued collective.

*Freedom through Health (1.122).* Here we have only one statement to be coded. This, despite the extent to which Parmenter (cf. chapter 6) saw health as absolutely fundamental to freedom. The one statement we have comes from one of the retired respondents:

R5, m: "...when my health is good and I have energy..."

This statement implies that perhaps sometimes his health is not good and he lacks energy. Clearly, for this respondent, health is necessary for him to pursue alternatives which are available to him. In later discussion, we will have more to say about some interesting relations between health and freedom. This, then, ends the presentation of these data.


### Discussion


The findings presented in this chapter need to be discussed in the context of those presented in Chapters 6 and 7, as well as in the context of some findings presented briefly below. Each of the sets of findings already presented have both strengths and weaknesses which can serve to critique and illuminate each other. Recall that Parmenter's autobiographical presentation was the result of a sustained and appropriately idiosyncratic inquiry into the experience of one individual; Zavalloni's materials were written one-way open-ended communications from a rather select group of European students in the early 1950s; Westcott's findings were based primarily on questionnaire data concerning experiences in settings which were rationally and theoretically derived. Only the present data are the results of extended interviews.

Parmenter's presentation (1980) has the advantage of being a systematic continuous narrative, following the development and variation of experienced freedom over a period of years and in a variety of settings; Zavalloni's interpretations (1962) have the advantage of being based on statements which were considered before they were written and were generated spontaneously without reference to any standard situations; Westcott's data (1982a) have the advantage of being systematized in such a way as to allow for quantification, and ease of aggregate presentation and analysis. They provide a measure of intensity of feeling, and an exploration of the dialectic between feeling free and feeling opposite to free. Not only were the present data generated by means of a dialogue between investigator and informant, but the coding was developed through dialogue with the data, informed by previously developed coding systems.

The present data could have been presented as individual narratives, but they were coded, that is, fragmented into significant statements and grouped. In this process, much idiosyncracy and context is lost. There is always the tension between dealing with the concrete in all its richness and dealing with the abstract derived by the imposition of some conceptual scheme on the concrete details. I have chosen something of a middle ground which partakes of both the advantages and disadvantages of each. For some, such a choice produces epistemological heartburn, but for others it merely represents a necessity in the pursuit of knowledge which is always transitional, always negotiable, and always open to revision.

The new material to be included in the discussion comes from a series of brief and structured interviews with informants between 6 and 19 years of age (Tothill, 1984). Tothill oriented her interviews around four questions:

a) Do you ever feel free?
b) When do you feel most free?
c) Is there something you are good at doing? How do you feel when you do it? Do you feel free?
d) What does the word "free" mean?

The first two questions are straightforward, but the third was introduced because in the pretest interviews, a large number of the responses to question b) from younger children involved "playing," "riding my bike," "having fun," etc. Earlier findings (Westcott, 1982a) showed the importance of engaging in skilled behaviour, so question c) was introduced as a follow-up to question b). The purpose of the final question was to elicit abstract definitions, which might be rather different from reported experience.

The aim of her study was primarily methodological – to determine whether young children could provide meaningful answers to the questions, to study the utility of the previously developed coding schemes, and to determine whether there were age-related differences in the kinds of responses given. To pursue these aims, Tothill coded the interview contents in several different ways. She attempted the three-fold conceptualization offered by Adler (1973), she used the categorizations which Westcott (1984) had derived from Zavalloni's (1962) data, and she attempted the grouping which Westcott (1982a) built into his questionnaire.

Her findings were preliminary and provocative and showed that children as young as six years of age did have meaningful concepts of freedom and experiences of freedom. She found that all of the previously described coding systems could be used, except that the most frequent conditions or experiences of freedom supplied by the younger children – "playing" or "having fun" – did not categorize easily in any of the schemes. She found age-related differences in the elaborateness of the responses, as well as some provocative differences in content.

She compared one sample ranging in age from 6 to 13 years (n = 23) with another sample ranging in age from 13-19 years (n = 13). In the Adler conceptualization, she found both groups gave a high frequency of responses having to do with circumstantial freedom, and few in either group gave responses related to acquired freedom. With respect to natural freedom (the self-generating of actions) 65% of the younger group described experiences of this kind, while 100% of the older sample did so. In a similar vein, when using the categories included in Westcott's questionnaire, only 48% of the younger informants made statements which could be construed as self-direction, while 100% of the older sample did so; 22% of the younger people cited the presence of alternatives as a contribution to experienced freedom, while 100% of the older people did so. When using the categories imposed on Zavalloni's responses, she found that about half the younger respondents found experienced freedom in independence and challenge, while 100% of the older sample did so. Interestingly, more than a quarter of the younger informants described experiencing freedom when going outside after an illness, while none of the older respondents did so, probably reflecting the usual round of childhood diseases.

Tothill provided a full inventory of the responses which she extracted from the interviews; Zavalloni provided a large number, but not his total set of responses; Westcott's full questionnaire was available. For the purposes of this discussion, all of the earlier materials were recoded into the system described earlier in this chapter. It was felt that Taylor's present coding system is the one most fully informed by previous research, and at the same time most responsive to the reports of the informants.

Taylor (1986) recoded Tothill's original statements into his coding system and provided some confirmation for the findings already presented. Specifically, the three code categories with the highest frequency of statements for both the younger and older of Tothill's samples were the same as the highest three code categories shown in Table 6—Freedom from Pressure (1.211), Freedom through Opportunity (1.111), and Self-Determination (3.2). While these three categories accounted for a total of 64% of the statements in the interviews analyzed by Taylor (1986) and reported earlier, they account for 67% of the statements of Tothill's older sample and for 86% of the statements from her younger sample. This may mean, reasonably enough, that the younger respondents have a less diversified conception of the circumstances that induce a feeling of freedom. It also appears to be a confirmation that several separate samples of respondents from essentially the same cultural and historical setting share these experiences.

Taylor also analyzed the 28 situations which make up Westcott's (1982a) questionnaire. He selected the three clusters which had the highest frequency of use (Cluster 1, Self-Direction; Cluster 2, Absence of Responsibility; Cluster 6, Presence of Alternatives) (See Westcott, 1982a p. 106) and found that eleven of the twelve specific situations described in these three clusters were easily recodable into the three major code categories of the present system: Freedom from Pressure, Freedom through Opportunity, and Freedom in Self-Determination. This is a further confirmation of the general centrality of these three types of situations in generating the experience of freedom.

But note in contrast, that none of these three kinds of situations produced the most intense experience of freedom in Westcott's findings. In fact, the two clusters in Westcott's data which produced the highest intensities of feeling free were the *least* frequently used. Recall also that even these least-used clusters were considered relevant nearly 80% of the time. Again, caution must be exercised to avoid confusing the frequency of the occurrence of various kinds of statements with the individual importance of those statements. We noted this with respect to the extremely low frequency of health as a contributor to experienced freedom in the present data as compared to the potential importance of this condition.

Taylor also recoded Zavalloni's (1962) work and found it somewhat more problematic. Zavalloni had a thesis to present, in contrast to the relatively open-ended nature of the studies by Westcott, Tothill and Taylor. The thesis had to do with moral education and the importance of training for individual decision making within the framework of high moral purpose. Zavalloni was concerned with the extent to which the students he studied were prevented from making guided decisions as preparation for future morally responsible lives. As noted earlier, Zavalloni reports that he received 173 usable responses, but in his book, he presented only a sampling of these (a total of 75) and used them to illustrate his thesis: that the over-restriction of individual decision making within a moral context, as represented by the experience of many of his boarding school respondents, can lead to excesses and irresponsibility when the constraints are removed. He argued that guided decision making and the appreciation of moral principles is a fundamental purpose of education.

And, indeed, when Zavalloni's examples are recoded into the present system, 27% of them fall into Freedom in Free Choice (3.1) and 20% fall into

Freedom in Social Responsibility and Moral Commitment (2.2), a total of 47%. Together, these categories accounted for only 6% of the statements made by respondents in Taylor's samples. However, in recoding Zavalloni's statements, the next three most frequently used categories are the ones we have already noted: Freedom from Pressure, Freedom in Self-Determination, and Freedom in Opportunity. When Zavalloni's selective bias is skimmed off and he has made his point, we still find these three central contributors to the experience of freedom. Again, we are speaking only of the frequency of statements referring to such conditions, and the only evidence we have concerning the intensity of feelings generated is in Westcott's data.

## Some protocols to illuminate the discussion further

As a final contribution to this discussion of direct experiential reports, presented below are six complete protocols, collected and analyzed by Merante (1984) in a study wholly independent of those already presented in this chapter. The protocols were solicited in written form in response to the question, "Under what conditions do you feel free?" Many submitted protocols were not usable because they became abstract treatises on human freedom or because they were excessively vague. Informants had to be repeatedly encouraged to stick to the specific question asked and to write at a personal and concrete level rather than a general or abstract level. Ultimately, following the methods suggested by Stones (in Kruger, 1981, Ch. 4) Merante reached conclusions about the conditions of freedom very like (and anticipating) the studies already reported in the present chapter.

The purpose of this presentation, however, is not the reporting of Merante's conclusions. Rather, it is to present his protocols as examples, and to indicate to the reader the ease with which the statements in the protocols can be assimilated to the code categories developed in the Taylor (1986) study which formed the bulk of this chapter. The second merit of Merante's protocols is that they are relatively compact, clear, and coherent, having been provided in written form by the informants. This makes them much different from interview transcripts. The third merit is that they come from contemporary North American university students, in contrast to the protocols provided by Zavalloni from predominantly European respondents in predominantly Roman Catholic boarding schools in the 1950s. This last makes them comparable to our other samples, both geographically and historically.

*Protocol #1.* This question is very difficult for me to answer. I feel free only in *one* episode in my life well, not one. Whenever I go to the cottage I feel free. Whenever I go to Lesat Lake which is located in the Muskoka Area, it is like heaven there. I feel so free and good. You see all the wilderness and the lake, it's magnificent. There are no laws to obey, not a lot of people. In fact, no people at all to bother you or to tell you what to do. No signs; no warnings; no laws. So you're free to do anything you want when you want. I wish sometimes when I'm feeling sad or when my day isn't going well to go up there and just be free and elated. It is so peaceful, warm, you can pick a spot on the lake and be free. No cares or worries. That's freedom.

*Protocol # 2.* When do I feel free?
– When I can do what I want without restrictions.
– When I have successfully completed a task that has   been difficult and a burden.
– Going for a walk to places I have never seen before.
– It feels as if there are no cares in the world.
– It feels like you are looking through a window where no one knows you are there and no one can hurt or touch you.

*Protocol #3.* I tend to feel freest if I am away from the city. I spend a fair bit of time in Muskoka at our family's cottage and it is probably there that I feel freest, possibly because it is the one place where I feel most at ease. The cottage is in the middle of a forest and up there the constrictions of the city disappear. Up north there are no rigid time constraints or rules to be adhered to. I am free to just sit and stare, which I often end up doing for hours, just watching the lake or the stars. I am also comfortable enough to try something new without worrying about reactions from other people, because judgement by others seem to be less frequent. I also feel free because of the openness of the forest as opposed to the concrete of the city. It seems that people become friendlier once they leave the city and head up north. It is far more likely that a stranger will talk to you rather than walking away and this gives me the freedom to just say hello and start up a conversation.

An entirely different situation in which I feel free is when I'm dancing. I am currently a member of a modern gymnastics club, where most of the activity resembles that of modern dance. Although most of the movements are choreographed by someone else, the time during which I am doing the routines gives me a feeling of being free. Part of this feeling arises from the sense of accomplishment after having finally learned the order of the full routine. The frustration of trying to memorize the proper order no longer hinders completion. With every routine, all that I hear is the music and I get totally involved in the dancing. At this point, everything else disappears from my thoughts, and to me, this temporary concentration on only the dance is a kind of freedom. While I am dancing it feels as though I am relaxed, even though the required movements are very precise.

*Protocol #4.* Conditions under which I feel free.
– in an intimate situation (but only when the partner is one that I know well or when I feel that I have mastery of the situation, this is somewhat like playing).

- when absorbed in work, intellectual or manual. When the work is complex enough to be challenging to me, but not overbearing to the point that I feel hopeless or lost.
- hiking (backpacking) in mountains. There is a sense of being lost and being part of nature. The mountains present themselves as magnificent. They present variety, challenge, but also serenity and harmony.
- when exercising (running). There is a point in running (after about 1.5 miles) when the body is loosened up and a running rhythm is achieved that I sense a feeling of elation and freedom (freedom feels like the dream of flying does).
- In exercise (running or backpacking) there is the feeling of flying. In backpacking it is being able to project myself to different parts of the scenery (a distant mountain top, or valley, or into a running stream). In running and the flying is where the ease and the rhythm of the movement. Similar sense of freedom happens when I am *absorbed* by a painting (the original Van Gogh's paintings did this in the most powerful manner). Here there is also the projection of myself into the painting and taking on the roles, the moods of the painting. But, this can be oppressive as well. However, the projection into the painting or an object gives a sense of flight of freedom.
- feel free when *released* from an oppressive situation (esp. when the oppression has strong emotive and intellectual components, or physical pain).

*Protocol #5.* The incident which firstly and most persistently comes to mind in which I have felt free is a moonlit night in early December/75 at a monastery on the coast of Maine. I was nearing the end of an intensive three month retreat during which time I had spent 10-16 hours a day practicing a Buddhist meditation indigenous to Southeast Asia.

Conscious thought had gradually become very immediate much of it ceasing altogether. Awareness of sensation, thought and awareness itself had been the object of three months of discipline.

As I walked through a field at dusk on one particular evening in December/75, and as the moon rose above the bare trees and the chilling air hit my skin, I noted the sensations, the thinking and the awareness of all this phenomena and was filled with an unprecedented sense of freedom. This experience included a great feeling of joy and peace as well as strength and sensitivity. This experience of freedom, and others which I have known, seem to involve a heightened sense of awareness of mind processes and a subsequent disidentification with them, at least in so far as being a discrete entity.

Similar feelings of freedom have also been felt when consciousness of myself has been removed, either by very strong pleasant sensations or by strong involvement in intellectual exercises. However these differ from the above because the experience of this is necessarily unconscious and so the feeling is known in retrospect (i.e., intellectually) only.

*Protocol #6.* The times that I have felt "free" have been times when I have not had to deal with mundane little jobs of everyday living. For instance the times I have felt most free have been during vacation and during school times. These have been times when I was unhampered in the pursuit of what was important to me. However freedom from daily drudgery is/has not been in itself sufficient. Equally important have been a sense of physical well being and a sense that those around me approved of me - a supportive environment as it were. Because the environment was supportive I could feel safe and could also feel trust towards the people around me. To summarize, I feel free under the following conditions. Freedom from menial boring jobs and involvement with pleasurable activities i.e., travel, study, solving a problem. Physical well-being. Support of those around me. Feeling of safety. My feeling I can trust those around me.

To me, feeling free means feeling I have both the opportunity and the self-confidence to undertake pleasurable and/or challenging activities that appeal to me. In other words when I feel free, I feel I can do practically anything that I wish to do.

**********

To say that these protocols provide further rich examples of the code categories developed in this chapter does not stretch credibility too far. We have a further confirmation concerning important dimensions of the conditions which contribute to experienced freedom, at least in the samples studied. In the next chapter we will have more to say about samples that haven't been studied.

## Conclusions

A variety of lessons can be learned from the methods and data presented in this chapter. First, it is entirely possible to engage in meaningful dialogue about the conditions of experienced freedom with children as young as six years. On the other hand, it is very difficult to get information about how it feels to feel free. It may be that we need to leave that to the poets and songsmiths. The few statements we were able to glean seemed almost like cliches — "light as a feather..." "...a weight was lifted..." "...in complete command..." and so on. But then, why shouldn't they come as cliches — accurate, representative, and common?

Second, the experience of freedom is induced by a fairly common set of conditions. While there is uniqueness, in the sense that any individual may have very special conditions under which he or she experiences freedom, there are also common themes, in the sense that considerable proportions of our informants in the various samples describe conditions for the experience of freedom which are similar. The similarity, of course, depends on the level of abstraction one selects in interpreting the results.

Third, in keeping with the tension between commonality and uniqueness, the frequency with which a particular kind of circumstance contributes to experienced freedom is not to be confused with the intensity of the feelings generated. For example, we may quite generally feel free when pressure is absent, or when we are offered a reasonable range of choices, but the feeling of freedom generated may be pallid compared to the feeling of freedom generated by the accomplishment of a skilled performance or the freedom experienced when one resolves a powerful moral dilemma or attains a special relationship with one's personal God. The latter is, of course, likely to be rarer, both individually and in the aggregate, than the former. We have some evidence on both of these points, and they should be kept clearly separate.

Fourth, it is evident that the contents of interviews and written statements on a subject as personal and complex as the experience of freedom can be interpreted or coded in various ways. We have shown a variety of these codings, and have suggested that perhaps the best method is to begin with some theoretical guidelines, and to develop a coding or interpretative system in dialogue with the specific materials presented.

It is also evident that when coding to abstract categories, however derived, the variety and particularity of the conditions for experienced freedom which informants provide is lost, and much of the personal and individual character of these experiences is lost. The individuality can be regained by recourse to the original statements, but even these statements are abstracted from the much richer texture and context of connected narrative about an individual life. Through abstraction and aggregation we gain a more general picture of the conditions which give rise to the experience of freedom, but we lose the details of the experience as lived by the individuals who provide the information. Full protocols can restore the rich individuality.

Finally, while it is not explicit in these findings, it is easily seen that the kind of interview conducted, and possibly the time of year an interview is conducted can influence the findings. The high school students were interviewed in the spring, when they were experiencing the upcoming pressures of exams and anticipating the summer holidays as well as choices or dilemmas about their subsequent plans. The explicit bias or thesis guiding Zavalloni's work led to a focus on the morality and responsibility of freedom and the success or failure of education in preparing people for the conduct of a life based on these considerations.

With respect to the content of the findings, the respondents provide plenty of examples of three fundamental features of the conditions of experienced freedom: a negative freedom — freedom from pressure; a positive freedom — freedom in opportunity; an experiential component — freedom through self-determination or the feeling of agency. These components align nicely with Adler's circumstantial freedom (which includes both non-interference and opportunity) and his notion of natural freedom — the capacity to initiate action. We found few examples of the acquired freedom of self-perfection; there were some, and they may be especially important, but the frequency was low.

Our general interpretations of the findings also align well with the Gibbs (1976) notions of optative freedom, conative freedom, and elective freedom, but once again, our findings tend to downplay his concept of natural freedom — involving the evaluative component of the pursuit of good ends.

But the evaluative features do not actually receive as short a shrift as implied here. We did find examples of freedom through self-perfection, the pursuit of higher rather than lower ends, particularly in members of Zavalloni's sample struggling with decisions about the religious or secular life. We also found examples of this with two of the secondary school respondents, both of whom described themselves as born-again Christians, and with one member of the retired sample, a former missionary. If we broaden our concept of self-perfection to include the struggle to achieve difficult ends and the freedom experienced in skill or achievement (all this by moving up a level of abstraction) this somewhat neglected aspect of experienced freedom attains greater status.

Just as there are alternative conceptualizations described in the philosophical literature in Chapter 1, we see here the possibility for alternative interpretations of the empirical findings reported in the last few chapters. In studies of the present kind, it becomes brilliantly clear that the facts do not speak for themselves, that there is inevitably individual subjective judgement, interpretation, and focussing at every step of the investigative process. We tend to think that the use of some of the treasured "objective" methodologies obviates this judgement process, and eliminates the more "subjective" features of the pursuit of truth, but it does not. Rather, it means that one has simply accepted or adopted such judgements made by others, explicitly or implicitly, and hallowed by tradition. In traditional methods and judgements, decisions and assumptions are typically buried and only come to light in the kind of sustained critiques reviewed in Chapter 5. In the present research, the decisions and judgements are entirely visible, can be disputed and critiqued at every point, and some of the consequences of alternative decisions can be anticipated. Knowledge so generated is explicitly open to revision — as all knowledge must necessarily be; research is not the pursuit of the incorrigible:

"Knowledge so conceived is not a series of self-consistent theories that converges toward an ideal view; it is not a gradual approach to the truth. It is rather an ever increasing ocean of mutually incompatible (and perhaps even incommensurable) alternatives, each single theory, each fairy tale, each myth that is part of the collection forcing the others into greater articulation and all of them contributing, via this process of competition, to the development of our consciousness. Nothing is ever settled, no view can ever be omitted from a comprehensive account" (Feyerabend, 1975, p. 30).

# PART V: FURTHER FACETS OF HUMAN FREEDOM

*Chapter Nine:  Loose Ends, Missed Opportunities, and Possible Futures*

# 9  Loose Ends, Missed Opportunities, and Possible Futures

## The plan

Throughout this work I have maintained a focus on human freedom as a personal experience or a personal achievement. I have tried to avoid much reference to specific political or social systems, although Chapters 1 and 2 necessarily made some reference to them. This restriction on my focus was originally inadvertent, but subsequently, was self-imposed in order to make the work manageable. It nonetheless represents a limitation which I would like to redress partially in this final chapter.

## Consciousness raised

My limited perspective was brought to my attention fairly early in my studies, but as I became aware of it I still did not have the resources to do very much about it.

My consciousness was raised in a rather abrupt fashion, as follows: Some years ago I was invited to give a colloquium at the University of Bristol, England, and was eager to do so. I was on sabbatical, and in residence as a Visiting Fellow of Wolfson College, Oxford; I was on the seminar circuit, so I had a lot of colloquia scheduled and a lot already behind me. This one was special for the kind of insight it gave me.

In the colloquium I presented a variety of the notions of human freedom which I have described in Chapter 1 of this book together with some of the very early findings of my own empirical studies described in Chapter 7. I presented nothing of the historical and anthropological thinking which appears in Chapter 2.

I had pretty well said my piece when a Chinese student raised his hand, and when recognized, launched into what I can only call an oration. He sustained this for five or seven minutes, and so far as I can recollect, he never even paused for breath. It was brilliant, and its topic was freedom through collectivization. He concluded by saying that I had presented only a middle class, capitalist bourgeois notion of freedom. He sat down, and there was a somewhat strained silence. The professor in charge of the seminar was the late, loved, Henri Tajfel. He broke the silence with one of his seismic chuckles, and commented: "And who better to present it than a member of the middle class capitalist bourgeoisie?" We all chuckled. Eventually.

And of course, they were both right. I had presented a very one sided notion. All my sources were either originally from western authors or translated into English. My perspective was narrow, and remains narrow, but now I do not think—as I did then—that I had a grip on the "real essence" of human freedom.

As we have seen, even within the relatively narrow confines of the people who have provided their own reports of experienced freedom, there is great diversity. In the anthropological reports provided in Chapter 2 and in the cross-cultural data presented at the end of Chapter 7 there is even more diversity. In the brief treatment of historical studies presented in Chapter 2 we noted that ancient conceptions of freedom are not the same as contemporary notions of freedom. Fromm has sensitized us to the idea that freedom, however conceived, is more or less attractive at different times in history and in different political and religious contexts. Freedom from restraint plays off against the dangers of experiment; freedom to decide is in conflict with the anxiety and uncertainty of deciding; freedom from interpersonal obligation or dependency is accompanied by existential loneliness; individuality has its attendant terrors of isolation. Parmenter alerts us to the difference between wanting to feel free and wanting to be free. Evidence provided in Chapter 7 shows that ordinary people can also detect the difference, and that people like feeling free more than they like being free.

It is evident that in the conduct of research on a topic as broad and diffuse as human freedom, the methods that one employs have a great effect on the kinds of information one can gain. I have been critical of the highly restricted and narrowly operationalized approach of the traditional psychological

194

laboratory. I have also noted that my own initial survey methods, while allowing more latitude for respondents than the studies of reactance and attribution, show the serious limitations of forcing or nudging respondents into preselected categories, regardless of the diversity of the sources of these categories. The material presented in Chapter 8 is, in my view, the most representative of the psychological conditions of experienced human freedom, and even that is limited by the narrow social and cultural sampling of respondents.

What can we draw from all this that can be of some use in the understanding of our own experience, the actions of others and the conduct of our own lives? What does all of this contribute to a scientific understanding of the nature and experience of human freedom? The reader will appreciate that with respect to human action and experience I use the term "scientific" in a broad sense. I mean "scientific" as an understanding which is rooted in systematic study and in empirical evidence which takes account of the historical and cultural context of the evidence, and treats human beings as if they were human beings.

One person's freedom is another person's bondage, and for any person, conditions supporting freedom at one time may mean bondage at another. Lee emphasized that freedom without constraint is quite impossible. While she offers this in the abstract, we find that concrete individuals, reporting concrete experience, find freedom through commitment — whether it be the commitment to a particular activity, as in dancing or swimming, or to a particular religious faith. While none of my informants provided a sociopolitical commitment as the basis for freedom, the oration in Bristol made exactly this point, and self-perfection — one of Adler's major sources of freedom — can be pursued through politics as well as through other channels.

## On freedom, privacy, and technology

Western cultures place a very high value on individuality, independence and privacy. That is why my sources led me to present that perspective on freedom. Indeed, Westin (1967) argues that privacy is absolutely fundamental to human freedom. He roots his contention in an evolutionary view of territoriality in lower species. However, it appears that notions of privacy in humans are actually of fairly recent origin, arising in the late middle ages, when the notion of an inner self which might be hidden or protected evolved (Baumeister, 1987). For Westin, it is this inner self and its protection which is central, rather than the fact of simple physical concealment. He details meticulously the technological developments which have, in recent years, made possible the extensive invasion of privacy, and for him, erosion of freedom. He is concerned with not only methods of physical surveillance, but those of psychological surveillance through personnel testing and information surveillance through elaborate data banks. Once an individual is deprived of personal discretion as to what information is to be revealed to whom, he argues that privacy is clearly gone, and freedom as well.

He conceives of this argument as a universal proposition, but it appears to be both historically and politically contingent. The organization of Chinese urban society, under Maoist philosophy, was designed to bring people together as much as possible, rather than to keep them apart. Individuality was shunned, and the loyalty was to the collective rather than to the individual inner self. Exposure of one's inner thoughts, so that errors could be corrected, was highly prized, and self-reliance was located in the collective rather than in the individual. Self-perfection was sought through the perfect integration of oneself in the progress of China (Sidel, 1974). Interdependency rather than independence is a common value in Eastern philosophies, and the sharing of both physical intimacy and psychological intimacy is fundamental.

This kind of sharing, this kind of self-revelation and intimacy, are also fundamental to the pursuit of perfection in the training for athletic prowess or for monastic orders. Constant surveillance of one's thoughts, one's habits, one's practices are necessary for the pursuit of freedom through the perfection of high religious, artistic, or athletic performance. From this perspective, not only is privacy not fundamental to freedom, privacy is incompatible with freedom.

So it is in psychotherapy, where a client may conceal "inner thoughts" — and obstruct progress. Heroic attempts to aid in self-disclosure may be made by the therapist, and it is ultimately through a breach of privacy that freedom is sought — freedom from pain, from compulsion, from incapacity. The confessional, designed for the exposure of inner thoughts and guilts, leads to forgiveness, and the development of intimate interpersonal relations through progressive self-disclosure may lead to security.

These last few examples are all matters of revelation of that inner self, but they are on some kind of a continuum of willingness. The ultimate value to the individual is in what is to be done with such revelations. When privacy is violated in a completely involuntary manner and the information is to be used against one, freedom does seem to be eroded. On the other hand, one may grudgingly self-disclose, and the information may be used to one's ultimate advantage. Further, one may eagerly disclose oneself, and the information may be used for or against one. These are all combinations of conditions which relate privacy to freedom in a complex set of ways. This theme is brought out in three enormously popular books originally published in 1971 (Reich, 1971; Slater, 1971; Toffler, 1971).

Slater (1971) places his intriguing analysis of American culture in the context of Viet Nam, the Chicago Democratic Primary, the Bay of Pigs, a series of assassinations, and the latest edition of Spock's *Baby and Child Care*. He makes the point that the tremendous and traditional focus in America on individuality, individualism and independence (See also Sampson, 1977) places person against person in an unrelenting competitiveness. This separates persons from each other, inevitably produces alienation from human contact, and results in isolation and loneliness. This is the loneliness of independence, of freedom, in which each individual family has its own private home, yard, power mower, barbecue, automobile, route to work, and so on. The privacy may go further, to where, ideally, each member of the family has his or her own room, TV, telephone, car, schedule, interests, friends, and life. Freedom is maximized by the intervention of technology—technology which supports and makes possible the separation of person from person, and provides mechanisms whereby people do not have to ask other people for anything. We have the electronic teller, the supermarket, the self-serve gas bar; the telephone replaces the letter and the electronic mail replaces the telephone, and bit by bit, as independence, privacy and freedom increase, more and more human contact is eliminated. Somehow these mechanical linkages are to be substitutes for human linkages.

Each of these steps is in concert with the notion of freedom as independence, individuality, and privacy; the cost borne is an absence of genuine human contact and interdependence. The human relationships are replaced by the electronic, the automated, the routinized, the high-speed.

Elaborate scenarios displaying the profound technological changes already with us and probable in the future, together with the ease, ignorance, and lack of foresight with which they are accepted, have been offered by Reich (1971) and Toffler (1971). They explore the positive, negative, and ambiguous impacts of technology on human life. That these impacts have a bearing on human freedom seems almost certain, but can be assessed only in the light of one's own experience of freedom. Are choices important? How about individuality, privacy, intimacy, personal perfection, non-interference, ease, escape from technologies? Whatever the conditions which contribute to one's experience of freedom, they are acquired or developed or granted through a trade-off with some other human values. Positive values are not necessarily compatible with each other, within a society or within an individual.

## On freedom and psychological well-being

There certainly is a wide and deep consciousness attesting to the notion that feeling free or being free is a wonderful state of affairs. This is reflected in popular songs and literature as well as in the relatively unguarded literature of psychotherapy and behaviour change, but the relation between freedom and psychological well-being has not been investigated empirically until recently (Enns, 1980).

Freedom and freedom-related concepts appear in almost all theories of psychotherapy and behaviour change. Such references become more frequent as one progresses from the more deterministic to the less deterministic theories, from classical psychoanalysis to ego analysis to behaviour and cognitive therapies to the humanistic theories.

From these literatures Enns derived four different kinds of theoretical uses of freedom and freedom-related concepts from the literature on psychotherapy and behaviour change, and described the following: *Reported freedom (either as an ontological state or as a phenomenal experience); reported self-control; reported self-transformation; reported belief in a philosophy of free will.* He constructed a 60-item questionnaire of face-valid items, with fifteen addressing each of these issues.

He included such items as "I feel free;" "I am free;" "I make up my mind to do something and do it;" "Try as I do, I can't overcome my bad habits;" "I find myself changing and developing in ways that are worthwhile;" "Free will is an illusion as people's behaviour is caused by external forces." He sought responses to statements such as these on a five point scale ranging from agree to disagree, and the questions were balanced for direction of response and as to explicitness or implicitness of the target concept. The responses of 211 university students were subjected to a multi-stage factor analysis which yielded three strong independent factors from the four conceptual categories which guided the design of the questionnaire.

The first factor loaded on reported freedom items, in both the ontological and experiential forms; the second factor loaded on both self-control and self-transformation items; the third factor loaded on the belief in free will items. These data confirm the findings reported earlier (Chapter 7) concerning the high correlation between reports of being free and feeling free in the same situations, and also provide statistical data supporting the earlier contention (Chapter 3) that it is a mistake to blur or gloss over the different conceptual and experiential facets of human freedom.

Enns then went on to relate the scores on the different factors to several selected indicators of psychological well-being. He used the MMPI-D scale as a general indicator, the Shostrom Personal Orientation Inventory as an index of self-actualization, an abbreviated form of the Internal-External scale, and finally the Jackson PRF-Desirability scale to control for social desirability of responses.

The reported freedom factor and the reported self-control/self-transformation factor both correlated negatively with the MMPI Depression scale and correlated positively with the Shostrom POI and Internal locus of control. The third factor, belief in free will, did not correlate with any of the indicators of psychological well-being (Enns and Westcott, 1983).

Thus, when examined directly, the general expectations embodied in the theoretical and speculative literature of psychotherapy and behaviour change are borne out: Experiencing oneself as free and as able to control and change oneself are experiences positively related to psychological well-being. But an explicit belief in the philosophical notion of free will is not related to psychological well-being. While Enns did not predict this last finding, he did anticipate it in describing the fundamental optimism of humanistic theorists of psychotherapy. He pointed out that those more strongly influenced by European existentialism, and an explicit commitment to a free-will philosophy such as May and Frankl, are very much less optimistic than the more

American-influenced theorists such as Rogers and Maslow (Enns, 1980, pp. 40-41). Freedom, taken seriously, as in existentialism, is by no means an unalloyed delight; freedom is fraught with anxiety and struggle, as Fromm and Sartre have made clear, and anxiety and struggle are not part of Western conceptions of psychological well-being.

### Freedom's just another word...

Throughout the interviewing I have done on the experience of human freedom, and throughout the many conversations I have had on the topic, I have never directly encountered a serious report of the kind make popular and poignant by Kris Kristofferson and Janis Joplin in the 1970s: "Freedom's just another word for nothing left to lose..." This kind of freedom is set in the context of a kind of abandoned desperation: "I'd give all of my tomorrows for just one yesterday..." and so on. In some respects, it is not unlike the report provided by Parmenter (Chapter 6) concerning the freedom he experienced when stripped of his identity, his telephone, his decisions, his past and his future upon induction into the army. But a more direct comparison is possible, as well. Gold (1974) describes dissenters in the Soviet Union who have been harassed and interrogated, blacklisted and fired, to the extent of developing "A blitheness of desperation; nothing more to lose." He quotes a physicist in Kiev: "At last, there are some free people in the Soviet Union. We don't care anymore" (p. 12). In effect, here we have a resolution of the "pressure" motif described in both Chapter 7 and Chapter 8: The resolution may be viewed as a primitive one in the form of denial, or it may be viewed as transcendent, in the form of a reorganization of perceptions or a realignment of values and priorities. It is obvious that the ways in which one interprets a situation can surely affect the extent to which one experiences oneself as free.

### On extreme conditions

There has been almost nothing said in this book about freedom among individuals suffering extreme privation or imprisonment. In Chapter 2, it was mentioned briefly, with reference to Lee (1963) who described prisoners in Nazi concentration camps, singing on their way to extermination — free, in that they were actively *doing* what could be done, however hopeless. Another view of prison camp life is offered by Solzhenitsyn (1963) in the context of Stalinist Russia. The prisoners did not live under continuous threat of death, but their lives were hedged about with privation, constant labour, and abusive domination by their warders.

The theme of freedom is woven through the novel, but in quite a peculiar way. There are less than a dozen references to freedom in the book, and many of them make it clear that for these prisoners freedom is a great deal less important than some other values. Without doubt, simple survival and making it through the day is the prime virtue along with a bit of pleasure or comfort.

Solzhenitsyn describes Shukhov staring at another prisoner who is smoking a cigarette. After two paragraphs of increasing lust, Shukhov "...thought he'd rather have this butt than his freedom" (p. 33). He goes on to describe the prisoners' privation of simple material things, and how this controlled their very thoughts:

> The prisoners were at their coldest and hungriest when they checked in through these gates in the evening, and their bowl of hot and watery soup without any fat was like rain in a drought. They gulped it down. They cared more for this bowlful than freedom, or for their life in years gone by and years to come" (p. 151).

> Even a prisoner's thoughts weren't free but kept coming back to the same thing, kept turning the same things over again" (p. 43).

This last refers to the constant concern over whether a piece of hidden bread will be discovered by the guards, where another prisoner got a warm shirt, whether one will be fortunate enough to be put on the sick list. Indeed, this last aspiration appears to be about the only reference to action which extricates a prisoner from imprisonment:

> "Now his one dream was to get sick for a couple of weeks, not fatally or anything that needed an operation, but just sick enough to be sent to the hospital. He'd lie there, he thought, for three weeks without moving, and even if the soup they gave you was a little thin it would still be great" (p. 23).

Freedom is perplexing to these prisoners, by no means the kind of unalloyed good it is often portrayed to be. Alyoshka asks Shukhov, "What d'you want your freedom for? What faith you have left will be choked in thorns. Rejoice that you are in prison. Here you can think of your soul" (p. 198).

> "Shukhov looked up at the ceiling and said nothing. He didn't know any longer himself whether he wanted freedom or not. At first he'd wanted it very much and every day he added up how long he still had to go. But then he got fed up with this. And as time went on he understood that they might let you out but they never let you home. And he didn't really know where he'd be better off. At home or here" (p. 199).

To the extent that Solzhenitsyn's picture is accurate—and we have good reason to believe it is—we have a description of the importance of freedom under conditions where mere survival is more important, where illness is liberating rather than restricting, and where freedom is clearly seen as something not wholly desirable, even if available. The ambiguity of freedom looms large, a point we have made repeatedly at a theoretical level, but have not been able to document with the clarity that Solzhenitsyn provides.

## On paradoxes

I have pointed repeatedly to the personal paradoxes inherent in the phenomena of human freedom: The contrasting pleasure and fear, the tension between abandon and constraint, the conflict between preserving choices and giving them up by making commitments. There is another kind of paradox, less personal but more sweeping, which is examined by Deese (1985). He addresses the fact that while the philosophies that inform and animate the social sciences have become more deterministic, the philosophies that inform and animate social practice have become more open, libertarian and voluntarist.

Deese traces the evolution of scientific thinking from the seventeenth century onward, and finds a progression toward a more and more fully deterministic view of the universe. In parallel, he traces the vagaries and fortunes of the notions of free will, volition, and reason in social philosophies, and finds these on a rising course as well. Not surprisingly, these contrasting perspectives, are seen to be on a collision course in the twentieth century.

He argues, as I did earlier, that any meaningful conception of human freedom must rest on the possibility of open rational choice, referred to earlier as "optative freedom" or "natural freedom". To the extent that modern social science operates on a fully deterministic foundation, modern social science cannot provide a comprehensive or comprehensible account of human action which articulates with social practice. As our society moves further and further to a liberalized free choice philosophy, and as the social sciences move further and further to a deterministic position, the conflict increases.

One area of social practice in which the conflict becomes explicit is in the determination of criminal responsibility and the subsequent decisions about what is to be done with or for individuals found to be responsible for their crimes. This issue is illustrated at the extreme in the contentious matter of the insanity defence (cf. Goldstein, 1967), but it is also a matter of more subtle distinctions. The problem is to determine in a court of law whether an individual is to be held responsible (essentially a legal or moral decision) for his or her actions, or whether an individual is to be seen as an example of an inevitable course of events (essentially a metaphysical decision). Of course, there is a spectrum involved — degrees of responsibility and inevitability. The judgement is to be made by a jury untutored in these subtleties, but nonetheless informed by the testimony of experts, or at least by persons with a bias one way or the other. Psychological and psychiatric experts will testify for both the prosecution and the defense, and on the basis of this testimony the attorneys will argue that there is or is not responsibility.

There are two features to the notion of legal responsibility — the cognitive and the volitional. The cognitive has to do with the ability to appreciate the nature of one's acts, and the volitional has to do with the capacity to control one's actions (Rogers, 1987). In practice, the relative importance of these two contributors is indeterminate at the present time and the relative weightings are to be negotiated (in the U.S.A.) by the American Psychological Association, the American Psychiatric Association and the American Bar Association. This is a striking example of the negotiated nature of truth (see also Schacht, 1985).

However, the American Psychological Association has already made its official position clear: In an *amicus* brief to the U.S. Supreme Court, in the case of Colorado *vs.* Connally, APA stated, "any action.... is the inevitable outcome of a set of antecedent and stimulus conditions" (Rogers, 1987, footnote 3, p. 841). This statement may mean only that when something happens or is done, it happens or is done as a result of all of the contributing conditions. If it means only that, then it means almost nothing. However, in the context of the determination of criminal responsibility, it surely seems to be an assertion of a fully deterministic position. There may be members of the APA who would object to being represented by such an official position, but it is on record. Deese (1985) would not support this position, I think, nor would the writers cited in Chapter 5, and it is precisely such a stance that renders social science explanations so often tangential to modern social practice.


### On the practice of human freedom


It seems evident to me that human freedom is something that an individual must pursue by activity. Freedom is not something which can be given or granted by some authority. There must be conditions for the practice of freedom, that is, certain conditions can be provided or denied by outside forces, but the conditions mean little if the individual does not engage with them. Here I am repeating MacCallum's (1967) argument that a coherent statement about freedom requires a statement about what a person is free from, what a person is free to do, and an acting agent. I am extending this argument into the psychological context to say that for freedom to be practiced or experienced there must be a set of surrounding conditions which allow or support an individual in engaging in agentic activity, and that such activity must be engaged in.

We have seen that for different individuals the surrounding conditions may be very diffuse or very specific, the activity may be very ambitious or very modest. We have also seen that for the samples of respondents studied directly, not much attention is given to the active agent aspect of this triad. This capacity to be an agent was to a large extent assumed, and seems to be a kind of background aspect to almost everyone's experience. For most people, focus is directed toward the external conditions of permission or allowance, and secondarily to the having or gaining of personal resources to make use of opportunities. This is the usual finding within studies of attribution of the causes of behaviour: When people explain themselves they focus on the external circumstances more often than they focus on their own personal attributes. The personal attributes are assumed as givens. But in any attempt to enhance one's personal experience of freedom, attention must be paid to one's personal resources: What do I know how to do? What am I good at? What kinds of opportunities can I make use of? Even under conditions of extreme privation, as those described by Lee (Chapter 2) and conditions of the less extreme sort described by Parmenter (Chapter 6) people could *do something*, could take some kind of advantage of their circumstances. In Chapter 7, high school athletes described taking advantage of many creative possibilities within the rules of the game, and others described taking advantage of the challenges of vague, uncertain or threatening situations, confident in the belief that they could cope. But for Shukhov and his fellow prisoners most action taken is in the service of what Solzhenitsyn sees as survival, rather than the pursuit of freedom.

We often think of human freedom in dramatic or heroic terms, but the studies here have focussed on day-to-day conditions and experiences of freedom. I have not heard anyone I interviewed say that he or she felt free when reading the Declaration of Independence or the Charter of Rights or when marking a ballot in a free democratic election. These, for my informants, are background givens. Nor have I had an informant tell me that being able to read a street sign made him or her feel free. Yet we know full well that when an individual comes up out of the subway and *can't* read the street signs, that individual can't be free in the mainstream of our society, can't feel free in a society which is so heavily based on such signs and symbols.

Freedom is practiced and experienced in many ways and in many contexts, and any single rule about human freedom is riddled with exceptions. Yet this does not make the phenomenon chaotic or incomprehensible. The confluence of opportunity, agent, and action seems to be the basis of human freedom both in practice and in experience. Matches between capacity and opportunity can be sought out or developed in efforts to enhance human experience.

## Finally

There is no really graceful way to end this book. There may be no way at all, except to stop writing. There is much more to be said, and much more will be said. In the course of this walk through the various literatures, I hope I have clarified some issues, untangled some confusions, and enriched some oversimplifications. I hope I have provided sufficient provocation so that I will have had some influence on the future study and understanding of human freedom.

# REFERENCES

Adair, J. and Spinner, B. (1981). Subjects' access to cognitive processes: demand characteristics and verbal report. *Journal for the Theory of Social Behaviour, 11*, 31-52.

Adams, D. (1931). A re-statement of the problems of learning. *British Journal of Psychology, XXII*, 150-176.

Adler, M. (1973). *The idea of freedom*. Westport, Conn: Greenwood Press.

Antaki, C. (Ed.). (1981). *The psychology of ordinary explanations of social behaviour*. London: Academic Press.

Atkinson, J. (1957). Motivational determinants of risk-taking behaviour. *Psychological Review, 64*, 359-372.

Austin, J. (1962). *Sense and sensibilia*. London: Oxford University Press.

Ayer, A. (1963). Freedom and necessity. In A.J. Ayer, *Philosophical Essays* (pp. 271-284). London: McMillan and Co. Ltd., New York: St. Martin's Press.

Bair, J. (1901). Development of voluntary control. *Psychological Review, 8*, 474-510.

Bakan, D. (1967). *On method*. San Francisco: Jossey-Bass.

Bartlett, J. (1955). *Familiar quotations*. Boston: Little, Brown and Company.

Basseches, M. (1984). Dialectical thinking as a meta-systematic form of cognitive organization. In M. Commons, F. Richards and C. Armon (Eds.), *Beyond formal operations* (pp. 216-238). New York: Praeger.

Baumeister, R. (1987). How the self became a problem: a psychological review of historical research. *Journal of Personality and Social Psychology, 52*, 163-176.

Bem, D. (1965). An experimental analysis of self-persuasion. *Journal of Experimental Social Psychology, 1,* 199-218.

Benn, S. and Weinstein, W. (1974). Freedom as the non-restriction of options: a rejoinder. *Mind, 83,* 435-439.

Berkowitz, L. and Donnerstein, E. (1982). External validity is more than skin deep. *American Psychologist, 37,* 245-257.

Berlin, I. (1958). *Two concepts of liberty.* Oxford: The Clarendon Press.

Berlin, I. (1969). *Four essays on liberty.* Oxford: Oxford University Press.

Bidney, D. (Ed.). (1963). *The concept of freedom in anthropology.* The Hague: Mouton and Co.

Blumenthal, A. (1980). Wundt and early American psychology. In R. Rieber (Ed.), *Wilhelm Wundt and the making of a scientific psychology* (pp. 117-135). New York: Plenum.

Boaz, F. (1940). Liberty among primitive people. In R. Anshen (Ed.), *Freedom: its meaning* (pp. 375-383). New York: Harcourt.

Braginski and Braginski. (1974). *Mainstream psychology: a critique.* New York: Holt, Rinehart and Winston.

Brandt, L. (1982). *Psychologists caught.* Toronto: University of Toronto Press.

Brehm, J. (1966). *A theory of psychological reactance.* New York: Academic Press.

Brehm, J. and Rozen, E. (1971). Attractiveness of old alternatives when a new, attractive alternative is introduced. *Journal of Personality and Social Psychology, 20,* 261-266.

Brehm, S. and Brehm, J. (1981). *Psychological reactance: a theory of freedom and control.* New York: Academic Press.

Broadbent, D. (1973). *In defense of empirical psychology.* London: Methuen.

Brown, S. (Ed.). (1974). *Philosophy of psychology.* New York: MacMillan.

Buchner, E. (1900). Volition as a scientific datum. *Psychological Review, 7,* 494-507.

Buss, A. (Ed.). (1979). *Psychology in social context.* New York: Irvington Publishers.

Campbell, C. (1938). In defense of free will. In C. Campbell (Ed.), *In defense of free will* (pp. 35-55). London: G. Allen and Unwin.

Canfield, J. (1962). The compatibility of free will and determinism. *Philosophical Review, 71,* 352-368.

Chanana, D. (1960). *Slavery in ancient India.* New Delhi: Peoples Publishing House.

Colaizzi, P. (1971). Analysis of the learner's perception of learning materials at various phases of the learning process. In A. Giorgi, W. Fischer, and R. Von Eckartsberg (Eds.), *Duquesne studies in phenomenological psychology* (Vol. 1, pp. 101-111). Pittsburgh: Duquesne University Press.

Colaizzi, P. (1978). Psychological research as the phenomenologist views it. In R. Valle and M. King (Eds.), *Existential-phenomenological alternatives for psychology* (pp. 48-71). New York: Oxford University Press.

Cotton, J. (1980). Verbal reports on mental processes: ignoring data for the sake of theory? *Personality and Social Psychology Bulletin*, 6, 278-281.

Cooper, H. (1986). An historical perspective on Gordon Allport: paradigmatic considerations for the functional autonomy of motives. Unpublished M.A. Thesis. Department of Psychology, York University, Toronto.

Cranston, M. (1967). *Freedom*, (3rd. Ed.). New York: Basic Books.

Danziger, K. (1979a). The positivist repudiation of Wundt. *Journal of the History of the Behavioral Sciences*, 15, 205-230.

Danziger, K. (1979b). The social origins of modern psychology. In A. Buss (Ed.), *Psychology in social context* (pp. 27-45). New York: Irvington Publishers.

Danziger, K. (1980). Wundt's theory of behaviour and volition. In R. Rieber (Ed.), *Wilhelm Wundt and the making of a scientific psychology* (pp. 89-115). New York: Plenum.

de Charms, R. (1968). *Personal causation*. New York: Academic Press.

de Charms, R. (1979). Personal causation and perceived control. In L. Perlmuter and R. Monty (Eds.), *Choice and perceived control* (pp. 29-39). Hillsdale, N.J.: Lawrence Erlbaum Associates.

Deese, J. (1985). *American freedom and the social sciences*. New York: Columbia University Press.

Dennett, D. (1984). *Elbow room: the varieties of free will worth wanting*. Cambridge, Mass.: The MIT Press.

Eddington, A. (1935). *New pathways in science*. Cambridge: Cambridge University Press.

Enns, K. (1980). Freedom-related variables and psychological well-being. Unpublished Ph.D. dissertation, York University, Toronto.

Enns, K. and Westcott, M. (1983, June). Should therapists encourage belief in both personal freedom and philosophical free will to improve treatment outcome? Paper presented at Canadian Psychological Association, Winnipeg, Manitoba.

Ericsson, K. and Simon, H. (1980). Verbal reports as data. *Psychological Review*, 87, 215-251.

Fancher, R. (1979). *Pioneers of psychology*. New York: W.W. Norton.

Feyerabend, P. (1975). *Against method*. London: NLB.

Ford, J. (1987). Whither volition? *American Psychologist*, 42, 1033-1034.

Fosdick, D. (1939). *What is freedom*? New York: Harper and Brothers.

Friedenberg, E. (1975). *The disposal of liberty and other industrial wastes*. Garden City, New York: Doubleday and Company.

Fromm, E. (1941). *Escape from freedom*. New York: Holt, Rinehart and Winston.

Gardner, J. (1982). *Mickelsson's ghosts*. Toronto: Random House.

Gergen, K. (1973). Social psychology as history. *Journal of Personality and Social Psychology, 26,* 309-320.

Gergen, K. (1978). Experimentation in social psychology: a reappraisal. *European Journal of Social Psychology, 8,* 507-527.

Gergen, K. (1982). *Toward transformation in social knowledge.* New York: Springer-Verlag.

Gergen, K. and Gergen, M. (1982). Explaining human conduct: form and function. In P. Secord (Ed.), *Explaining human behavior* (pp. 127-154). Beverly Hills, Calif.: Sage Publications.

Gibbs, B. (1976). *Freedom and liberation.* Sussex: Sussex University Press.

Gilbert, A. (1970). What ever happened to the will in American psychology? *Journal of the History of the Behavioural Sciences, 6,* 52-58.

Gilbert, L. (1970). Untitled. Unpublished Ms. Whitman College, Walla Walla, Washington.

Giorgi, A. (1970). *Psychology as a human science.* New York: Harper and Row.

Giorgi, A. (1971). Phenomenology and experimental psychology: I. In A. Giorgi, W. Fischer, and R. Von Eckartsberg (Eds.), *Duquesne Studies in phenomenological psychology* (Vol. 1, pp. 6-16). Pittsburgh: Duquesne University Press.

Giorgi, A. (1982). A disclaimer. *American Psychologist, 37,* 1410.

Glass, D., Singer, J., and Friedman, L. (1969). Psychic cost of adaptation to an environmental stressor. *Journal of Personality and Social Psychology, 12,* 200-210.

Gold, H. (1974, April 18). The dissenters Solzhenitsyn left behind. *Newsweek,* pp. 12-13.

Goldstein, A. (1967). *The insanity defense.* New Haven: Yale University Press.

Gouldner, A. (1960). The norm of reciprocity: a preliminary statement. *American Sociological Review, 25,* 161-168.

Greeno, J. (1982). Response to "The hegemony of natural scientific conceptions of learning." *American Psychologist, 37,* 332-334.

Gurwitz, S. and Panciera, L. (1975). Attributions of freedom by actors and observers. *Journal of Personality and Social Psychology, 32,* 531-539.

Hamilton, W. (1928). Freedom and economic necessity. In H. Kallen (Ed.), *Freedom in the modern world* (pp. 25-49). New York: Coward-McCann, Inc.

Hampshire, S. (1965). *Thought and action.* London: Chatto and Windus.

Harré, R. (1981). The posivist-empiricist approach and its alternative. In P. Reason and J. Rowan (Eds.), *Human Inquiry* (pp. 3-18). London: John Wiley and Sons Ltd.

Harré, R. (1984). *Personal being.* Cambridge: Harvard University Press.

Harré, R. and Secord, P. (1972). *The explanation of social behaviour.* Oxford: Blackwell.

Harris, B. and Harvey, J. (1981). Attribution theory: From phenomenal causality to the intuitive social scientist and beyond. In C. Antaki (Ed.), *The psychology of ordinary explanations of social behaviour* (pp. 57-95). London: Academic Press.

Harvey, J. (1976). Attribution of freedom. In J. Harvey, J. Ickes, and R. Kidd (Eds.), *New directions in attribution research* (Vol. I, pp. 73-96). Hillsdale, N.J.: Lawrence Erlbaum Associates.

Harvey, J. and Harris, B. (1975). Determinants of perceived choice and expectancy about feelings of internal control. *Journal of Personality and Social Psychology, 31*, 101-106.

Harvey, J., Harris, B., and Barnes, R. (1975). Actor-observer differences in the perceptions of responsibility and freedom. *Journal of Personality and Social Psychology, 32*, 22-28.

Harvey, J., Harris, B. and Lightner, J. (1979). Perceived freedom as a central concept in psychological theory and research. In L. Perlmuter and R. Monty (Eds.), *Choice and perceived control* (pp. 275-300). Hillsdale, N.J.: Erlbaum Associates.

Harvey, J., and Jellison, J. (1974). Determinants of perceived choice, number of options, and perceived time in making a selection. *Memory and Cognition, 2*, 539-544.

Harvey, J., and Johnston, S. (1973). Determinants of the perception of choice. *Journal of Experimental Social Psychology, 9*, 164-179.

Harwood, M. (1983, January 23). The universe and Dr. Hawking, *The New York Times Magazine*, 16-19, 53-64.

Hayes, S. Contextual determinants of "volitional action": a reply to Howard and Conway. *American Psychologist, 42*, 1029-1030.

Hebb, D. (1960). Call for Dr. Finagle. (Review of Miller, G., Galanter, E., and Pribram, K. (1960) *Plans and the structure of behavior*. New York: Henry Holt). *Contemporary Psychology, 5*, 209-211.

Heider, F. (1944). Social perception and phenomenal causality. *Psychological Review, 51*, 358-374.

Heider, F. (1958). *The psychology of interpersonal relations*. New York: Wiley.

Heider, F. and Simmel, M. (1944). An experimental study of apparent behavior. *American Journal of Psychology, 57*, 243-259.

Hershberger, W. (1987). Of course there can be an empirical science of volitional action. *American Psychologist, 42*, 1032-1033.

Howard, G. and Conway, C. (1986). Can there be an empirical science of volitional action? *American Psychologist, 41*, 1241-1251.

Howard, G. and Conway, C. (1987). The next steps toward a science of agency. *American Psychologist, 42*, 1034-1035.

Hume, D. (1978). *A treatise on human nature*. Oxford: Oxford University Press (original 1888).

Irwin, F. (1942). The concept of volition in experimental psychology. In F. Clarke, and M. Nahm (Eds.), *Philosophical essays in honor of Edgar Arthur Singer, Jr.* (pp. 115-137). Philadelphia: University of Pennsylvania Press.

James, W. (1890). *The principles of psychology* (Two volumes). New York: Henry Holt.

Jellison, J. and Harvey, J. (1973). Determinants of perceived choice and the relationship between perceived choice and perceived competence. *Journal of Personality and Social Psychology, 28,* 376-382.

Johnson, R. (1975). *In quest of a new psychology.* New York: Human Sciences Press.

Jones, E., Davis, K., and Gergen, K. (1961). Role playing variations and their informational value for person perception. *Journal of Abnormal and Social Psychology, 63,* 302-310.

Jones, E., and Harris, V. (1967). The attribution of attitudes. *Journal of Experimental Social Psychology, 3,* 1-24.

Kahneman, D. (1973). *Attention and effort.* Englewood Cliffs, N.J.: Prentice Hall.

Keen, E. (1975). *A primer in phenomenological psychology.* New York: Holt, Rinehart and Winston.

Kelley, H. (1967). Attribution theory in social psychology. In D. Levine (Ed.), *Nebraska symposium on motivation* (pp. 192-238). Lincoln: University of Nebraska Press.

Kelly, G. (1955). *The psychology of personal constructs* (Two volumes). New York: Norton.

Kimble, G. and Perlmuter, L. (1970). The problem of volition. *Psychological Review, 77,* 361-384.

Koch, S. (1981). The nature and limits of psychological knowledge: lessons of a century qua "science". *American Psychologist, 36,* 257-269.

Kruger, D. (1981). *An introduction to phenomenological psychology.* Pittsburgh: Duquesne University Press.

Lamiell, J. and Durbeck, P. (1987). Whence cognitive prototypes in impression formation? some empirical evidence for dialectical reasoning as a generative process. *The Journal of Mind and Behavior, 8,* 223-244.

Leach, E. (1963). Law as a condition of freedom. In D. Bidney (Ed.), *The concept of freedom in anthropology* (pp. 74-90). The Hague: Mouton and Co.

Lee, D. (1959). *Freedom and culture.* Englewood Cliffs, N.J.: Prentice Hall (Spectrum).

Lee, D. (1963). Freedom and social constraint. In D. Bidney (Ed.), *The concept of freedom in anthropology* (pp. 61-73). The Hague: Mouton and Co.

Lefcourt, H. (1973). The function of the illusions of control and freedom. *American Psychologist, 28,* 417-425.

MacCallum, G. (1967). Negative and positive freedom. *Philosophical Review, 76,* 312-334.

Malinowski, B. (1944). *Freedom and civilization.* New York: Roy Publishers.

Mandler, G. and Kessen, W. (1974). The appearance of free will. In S. Brown (Ed.), *Philosophy of Psychology* (pp. 305-324). New York: MacMillan.

Martin, A. (1922). An experimental study of the factors and types of voluntary choice. *Archives of Psychology, 51,* 1-116.

Merante, T. (1984). The phenomenology of freedom: an empirical study. Unpublished manuscript, Department of Psychology, York University, Toronto.

Miller, A. (Ed.). (1972). *The social psychology of psychological research.* New York: Free Press.

Miller, G., Galanter, E., and Pribram, K. (1967). *Plans and the structure of behavior.* New York: Wiley.

Mook, D. (1983). In defense of external validity. *American Psychologist, 38,* 379-387.

Morris, P. (1981). The cognitive psychology of self-reports. In C. Antaki (Ed.), *The psychology of ordinary explanations of social behaviour* (pp. 183-204). London: Academic Press.

Muller, H. (1963). Freedom and justice in history. In D. Bidney (Ed.), *The concept of freedom in anthropology* (pp. 272-291). The Hague: Mouton and Co.

Murphy, G. (1947). *Personality.* New York: Harper Brothers.

Murphy, G. (1971). William James on the will. *Journal of the History of the Behavioural Sciences, 7,* 249-260.

Nisbett, R. and Wilson, T. (1977). Telling more than we can know: verbal reports on mental processes. *Psychological Review, 84,* 231-259.

Nowell-Smith, P. (1948). Free will and moral responsibility. *Mind, LVII,* 45-61.

Ofstad, H. (1967). Recent work on the free-will problem. *American Philosophical Quarterly, 4,* 179-207.

Orwell, E. (1949). *Nineteen eight-four.* New York: Harcourt Brace.

Parent, W. (1974a). Freedom as the non-restriction of options. *Mind, 83,* 432-435.

Parent, W. (1974b). Some recent work on the concept of liberty. *American Philosophical Quarterly, 11,* 149-167.

Parmenter, R. (1980). *School of the soldier.* New York: Profile Press.

Platt, J. (1973). Social traps. *American Psychologist, 28,* 641-651.

Pospisil, L. (1958). *Kapauko Papuans and their law.* New Haven: Yale University Publications in Anthropology, No. 54.

Quarrington, P. (1984). *Home Game.* New York: Penguin Books.

Reason, P. and Rowan, J. (Eds.). (1981). *Human inquiry.* Chichester, England: Wiley.

Reich, C. (1971). *The greening of America.* Toronto: Bantam Books.

Rich, M. (1979). Verbal reports on mental processes: issues of accuracy and awareness. *Journal for the Theory of Social Behaviour, 9,* 29-37.

Rogers, R. (1987). APA's position on the insanity defense: empiricism vs. emotionalism. *American Psychologist, 42*, 840-848.

Royce, J. (1970). Historical aspects of free choice. *Journal of the History of the Behavioral Sciences, 6*, 48-51.

Rychlak, J. (1975). Psychological science as a humanist views it. In W. Arnold (Ed.), *Nebraska symposium on motivation* (pp. 205-279). Lincoln, Nebraska: University of Nebraska Press.

Rychlak, J. (1977). *The psychology of rigorous humanism*. New York: Wiley-Interscience.

Rychlak, J. (1980). Concepts of free will in modern psychological science. *The Journal of Mind and Behavior, 1*, 9-32.

Rychlak, J. (1987). Can the strength of past associations account for the direction of thought? *The Journal of Mind and Behavior, 8*, 185-193.

Sampson, E. (1977). Psychology and the American ideal. *Journal of Personality and Social psychology, 35*, 767-782.

Sampson, E. (1978). Scientific paradigms and social values: wanted − a scientific revolution. *Journal of Personality and Social Psychology, 36*, 1332-1343.

Sarason, S. (1981). *Psychology misdirected*. New York: Free Press.

Sartre, J-P. (1956). *Being and nothingness*. (Tr. H. Barnes). New York: Philosophical Library.

Schacht, T. (1985). DSM-III and the politics of truth. *American Psychologist, 40*, 513-521.

Secord, P. (Ed.). (1982). *Explaining human behavior*. Beverly Hills, California: Sage Publications, Inc.

Shaw, G. (1931). *The complete plays of Bernard Shaw*. London: Constable and Co. Ltd.

Shevrin, H. and Dickman, S. (1980). The psychological unconscious: a necessary assumption for all psychological theory? *American Psychologist, 35*, 421-434.

Shotter, J. (1975). *Images of man in psychological research*. London: Methuen.

Shotter, J. (1981). Telling and reporting: prospective and retrospective uses of self-ascriptions. In C. Antaki (Ed.), *The psychology of ordinary explanations of social behaviour* (pp. 157-181). London: Academic Press.

Sidel, R. (1974). Families of Fengsheng: urban life in China. Markham, Ontario: Penguin.

Siegel, S. (1956). Non-parametric statistics for the behavioral sciences. N.Y.: McGraw Hill.

Silverman, I. (1977). Why social psychology fails. *Canadian Psychological Review, 18*, 353-358.

Skinner, B. (1971). *Beyond freedom and dignity*. New York: Alfred A. Knopf.

Slater, P. (1971). *The pursuit of loneliness*. Boston: Beacon Press.

Slife, B. (1987). Can cognitive psychology account for metacognitive functions of mind? *The Journal of Mind and Behavior, 8*, 195-208.

Smith, M. (1972). Is social psychology advancing? *Journal of Experimental Social Psychology*, *8*, 86-96.

Smith, E. and Miller, F. (1978). Limits on perception of cognitive processes: a reply to Nisbett and Wilson. *Psychological Review*, *85*, 355-362.

Solomon, R. (1980). The opponent-process theory of motivation. *American Psychologist*, *35*, 691-712.

Solzhenitsyn, A. (1963). *One day in the life of Ivan Denisovich*. New York: Frederick A. Praeger, Inc.

Staats, A. (1987). Humanistic volition versus behavioristic determinism: disunified psychology's schism problem and its solution. *American Psychologist*, *42*, 1030-1032.

Stebbing, L. (1937). *Philosophy and the physicists*. London: Methuen.

Steiner, I. (1970). Perceived freedom. In L. Berkowitz (Ed.), *Advances in Experimental Social Psychology* (Vol. 5, pp. 187-248). New York: Academic Press.

Steiner, I. (1979). Three kinds of reported choice. In L. Perlmuter and R. Monty (Eds.), *Choice and perceived control*. (pp. 17-27). Hillsdale, N.J.: Lawrence Erlbaum Associates.

Steiner, I. (1980). The attribution of choice. In M. Fishbein (Ed.), *Progress in Social Psychology* (pp. 1-47). Hillsdale, N.J.: Lawrence Erlbaum Associates.

Steiner, I., and Field, W. (1960). Role assignment and interpersonal influence. *Journal of Abnormal and Social Psychology*, *61*, 239-245.

Stones, C. (1981). Research: toward a phenomenological praxis. In Kruger, D. *An introduction to phenomenological psychology* (pp. 113-139). Pittsburgh: Duquesne University Press.

Strawson, P. (1959). *Individuals*. London: Methuen.

Strunk, O. (1970). Values move will: the problem of conceptualization. *Journal of the History of the Behavioral Sciences*, *6*, 59-63.

Taylor, G. (1986). A phenomenological investigation into the structure of experienced freedom. Unpublished B.A. Honours Thesis, Department of Psychology, York University, Toronto.

Tesser, A., Gatewood, R., and Driver, M. (1968). Some determinants of gratitude. *Journal of Personality and Social Psychology*, *9*, 233-236.

Thines, G. (1977). *Phenomenology and the science of behaviour*. London: George Allen and Unwin.

Toffler, A. (1971). *Future shock*. Toronto: Bantam Books.

Tothill, S. (1984). A developmental investigation of the phenomenology of freedom. Unpublished B.A. Honours Thesis, Department of Psychology, York University, Toronto.

Valle, R. and King, M. (Eds.). (1978). *Existential-phenomenological alternatives for psychology*. New York: Oxford University Press.

Viney, D. (1986). William James on free will and determinism. *The Journal of Mind and Behavior*, *7*, 555-566.

Von Mering, O. (1963). The experience of individual freedom. In D. Bidney (Ed.), *The concept of freedom in anthropology* (pp. 106-130). The Hague: Mouton and Co.

Walster, E., Walster, G., Piliavin, J., and Schmidt, L. (1973). Playing hard to get: understanding an elusive phenomenon. *Journal of Personality and Social Psychology, 26,* 113-121.

Watson, G. (Ed.). (1982). *Free will.* Oxford: Oxford University Press.

Westcott, M. (1977). Free will: an exercise in metaphysical truth or psychological consequences. *Canadian Psychological Review, 18,* 249-263.

Westcott, M. (1978). Toward psychological studies of human freedom. *Canadian Psychological Review, 19,* 277-290.

Westcott, M. (1981). Direct and dialectical semantics of human freedom. *Et cetera: A Review of General Semantics, 38,* 64-75.

Westcott, M. (1982a). Quantitative and qualitative aspects of experienced freedom. *The Journal of Mind and Behavior, 3,* 99-126.

Westcott, M. (1982b, July). On being free and feeling free. Presentation at the International Congress of Applied Psychology, Edinburgh.

Westcott, M. (1984). Natural science and human science approaches to the study of human freedom. *The Journal of Mind and Behavior, 5,* 11-28.

Westcott, M. (1985). Volition is a nag. In F. Brush and J. Overmier (Eds.), *Affect, conditioning, and cognition: essays on the determinants of behavior* (pp. 353-367). Hillsdale, N.J.: Lawrence Erlbaum Associates.

Westin, A. (1967). *Privacy and freedom.* New York: Atheneum.

Westland, G. (1978). *Current crises of psychology.* London: Heinemann.

White, P. (1980). Limitations on verbal reports of internal events: a refutation of Nisbett and Wilson and of Bem. *Psychological Review, 87,* 105-112.

White, T. (1982). *America in search of itself.* New York: Harper and Row.

Wicklund, R. (1974). *Freedom and reactance.* Potomac, Maryland: Lawrence Erlbaum Associates.

Williams, R. (1987). Can cognitive psychology offer a meaningful account of meaningful human action? *The Journal of Mind and Behavior, 8,* 209-222.

Wittfogel, K. (1957). *Oriental despotism.* New Haven: Yale University Press.

Woodworth, R. (1906). The cause of voluntary movement. In R. Woodworth, *Studies in philosophy and psychology* (pp. 351-392). Boston: Houghton Mifflin.

Worchel, S. (1971). The effect of simple frustration, violated expectancy, and reactance on the instigation to aggression. Unpublished Ph.D. Dissertation, Duke University.

Worchel, S. (1974). The effect of three types of arbitrary thwarting on the instigation to aggesssion. *Journal of Personality, 42,* 300-318.

Wortman, C. and Brehm, J. (1975). Responses to uncontrollable outcomes: an integration of reactance theory and the learned helplessness model. In L. Berkowitz (Ed.), *Advances in experimental social psychology* (Vol. 8, pp. 277-336). New York: Academic Press.

Zavalloni, R. (1962). *Self determination: the psychology of personal freedom*. Chicago: Forum Books; Chicago: The Franciscan Press.

# Appendix

Complete listing of the situational descriptions included in the questionnaire.

Numbering is as in the questionnaire.

*Cluster 1.    Self Direction*

  5.   I am in a situation where I am the one who determines what I will do.

  8.   I have been accepted into the Individualized Studies Programme at my University and have devised my own plan of study. Step by step I am working steadily through that plan, completing the necessary stages in the pursuit of my degree.

13.   I am taking successful steps in working my way to a longterm goal.

24.   As the end of term approaches I am well caught up in my regular work. I plan to spend the time between the end of classes and the beginning of exams in both study and relaxation. I am in the process of setting my own priorities and making a schedule for myself which will include both.

*Cluster 2.    Absence of Responsibility*

12.   All of the week's duties, tasks, and responsibilities have been met and completed. The weekend is at hand, with no dates to be kept or promises to fulfill; there are no obligations which must be kept for the next several days, either to others, or work or school.

16.   I'm at home on a quiet afternoon with nothing to do. I'm warm and comfortable with plenty to eat and no need to leave the house. My

friends are not around; there are no books here I haven't read; there's not much of interest on the T.V. I'm going to spend the entire day doing nothing in particular.

19. Sometimes I am not actively engaged in any particular activity, and I have nothing to do.

22. Sometimes I have no responsibilities.

*Cluster 3.    Release from Noxious Stimulation*

3. All day long I have had a nagging headache, and I have just realized that it is gone.

10. A problem or an irritation or a frustration has been bothering me for a long time, and suddenly I realize that it is no longer there.

20. I have been planning an outing with a group of my friends, but none of us has been able to get the tickets we wanted, and the outing may fall flat. I am feeling quite upset and disappointed about our plans being spoiled, when I receive a phone call from the ticket agency informing me of six cancellations. Tickets for me and my friends are now available.

25. I have been trying to accomplish something for a long time, but there have been repeated obstructions preventing the attainment of my goal. Suddenly without any action on my part, I find the obstacles have been cleared away.

*Cluster 4.    Recognition of Limits*

4. As a new student at University, I was rather unsure of my programme's guidelines of study, course requirements, etc. After meeting with my advisor, though, I have a clear picture of the boundaries within which I can operate in pursuing my degree.

7. In a given situation, I realize that I really know the limits within which I can operate (i.e., the restrictions and opportunities of the situation are clear to me).

21. Getting all "A" marks on my grade report is something I would really like to achieve. With some difficult courses, and additional work responsibilities, though, it seems a very unlikely outcome for the present term. A "B" average though, does seem reasonable and within my realistic reach. By lowering my aims I go for the more certainly attainable goal.

26. Sometimes I restrict or reduce my desires to fit with what I believe a situation allows and to what I believe my abilities to be.

*Cluster 5.    Active Decision Making*

2. It's 12:00, and I've gone to the local cafeteria for a lunch break. I'm standing in line looking over the array of sandwiches, soups and salads. I am deciding what to buy for lunch.

11. I am deciding between two fairly trivial choices (e.g., like which of two shirts to wear).

18. I have been accepted at two very reputable universities and I must decide between them. I am in the process of comparing them with respect to their advantages and disadvantages — quality of programme, tuition and living costs, social life, location, etc. Both are very appealing to me. Of course, I can only attend one of them, and I am deciding which it will be.

23. I am faced with two important, valuable and apparently equal choices. I am now deciding between them.

*Cluster 6. Presence of Alternatives*

9. Every year when I go through the university calendar and lecture schedule, I find a very large number of attractive courses which are open to me.

14. Sometimes I know there are attractive opportunities open to me which remain open, even though I don't have to immediately decide to take advantage of any of them.

17. I realize that there are many alternatives open to me in a situation, but I have not yet made any decisions about these alternatives.

27. An ad in the newspaper advertises a vacation package to a place I would very much like to visit some day. The travel plan advertised remains in effect for the next year. Although I have enough money and time to take a trip, I haven't taken any action yet to pursue it. Time remains to either take advantage of the travel plan, stay at home, or spend my vacation in another way. The opportunity remains available, but I do not act on it.

*Cluster 7. Exercise of Skilled Behaviour*

1. I am doing something at which I am skilled — something I do very well.

6. Working with the Help-Repair Organization, I have become very good at fixing and re-finishing broken furniture, discarded clothing, etc. Now, faced with the task of a repair, I am able to manage well and efficiently.

15. I am engaged in an activity at which I am skilled (e.g., writing an essay, repairing a radio, making lasagne). In the middle of the project I find that it is more complicated or demanding than I had first expected (e.g., one of my references contradicts everything I have written so far, the wiring diagram I have is for a different circuit, I don't have any ricotta). Nonetheless, I meet the extra demands and challenges successfully.

28. At times, I engage in activities with skill and confidence in my ability to perform well.

# Index of Names

Joplin, J., 199

Kahneman, D., 109, *209*
Kallen, H., *207*
Keen, E., 99, *209*
Kelley, H., 82, 84, *209*
Kelly, G., 151, *209*
Kessen, W., 111, 112, *210*
Kidd, R., *208*
Kimble, G., 109, 110, 111, *209*
King, M., 99, *206, 209*
Koch, S., 98, 99, 104, 112, 119, *209*
Kristofferson, K., 199
Kruger, D., 99, 185, *209, 212*

Lamiell, J., 104, 151, *209*
Leach, E., 28, 29, *209*
Lee, D., 3, 8, 28, 29, 35, 37, 38, 40, 68, 131, 195, 199, *209*
Lefcourt, H., 8, 112, 150, *209*
Levine, D., *209*
Lightner, J., 88, 89, 90, *208*
Luther, M., 21, 42, 57,

MacCallum, G., 23, 24, 26, 139, 147, 155, 167, 202, *209*
Malcolm, X., 3
Malinowski, B., 3, 8, 30, 31, 32, 41, *210*
Mandler, G., 111, 112, *210*
Martin, A., 92, *210*
Marx, K., 3
Maslow, A., 199
May, R., 3, 188
Merante, T., 185, *210*
Mill, J., 10
Miller, A., 98, *210*
Miller, F., l05 *212*
Miller, G., 108, 109, *210*
Monty, R., *212*
Mook, D., 99, *210*
Morris, P., 105, *210*
Muller, H., 32, *210*

Munsterberg, H., 114
Murphy, G., 17, 108, *210*

Nahm, M., *209*
Nisbett, R., 105, *210*
Nowell-Smith, P., 16, *210*

Ofstad, H., 8, *210*
Orwell, G., 28, *210*

Panciera, L., 85, 86, *207*
Parent, W., 8, 22, 24, 26, 139, 148, 155, *210*
Parmenter, R., 3, 117, 120-127, 158, 181, 182, 194, 199, *210*
Perlmuter, L., 109,. 110, 111, *209, 212*
Piliavin, J., 55, *213*
Platt, J., 150, 210
Pospisil, L., 29, *210*
Pribram, K., 108, 109, *210*

Quarrington, P., 25, *210*

Rawls, J., 3
Reason, P., 98, 99, *207, 210*
Reich, C., 196, 197, *210*
Rich, M., 105, *210*
Richards, F., *204*
Rieber, R., *206*
Rogers, C., 3, 199
Rogers, R., 201, 202, *211*
Royce, J., 109, *211*
Rowan, J., 98, 99, *207, 210*
Rozen, E., 69, 71, *205*
Rychlak, J., 81, 98, 99, 104, 151, *211*

Sampson, E., 98, 196, *211*
Sarason, S., 98, *211*
Sartre, J-P., 3, 24, 25, 26, 38, 199, *211*

# Index of Subjects